MUNCHKIN

VOLUME TWO

BOOM! BOX

STEVE JACKSON GAMES

STEVE
JACKSON
GAMES

MUNCHKIN Volume Two, May 2016. Published by BOOM! Box,
a division of Boom Entertainment, Inc. *Munchkin*, the *Munchkin*
characters, and the names of all products published by Steve Jackson
Games Incorporated are trademarks or registered trademarks of
Steve Jackson Games Incorporated, used under license by Boom
Entertainment, Inc. All rights reserved. The *Munchkin* comic is copyright
© 2016 by Steve Jackson Games Incorporated. All rights reserved.
Originally published in single magazine form as MUNCHKIN No. 5-8.
™ & © 2015 Steve Jackson Games. All rights reserved. BOOM! Box™
and the BOOM! Box logo are trademarks of Boom Entertainment, Inc.,
registered in various countries and categories. All characters, events,
and institutions depicted herein are fictional. Any similarity between any
of the names, characters, persons, events, and/or institutions in this
publication to actual names, characters, and persons, whether living or
dead, events, and/or institutions is unintended and purely coincidental.
BOOM! Box does not read or accept unsolicited submissions of ideas,
stories, or artwork.

A catalog record of this book is available from OCLC and from the BOOM!
Studios website, www.boom-studios.com, on the Librarians page.

BOOM! Studios, 5670 Wilshire Boulevard, Suite 450, Los Angeles, CA
90036-5679. Printed in China. First Printing.

ISBN: 978-1-60886-805-6, eISBN: 978-1-61398-476-5

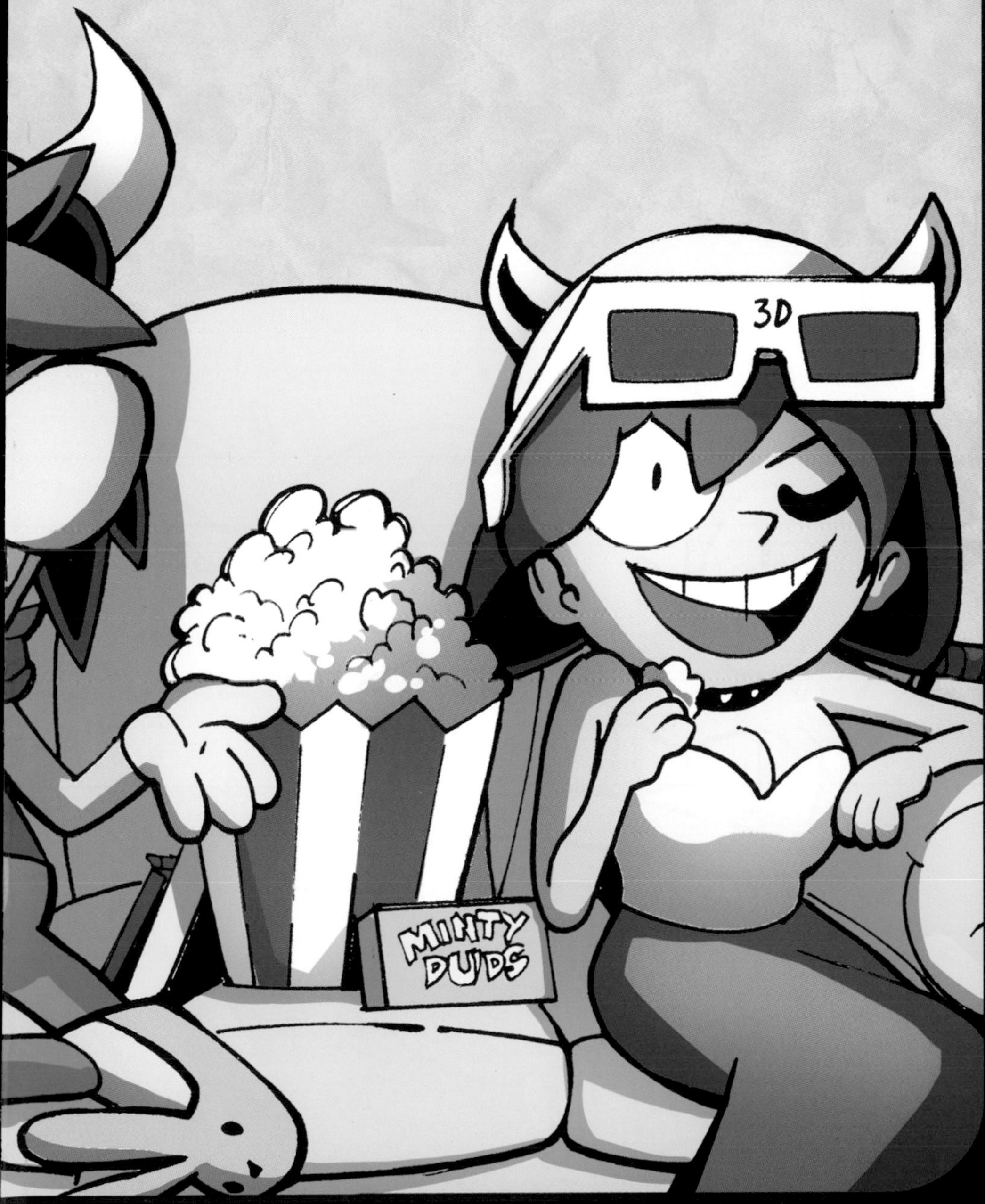
3D
MINTY DUDS

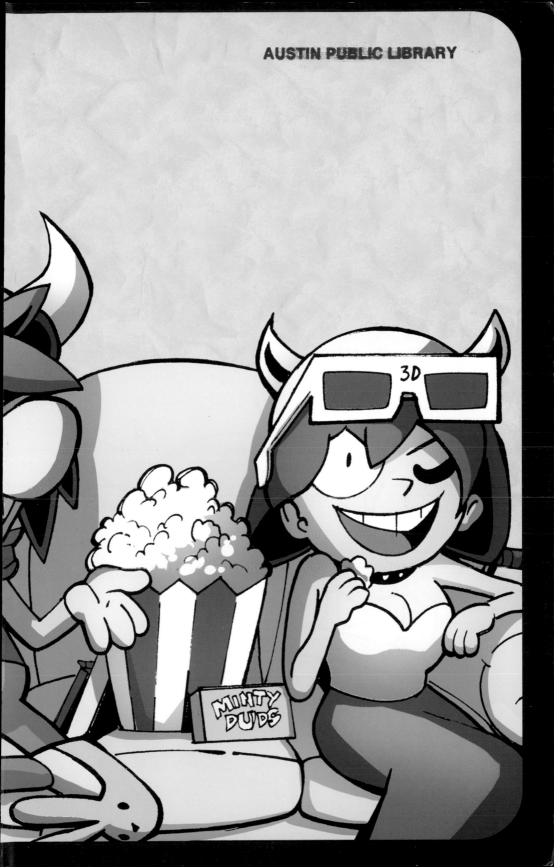

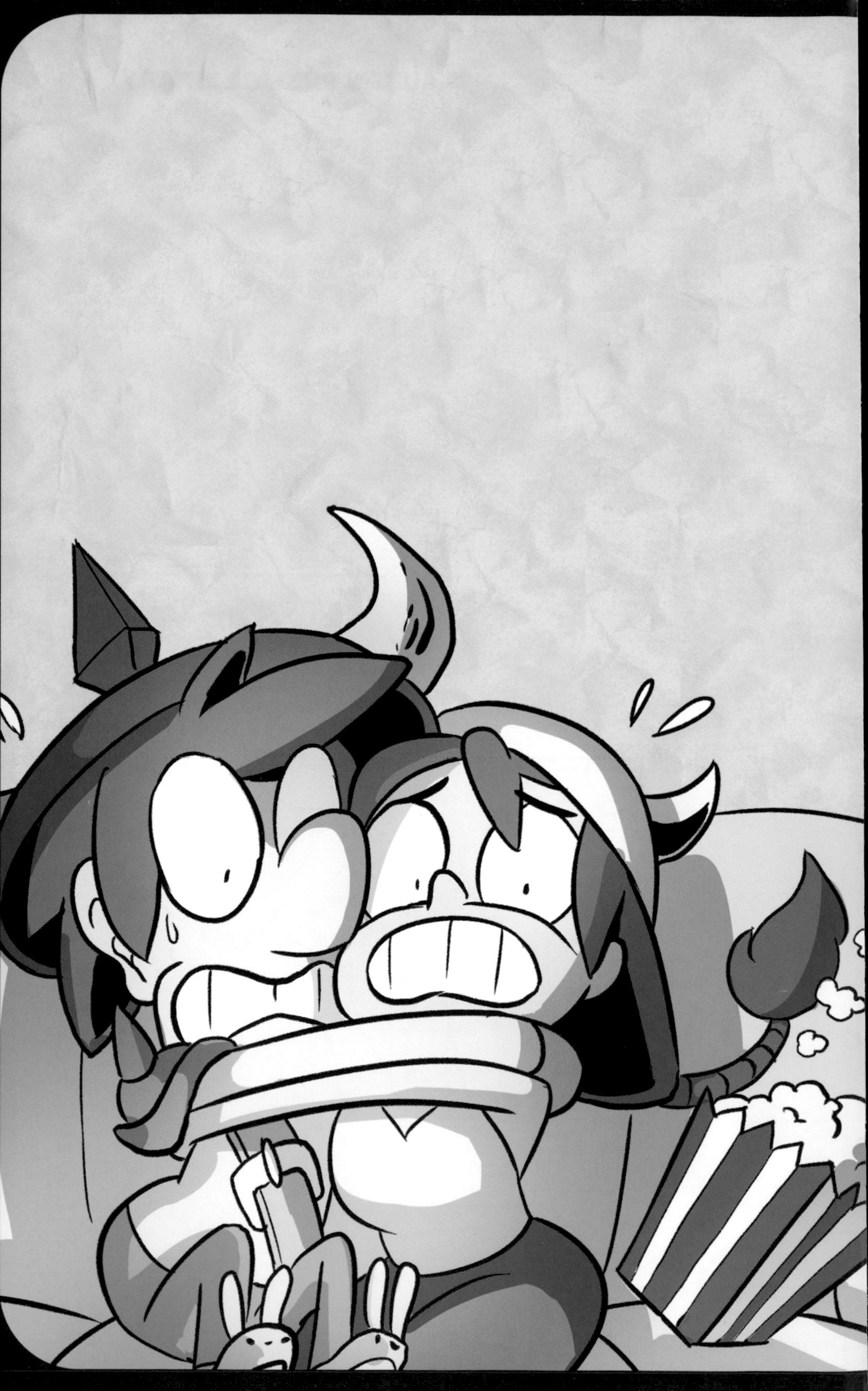

Munchkin®

Written by
Tom Siddell

Illustrated by
Ian McGinty
(chapters 5, 8)
and Mike Luckas
(chapters 6, 7)

Inks by
Nick Nix
(chapter 6)

Colors by
Fred Stresing
(chapters 5, 6, 8)
and Katy Farina
(chapters 6, 7)

Letters by
Jim Campbell

"Munchkin Minis"

"Chick-on-Head"
Written by
Shannon Campbell
Illustrated by
Rian Sygh

"Death & Taxes"
Written by
Derek Fridolfs
Illustrated by
Rian Sygh
Colors by
Fred Stresing

"Duck Die Nasty"
Written by
Derek Fridolfs
Illustrated by
Fred Stresing

"For Love or Money"
Written by
Derek Fridolfs
Illustrated by
Rian Sygh

Designer
Kara Leopard

Associate Editor
Jasmine Amiri

Editor
Shannon Watters

Special thanks to Steve Jackson, Phil Reed, Andrew Hackard and all of the amazing folks at Steve Jackson Games.

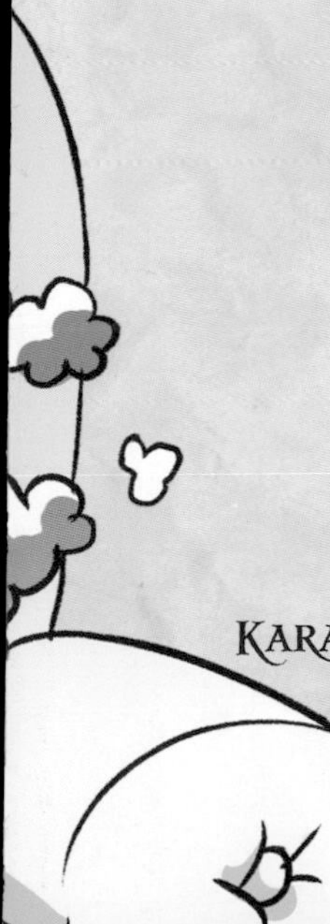

CHAPTER
FIVE

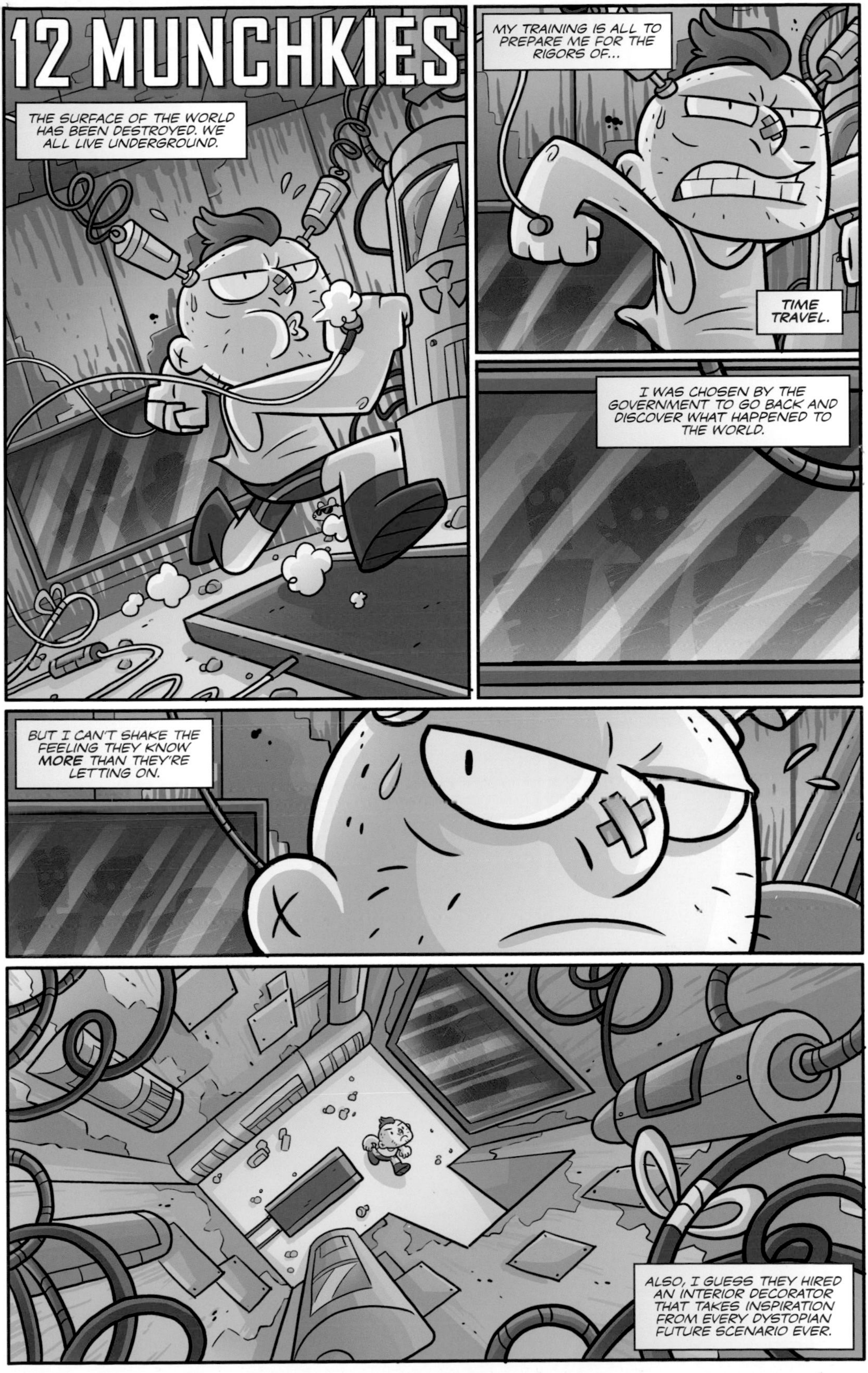
12 MUNCHKIES
THE SURFACE OF THE WORLD HAS BEEN DESTROYED. WE ALL LIVE UNDERGROUND.
MY TRAINING IS ALL TO PREPARE ME FOR THE RIGORS OF...
TIME TRAVEL.
I WAS CHOSEN BY THE GOVERNMENT TO GO BACK AND DISCOVER WHAT HAPPENED TO THE WORLD.
BUT I CAN'T SHAKE THE FEELING THEY KNOW MORE THAN THEY'RE LETTING ON.
ALSO, I GUESS THEY HIRED AN INTERIOR DECORATOR THAT TAKES INSPIRATION FROM EVERY DYSTOPIAN FUTURE SCENARIO EVER.

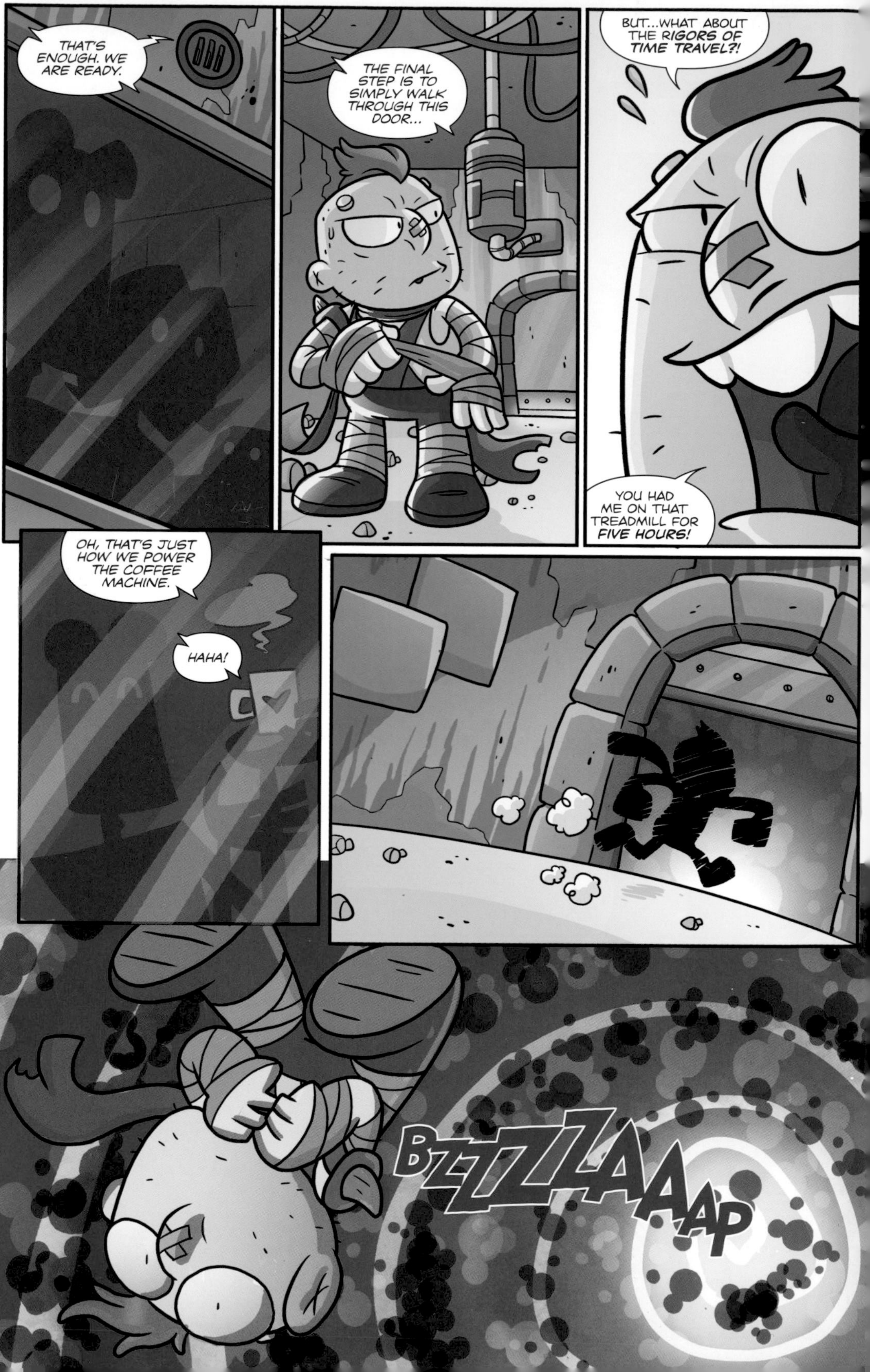
THAT'S ENOUGH. WE ARE READY.
THE FINAL STEP IS TO SIMPLY WALK THROUGH THIS DOOR...
BUT...WHAT ABOUT THE RIGORS OF TIME TRAVEL?!
YOU HAD ME ON THAT TREADMILL FOR FIVE HOURS!
OH, THAT'S JUST HOW WE POWER THE COFFEE MACHINE.
HAHA!
BZZZZAAAAP

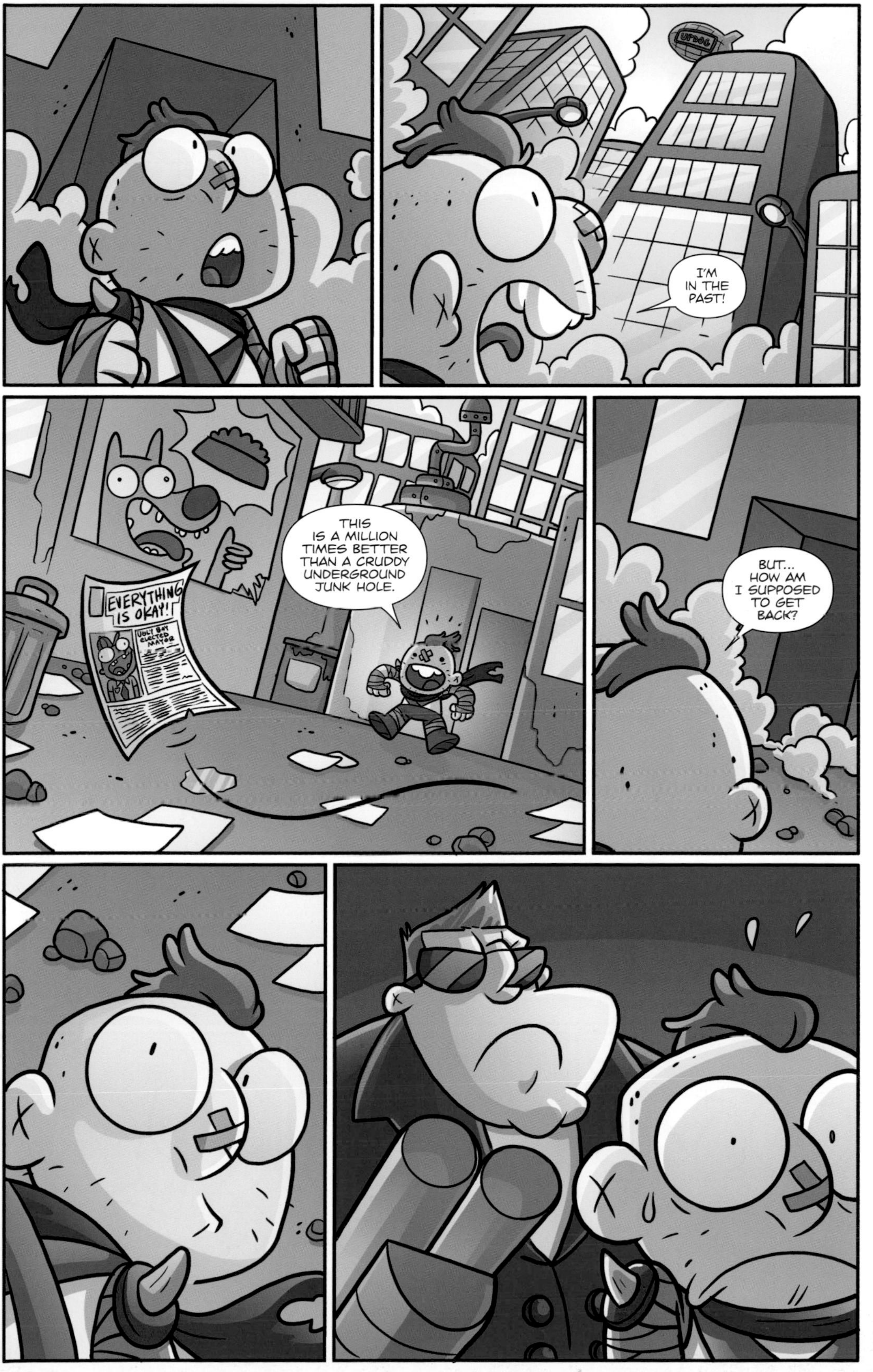
UPDOG
I'M IN THE PAST!
EVERYTHING IS OKAY!
THIS IS A MILLION TIMES BETTER THAN A CRUDDY UNDERGROUND JUNK HOLE.
BUT... HOW AM I SUPPOSED TO GET BACK?

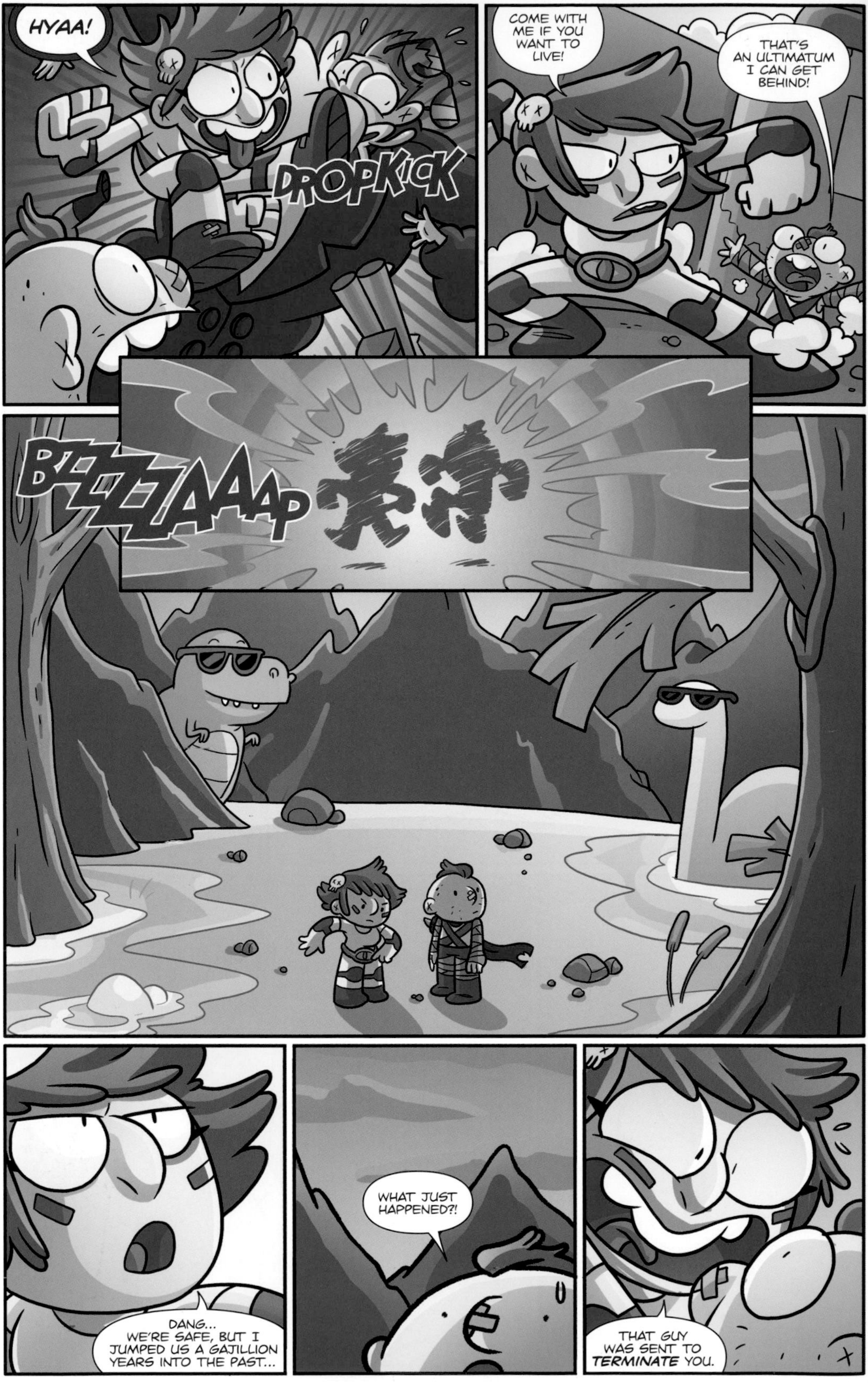
HYAA!
DROPKICK
COME WITH ME IF YOU WANT TO LIVE!
THAT'S AN ULTIMATUM I CAN GET BEHIND!
BZZZZAAAAP
DANG... WE'RE SAFE, BUT I JUMPED US A GAJILLION YEARS INTO THE PAST...
WHAT JUST HAPPENED?!
THAT GUY WAS SENT TO *TERMINATE* YOU.

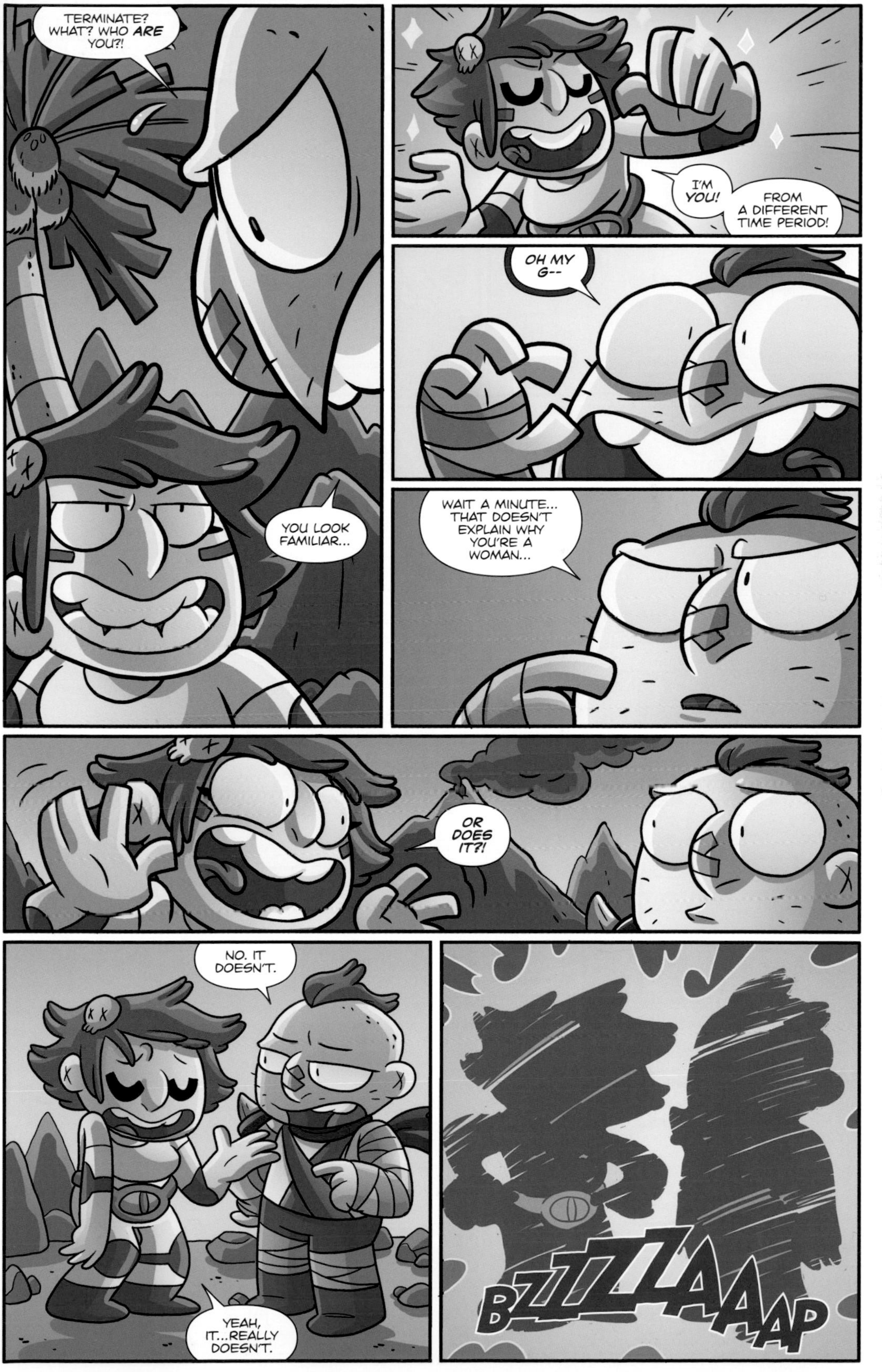
TERMINATE? WHAT? WHO **ARE** YOU?!
YOU LOOK FAMILIAR...
I'M *YOU!*
FROM A DIFFERENT TIME PERIOD!
OH MY G--
WAIT A MINUTE... THAT DOESN'T EXPLAIN WHY YOU'RE A WOMAN...
OR DOES IT?!
NO. IT DOESN'T.
YEAH, IT...REALLY DOESN'T.
BZZZZAAAAP

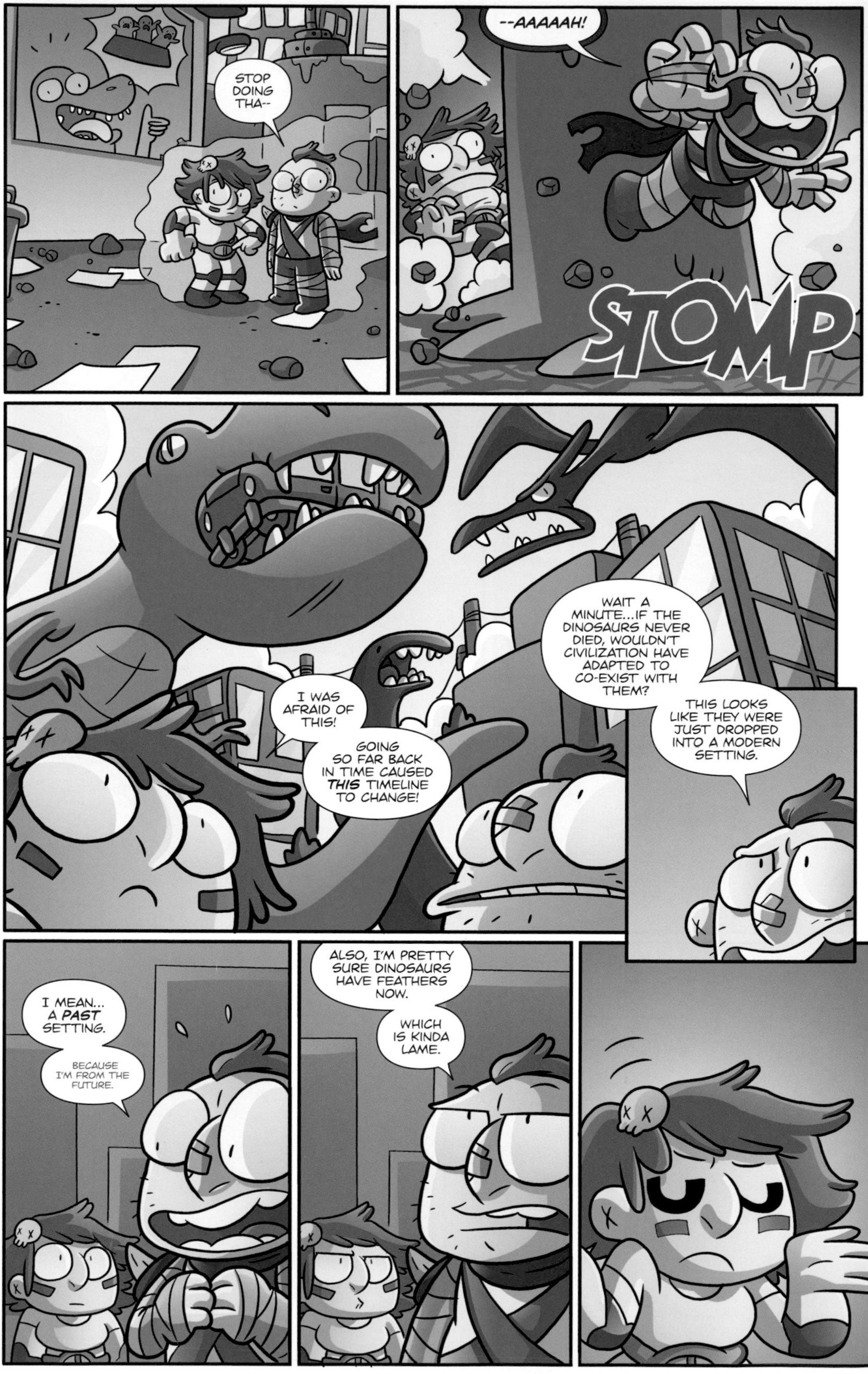
STOP DOING THA--
--AAAAAH!
STOMP
WAIT A MINUTE...IF THE DINOSAURS NEVER DIED, WOULDN'T CIVILIZATION HAVE ADAPTED TO CO-EXIST WITH THEM?
I WAS AFRAID OF THIS!
GOING SO FAR BACK IN TIME CAUSED ***THIS*** TIMELINE TO CHANGE!
THIS LOOKS LIKE THEY WERE JUST DROPPED INTO A MODERN SETTING.
I MEAN... A ***PAST*** SETTING.
BECAUSE I'M FROM THE FUTURE.
ALSO, I'M PRETTY SURE DINOSAURS HAVE FEATHERS NOW.
WHICH IS KINDA LAME.

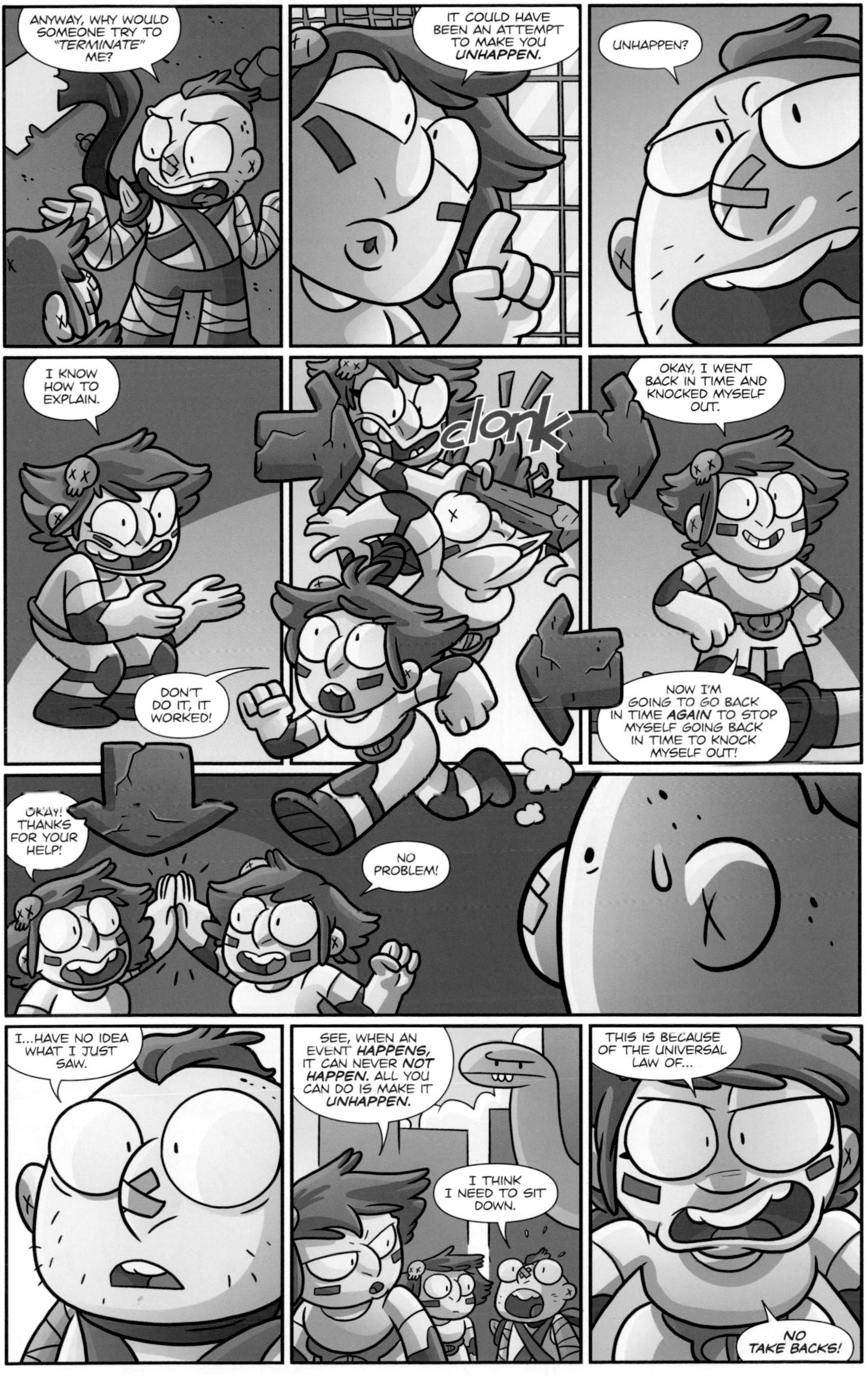
ANYWAY, WHY WOULD SOMEONE TRY TO "TERMINATE" ME?
IT COULD HAVE BEEN AN ATTEMPT TO MAKE YOU UNHAPPEN.
UNHAPPEN?
I KNOW HOW TO EXPLAIN.
CLONK
OKAY, I WENT BACK IN TIME AND KNOCKED MYSELF OUT.
DON'T DO IT, IT WORKED!
NOW I'M GOING TO GO BACK IN TIME AGAIN TO STOP MYSELF GOING BACK IN TIME TO KNOCK MYSELF OUT!
OKAY! THANKS FOR YOUR HELP!
NO PROBLEM!
I...HAVE NO IDEA WHAT I JUST SAW.
SEE, WHEN AN EVENT HAPPENS, IT CAN NEVER NOT HAPPEN. ALL YOU CAN DO IS MAKE IT UNHAPPEN.
I THINK I NEED TO SIT DOWN.
THIS IS BECAUSE OF THE UNIVERSAL LAW OF...
NO TAKE BACKS!

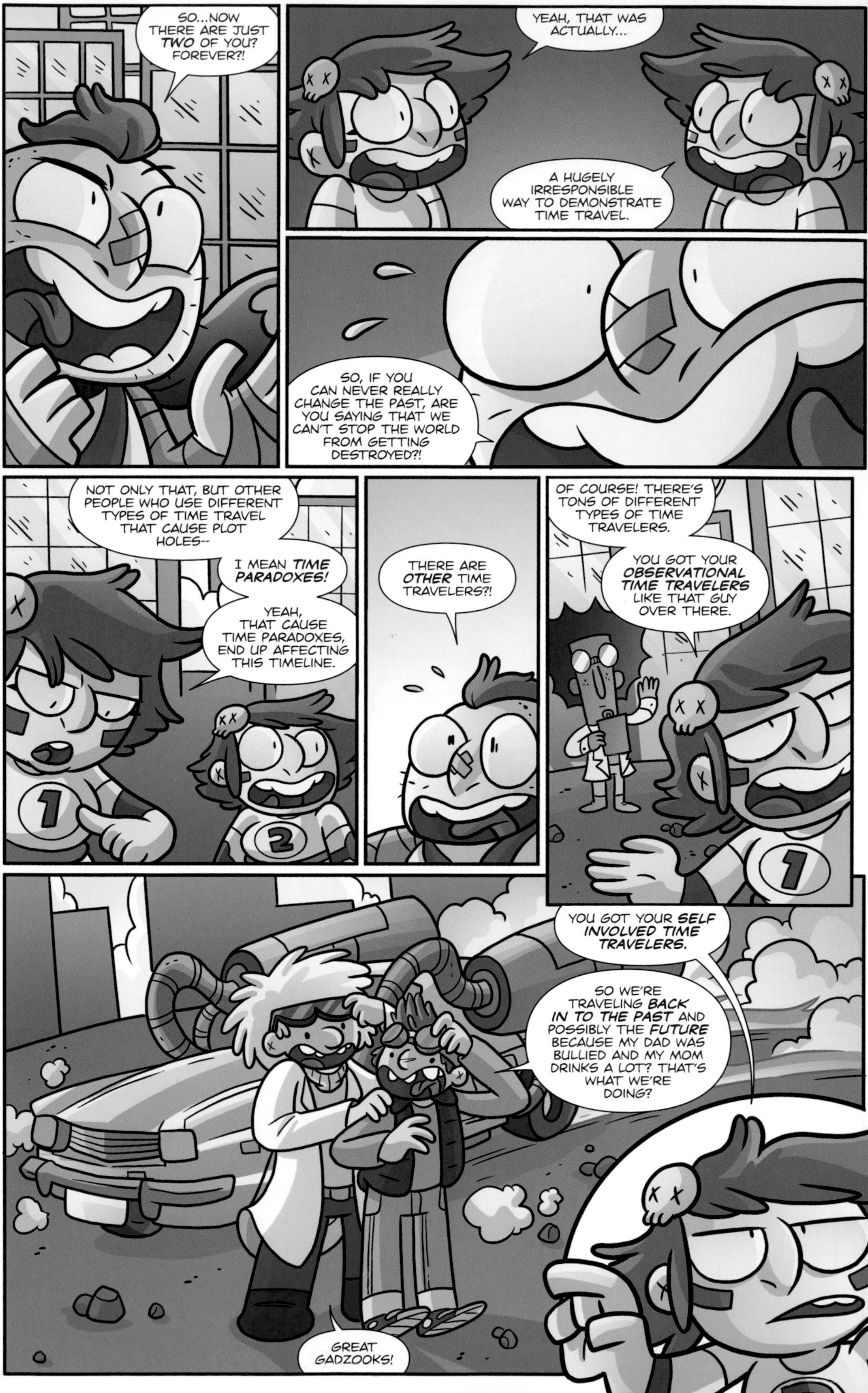
SO...NOW THERE ARE JUST TWO OF YOU? FOREVER?!
YEAH, THAT WAS ACTUALLY...
A HUGELY IRRESPONSIBLE WAY TO DEMONSTRATE TIME TRAVEL.
SO, IF YOU CAN NEVER REALLY CHANGE THE PAST, ARE YOU SAYING THAT WE CAN'T STOP THE WORLD FROM GETTING DESTROYED?!
NOT ONLY THAT, BUT OTHER PEOPLE WHO USE DIFFERENT TYPES OF TIME TRAVEL THAT CAUSE PLOT HOLES--
I MEAN TIME PARADOXES!
YEAH, THAT CAUSE TIME PARADOXES, END UP AFFECTING THIS TIMELINE.
THERE ARE OTHER TIME TRAVELERS?!
OF COURSE! THERE'S TONS OF DIFFERENT TYPES OF TIME TRAVELERS.
YOU GOT YOUR OBSERVATIONAL TIME TRAVELERS LIKE THAT GUY OVER THERE.
YOU GOT YOUR SELF INVOLVED TIME TRAVELERS.
SO WE'RE TRAVELING BACK IN TO THE PAST AND POSSIBLY THE FUTURE BECAUSE MY DAD WAS BULLIED AND MY MOM DRINKS A LOT? THAT'S WHAT WE'RE DOING?
GREAT GADZOOKS!

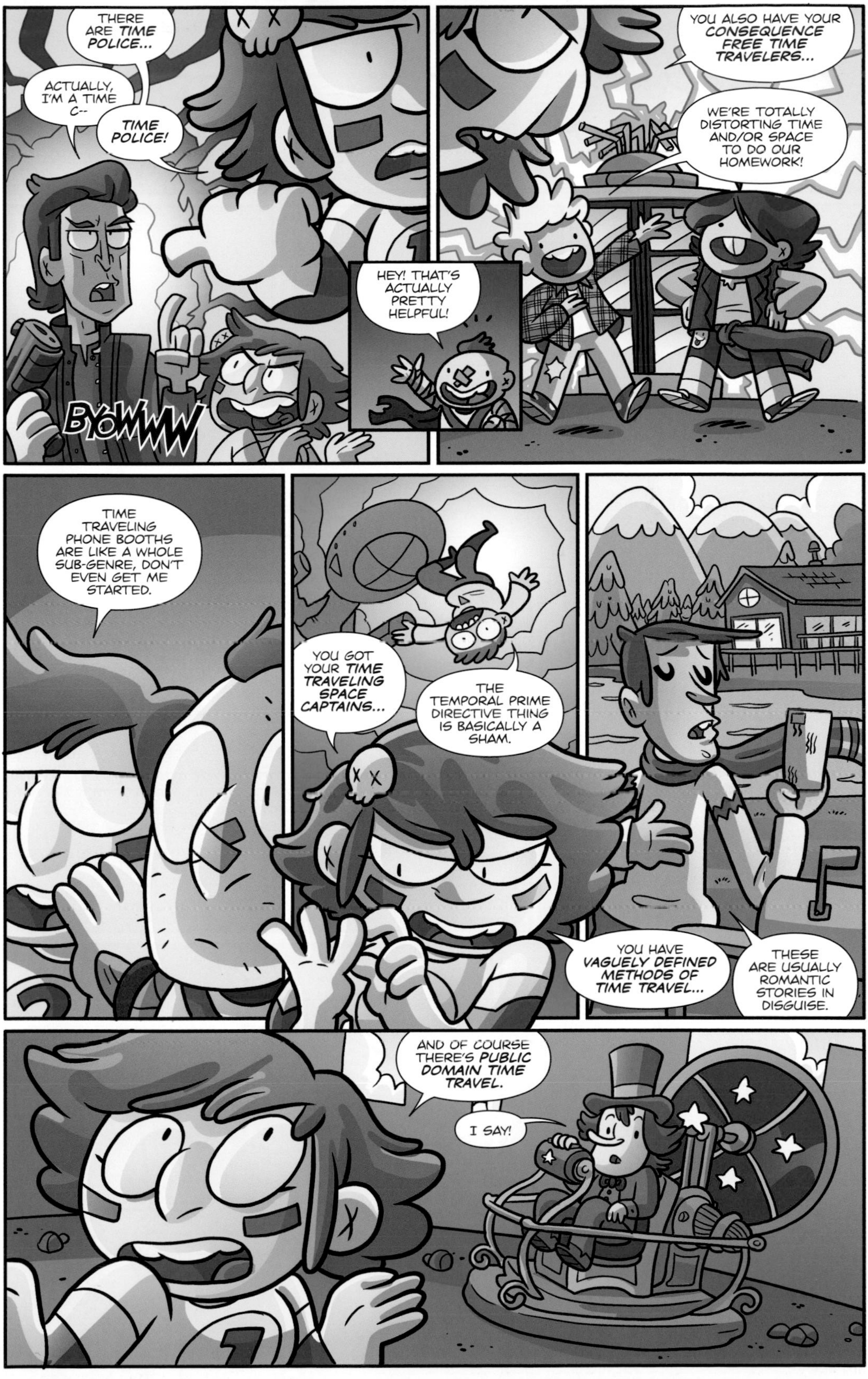
THERE ARE TIME POLICE...
ACTUALLY, I'M A TIME C--
TIME POLICE!
BYOWWW
YOU ALSO HAVE YOUR CONSEQUENCE FREE TIME TRAVELERS...
WE'RE TOTALLY DISTORTING TIME AND/OR SPACE TO DO OUR HOMEWORK!
HEY! THAT'S ACTUALLY PRETTY HELPFUL!
TIME TRAVELING PHONE BOOTHS ARE LIKE A WHOLE SUB-GENRE, DON'T EVEN GET ME STARTED.
YOU GOT YOUR TIME TRAVELING SPACE CAPTAINS...
THE TEMPORAL PRIME DIRECTIVE THING IS BASICALLY A SHAM.
YOU HAVE VAGUELY DEFINED METHODS OF TIME TRAVEL...
THESE ARE USUALLY ROMANTIC STORIES IN DISGUISE.
AND OF COURSE THERE'S PUBLIC DOMAIN TIME TRAVEL.
I SAY!

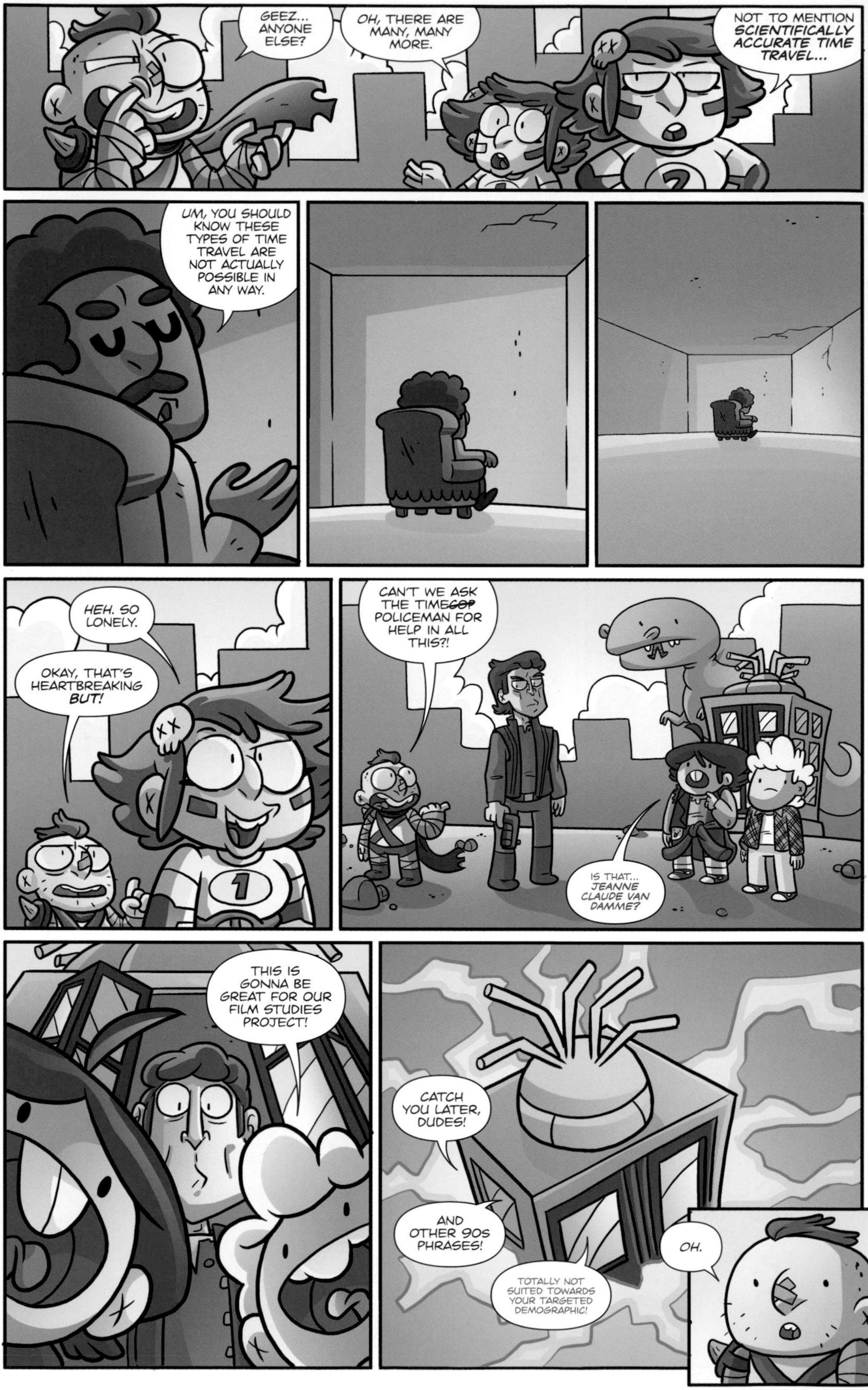
GEEZ... ANYONE ELSE?
OH, THERE ARE MANY, MANY MORE.
NOT TO MENTION SCIENTIFICALLY ACCURATE TIME TRAVEL...
UM, YOU SHOULD KNOW THESE TYPES OF TIME TRAVEL ARE NOT ACTUALLY POSSIBLE IN ANY WAY.
HEH. SO LONELY.
OKAY, THAT'S HEARTBREAKING BUT!
CAN'T WE ASK THE TIME~~COP~~ POLICEMAN FOR HELP IN ALL THIS?!
IS THAT... JEANNE CLAUDE VAN DAMME?
THIS IS GONNA BE GREAT FOR OUR FILM STUDIES PROJECT!
CATCH YOU LATER, DUDES!
AND OTHER 90s PHRASES!
TOTALLY NOT SUITED TOWARDS YOUR TARGETED DEMOGRAPHIC!
OH.

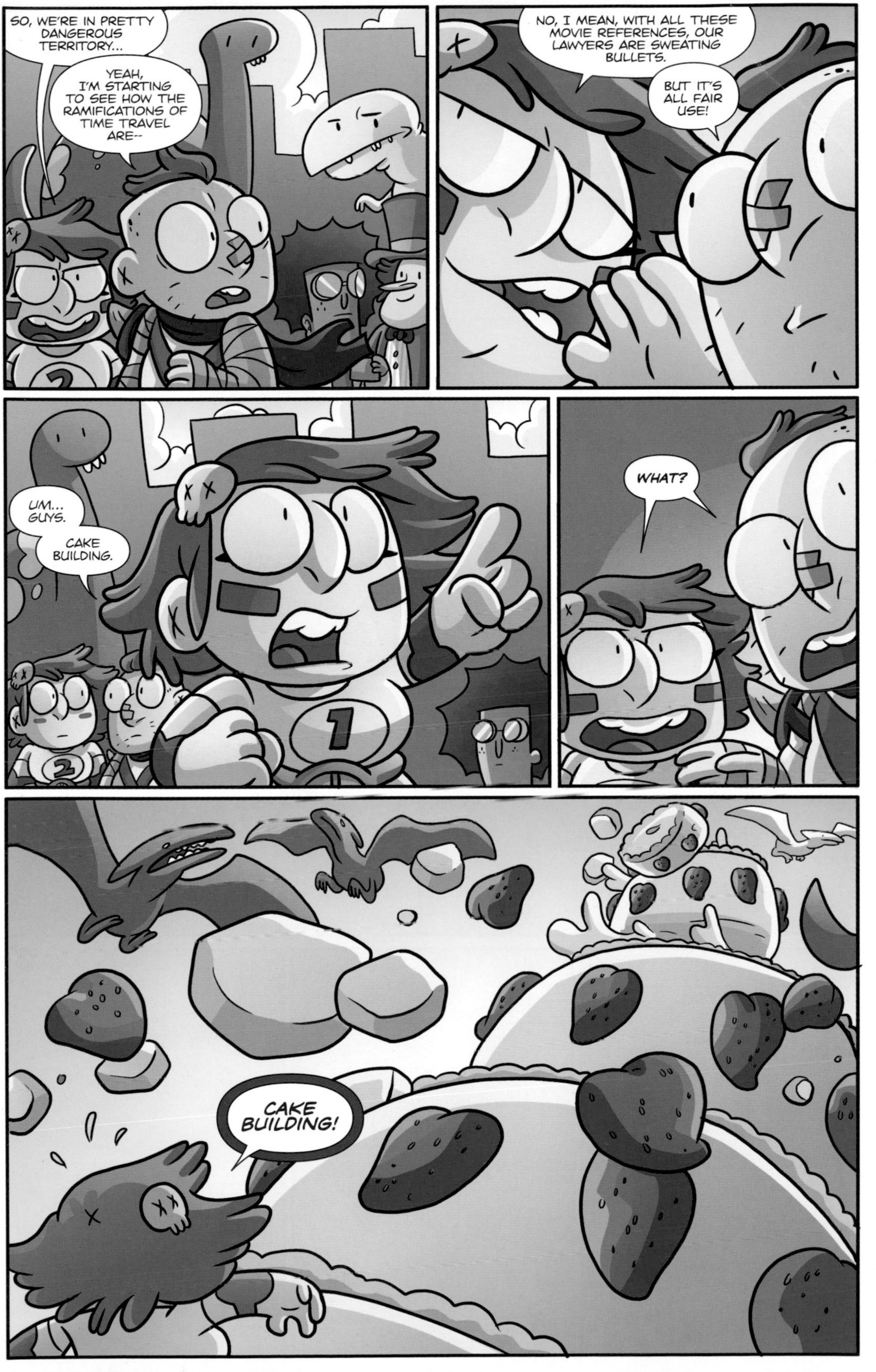
SO, WE'RE IN PRETTY DANGEROUS TERRITORY...
YEAH, I'M STARTING TO SEE HOW THE RAMIFICATIONS OF TIME TRAVEL ARE--
NO, I MEAN, WITH ALL THESE MOVIE REFERENCES, OUR LAWYERS ARE SWEATING BULLETS.
BUT IT'S ALL FAIR USE!
UM... GUYS.
CAKE BUILDING.
WHAT?
CAKE BUILDING!

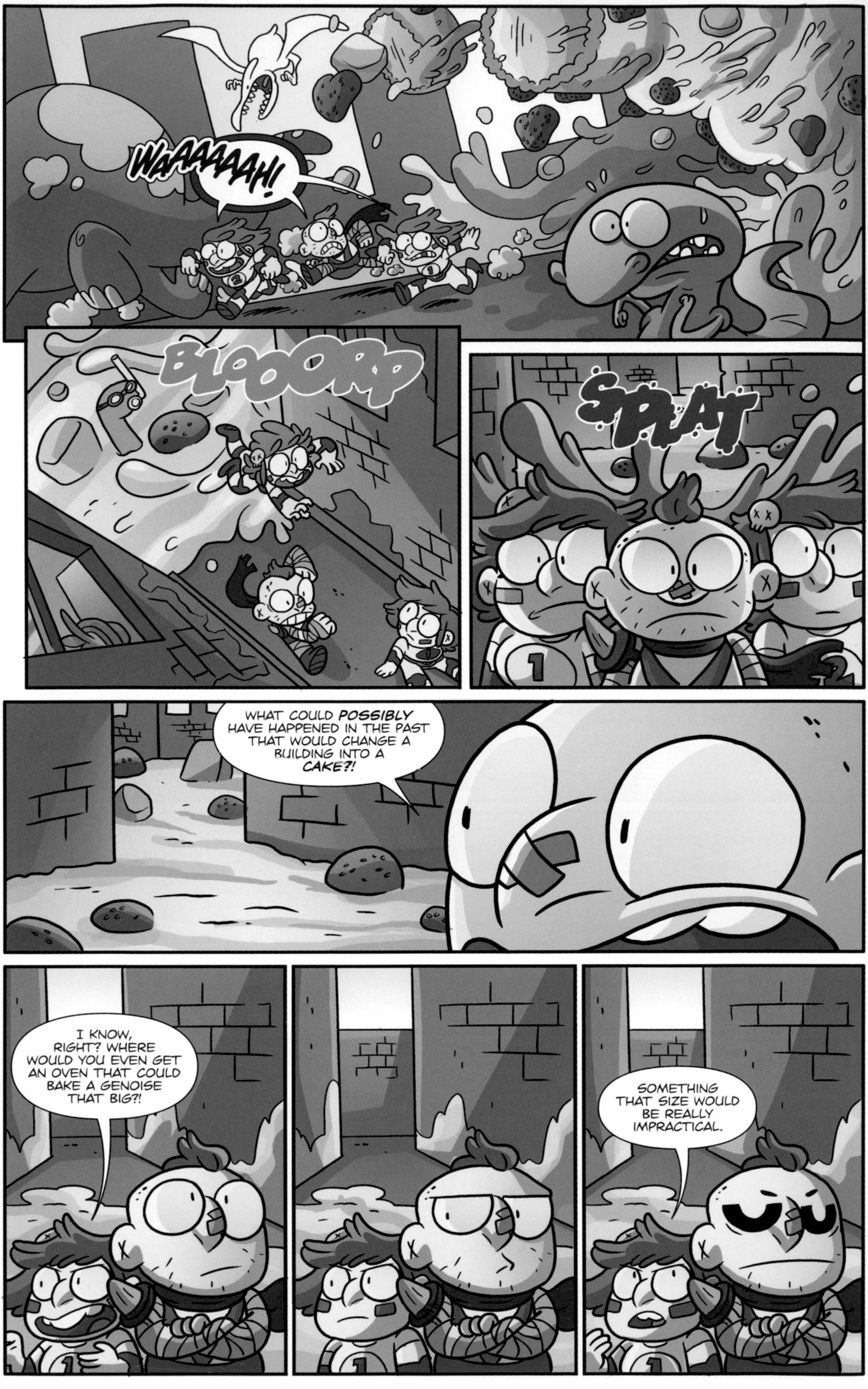
WAAAAAAH!
BLOOORP
SPLAT
WHAT COULD POSSIBLY HAVE HAPPENED IN THE PAST THAT WOULD CHANGE A BUILDING INTO A CAKE?!
I KNOW, RIGHT? WHERE WOULD YOU EVEN GET AN OVEN THAT COULD BAKE A GENOISE THAT BIG?!
SOMETHING THAT SIZE WOULD BE REALLY IMPRACTICAL.

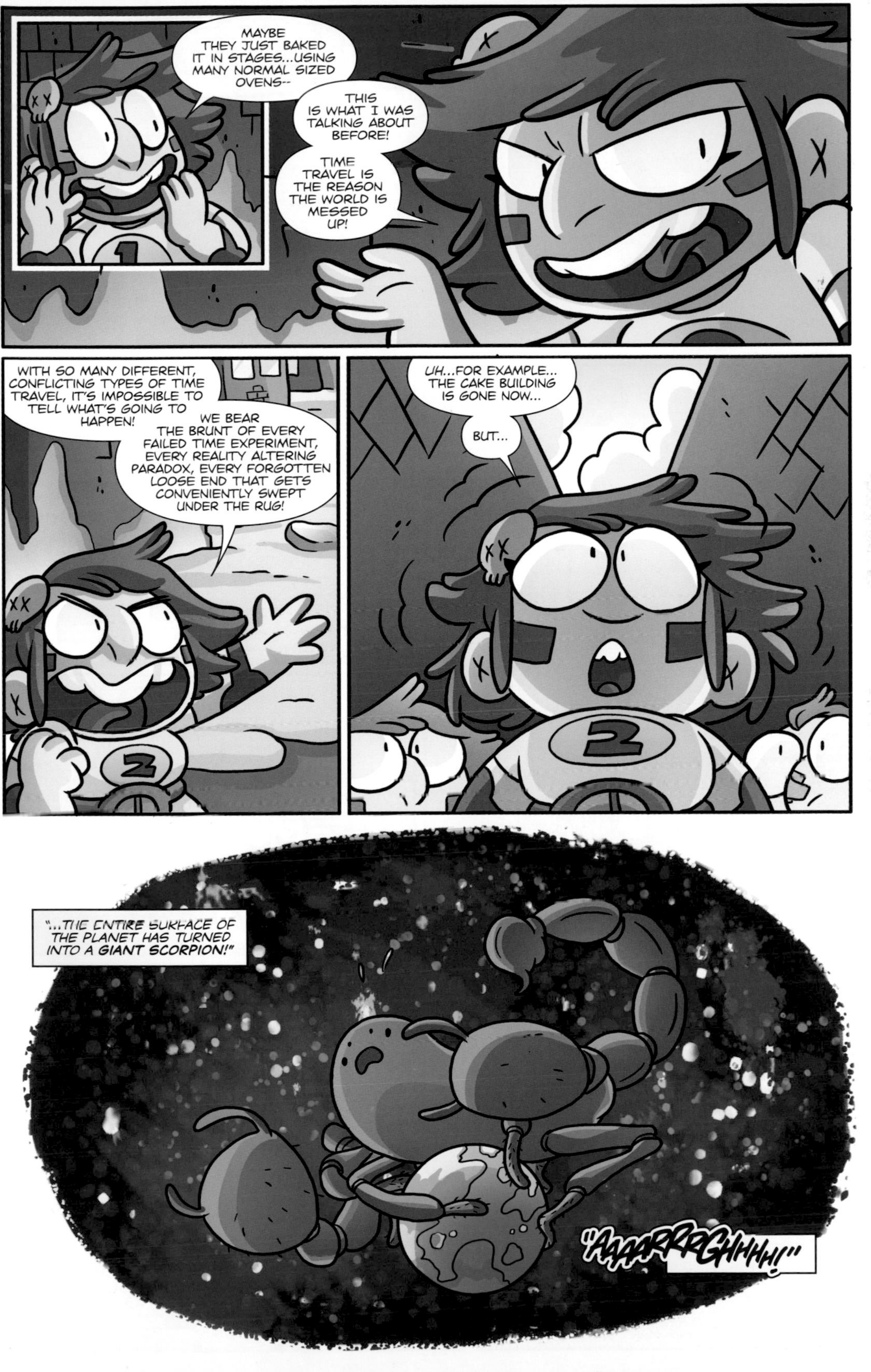
MAYBE THEY JUST BAKED IT IN STAGES...USING MANY NORMAL SIZED OVENS--
THIS IS WHAT I WAS TALKING ABOUT BEFORE!
TIME TRAVEL IS THE REASON THE WORLD IS MESSED UP!
WITH SO MANY DIFFERENT, CONFLICTING TYPES OF TIME TRAVEL, IT'S IMPOSSIBLE TO TELL WHAT'S GOING TO HAPPEN!
WE BEAR THE BRUNT OF EVERY FAILED TIME EXPERIMENT, EVERY REALITY ALTERING PARADOX, EVERY FORGOTTEN LOOSE END THAT GETS CONVENIENTLY SWEPT UNDER THE RUG!
UH...FOR EXAMPLE... THE CAKE BUILDING IS GONE NOW...
BUT...
"...THE ENTIRE SURFACE OF THE PLANET HAS TURNED INTO A GIANT SCORPION!"
"AAAARRRGHHHH!"

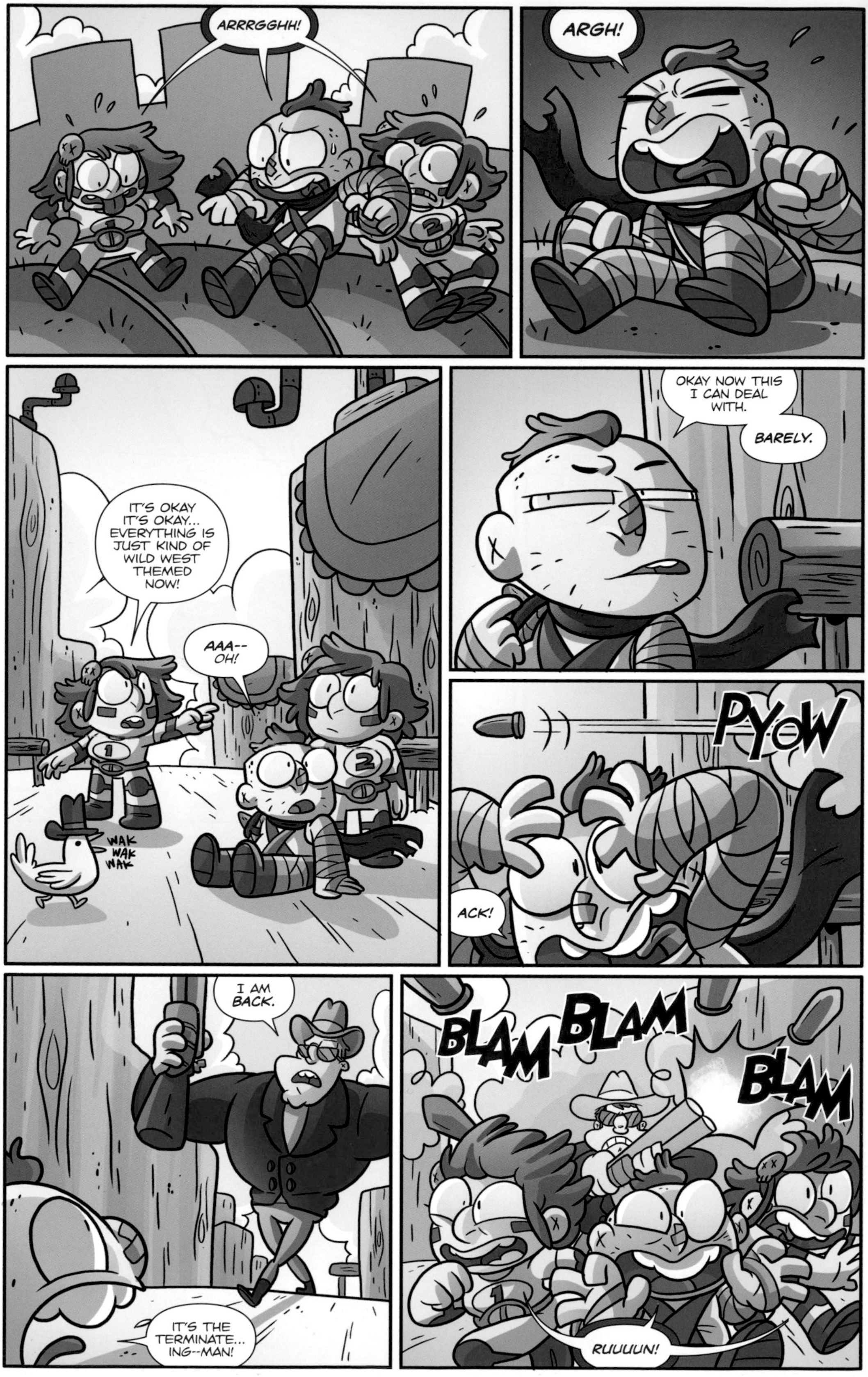
ARRRGGHH!
ARGH!
IT'S OKAY IT'S OKAY... EVERYTHING IS JUST KIND OF WILD WEST THEMED NOW!
AAA-- OH!
WAK WAK WAK
OKAY NOW THIS I CAN DEAL WITH.
BARELY.
PYOW
ACK!
I AM BACK.
IT'S THE TERMINATE... ING--MAN!
BLAM BLAM
BLAM
RUUUUN!

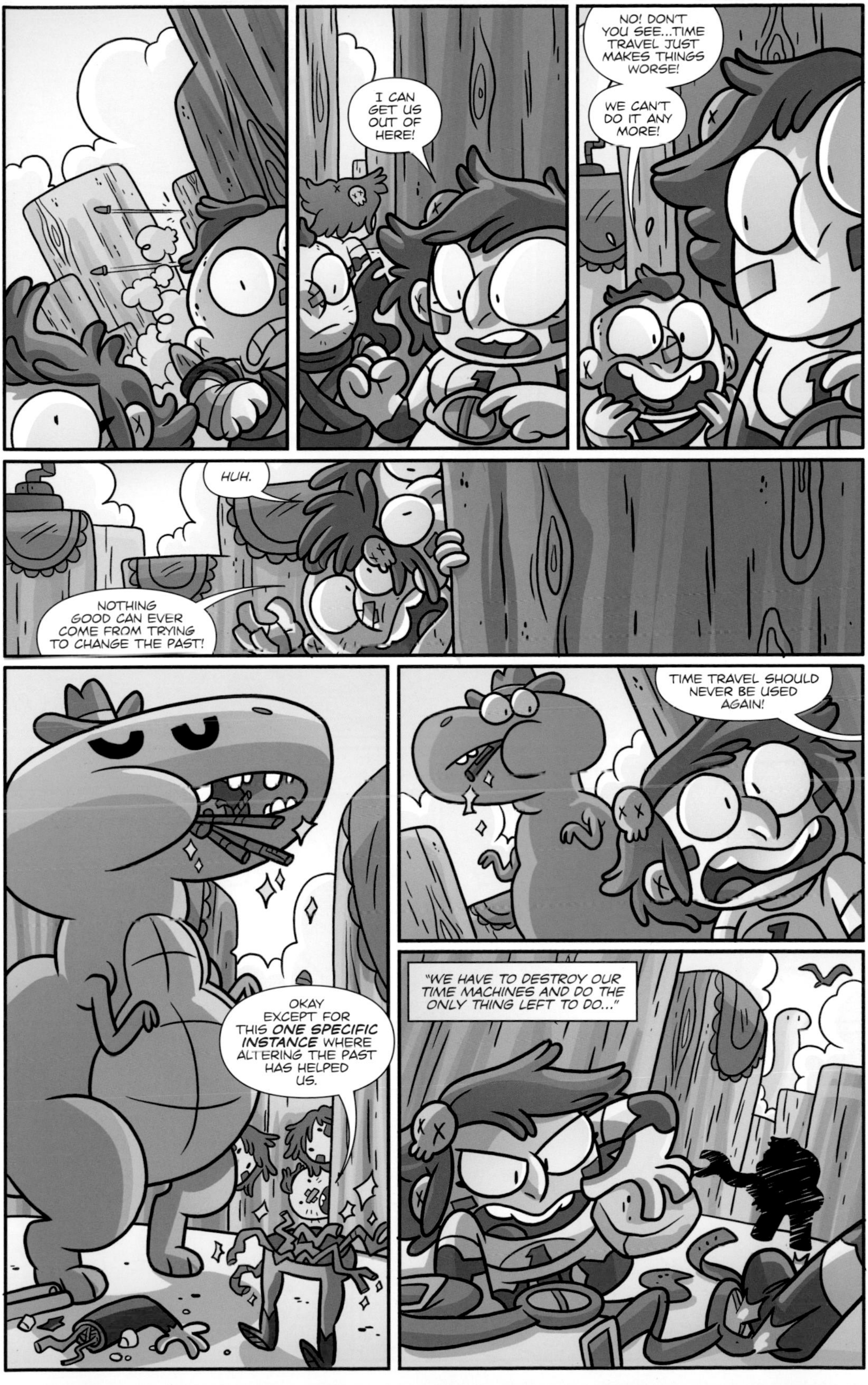
I CAN GET US OUT OF HERE!
NO! DON'T YOU SEE...TIME TRAVEL JUST MAKES THINGS WORSE!
WE CAN'T DO IT ANY MORE!
HUH.
NOTHING GOOD CAN EVER COME FROM TRYING TO CHANGE THE PAST!
TIME TRAVEL SHOULD NEVER BE USED AGAIN!
OKAY EXCEPT FOR THIS **ONE SPECIFIC INSTANCE** WHERE ALTERING THE PAST HAS HELPED US.
"WE HAVE TO DESTROY OUR TIME MACHINES AND DO THE ONLY THING LEFT TO DO..."

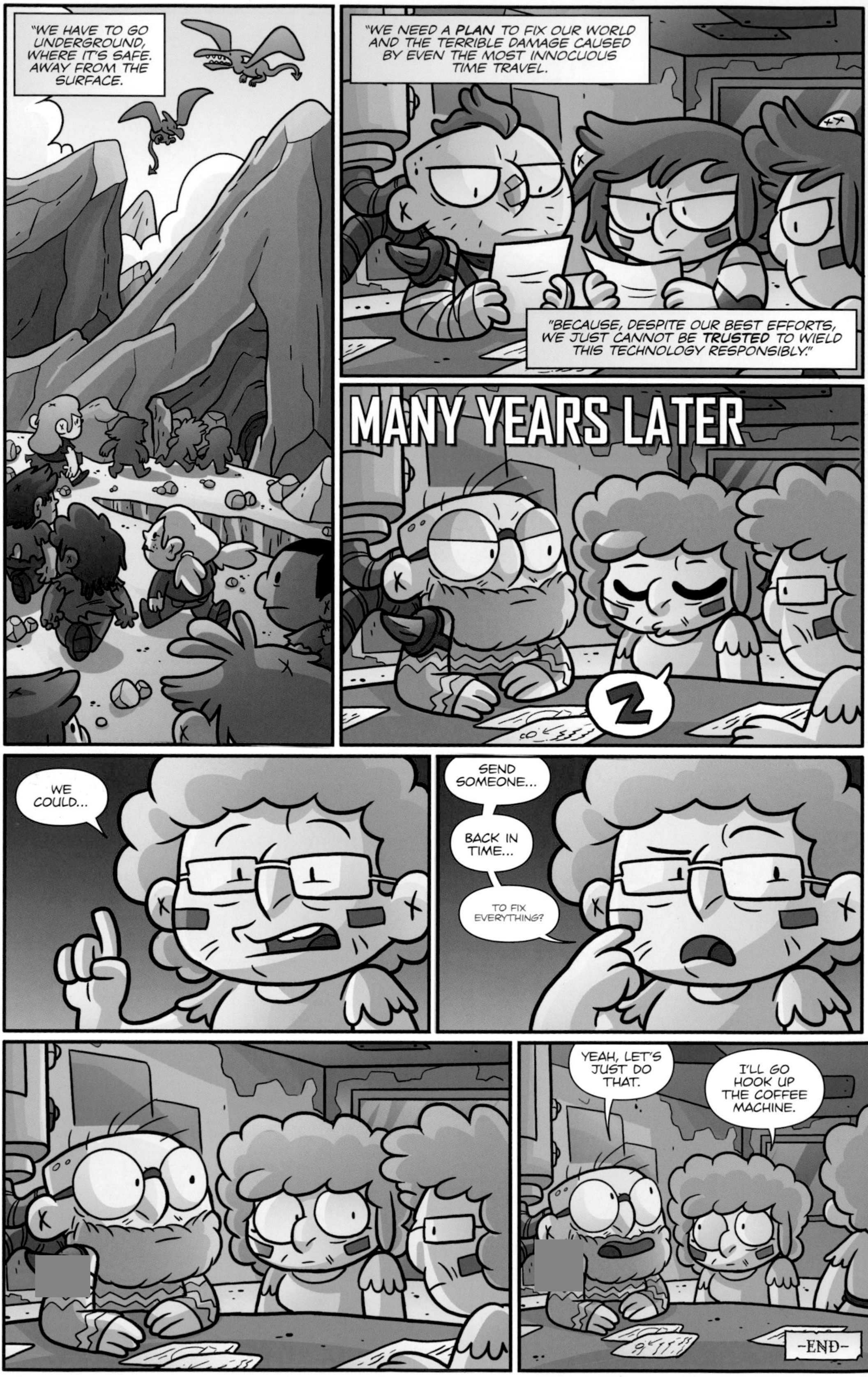
"WE HAVE TO GO UNDERGROUND, WHERE IT'S SAFE. AWAY FROM THE SURFACE.
"WE NEED A PLAN TO FIX OUR WORLD AND THE TERRIBLE DAMAGE CAUSED BY EVEN THE MOST INNOCUOUS TIME TRAVEL.
"BECAUSE, DESPITE OUR BEST EFFORTS, WE JUST CANNOT BE TRUSTED TO WIELD THIS TECHNOLOGY RESPONSIBLY."
MANY YEARS LATER
Z
WE COULD...
SEND SOMEONE...
BACK IN TIME...
TO FIX EVERYTHING?
YEAH, LET'S JUST DO THAT.
I'LL GO HOOK UP THE COFFEE MACHINE.
-END-

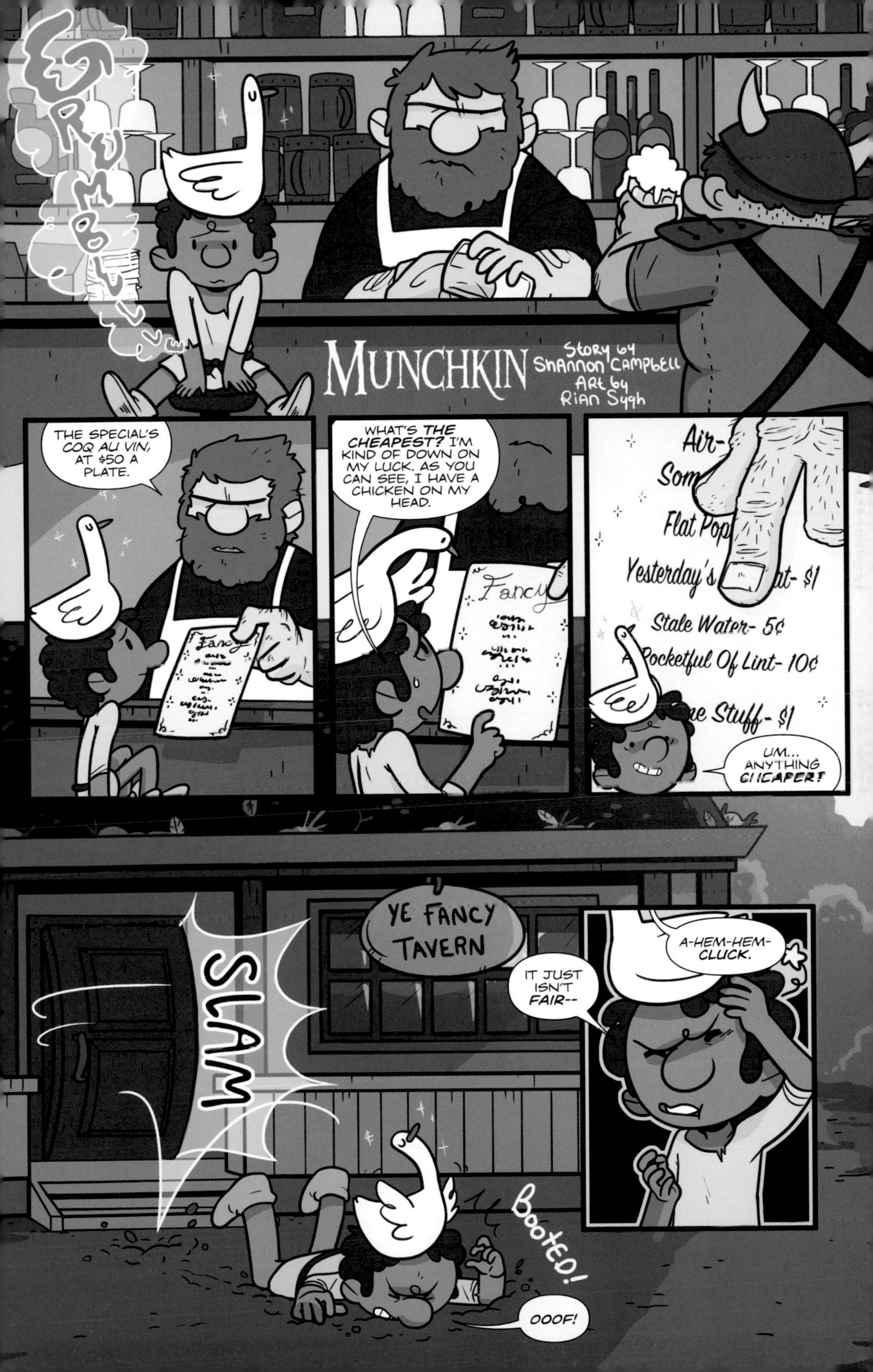
GRUMBULLULL
MUNCHKIN
Story by Shannon Campbell
Art by Rian Sygh
THE SPECIAL'S COQ AU VIN, AT $50 A PLATE.
Fancy
WHAT'S THE CHEAPEST? I'M KIND OF DOWN ON MY LUCK. AS YOU CAN SEE, I HAVE A CHICKEN ON MY HEAD.
Fancy
Air-
Som
Flat Pop
Yesterday's at- $1
Stale Water- 5¢
Pocketful Of Lint- 10¢
e Stuff- $1
UM... ANYTHING CHEAPER?
YE FANCY TAVERN
SLAM
BOOTED!
OOOF!
IT JUST ISN'T FAIR--
A-HEM-HEM-CLUCK.

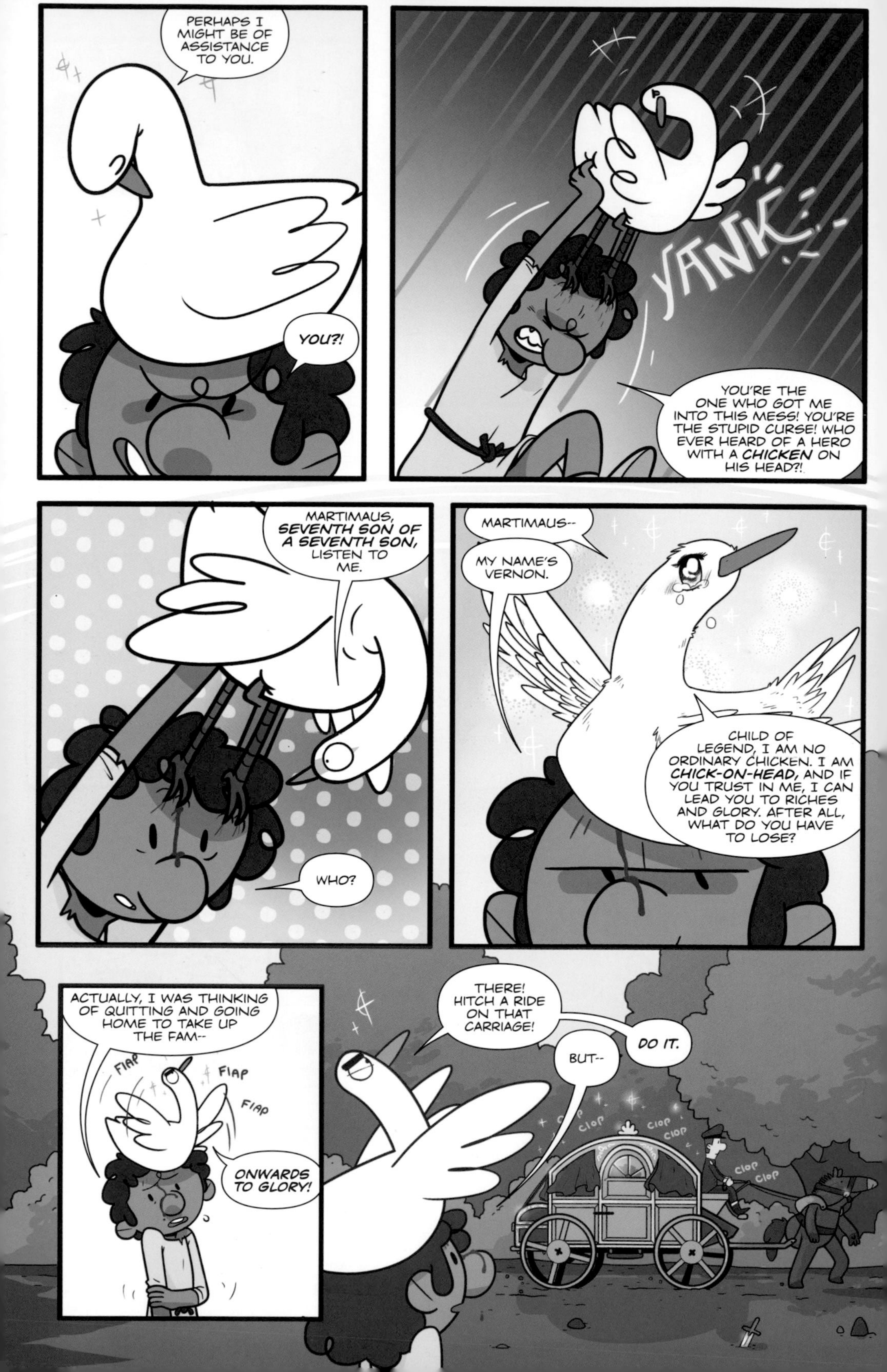
PERHAPS I MIGHT BE OF ASSISTANCE TO YOU.
YOU?!
YANK
YOU'RE THE ONE WHO GOT ME INTO THIS MESS! YOU'RE THE STUPID CURSE! WHO EVER HEARD OF A HERO WITH A CHICKEN ON HIS HEAD?!
MARTIMAUS, SEVENTH SON OF A SEVENTH SON, LISTEN TO ME.
WHO?
MARTIMAUS--
MY NAME'S VERNON.
CHILD OF LEGEND, I AM NO ORDINARY CHICKEN. I AM CHICK-ON-HEAD, AND IF YOU TRUST IN ME, I CAN LEAD YOU TO RICHES AND GLORY. AFTER ALL, WHAT DO YOU HAVE TO LOSE?
ACTUALLY, I WAS THINKING OF QUITTING AND GOING HOME TO TAKE UP THE FAM--
FLAP
FLAP
FLAP
ONWARDS TO GLORY!
THERE! HITCH A RIDE ON THAT CARRIAGE!
DO IT.
BUT--
CLOP
CLOP
CLOP
CLOP
CLOP
CLOP

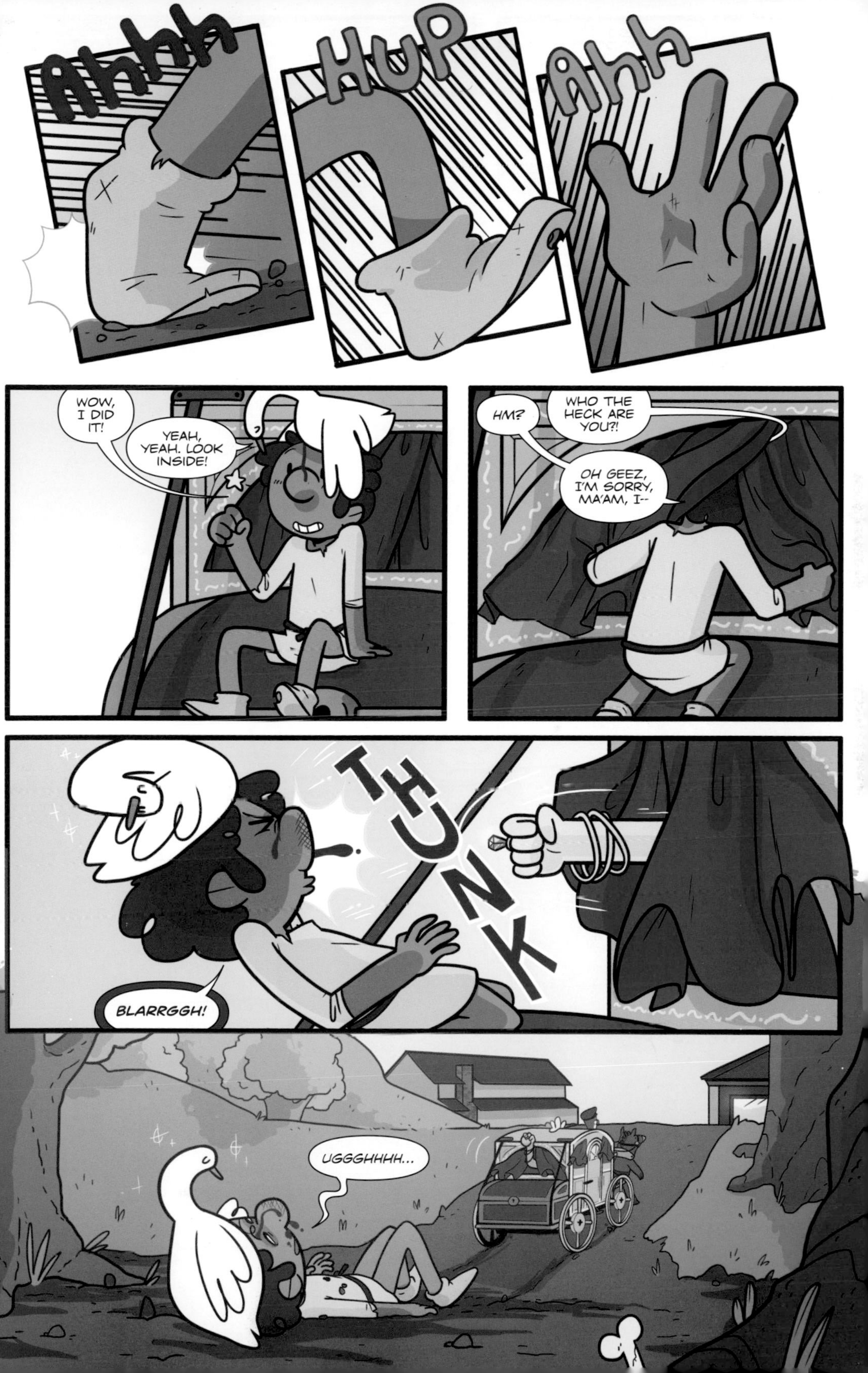
AHHH
HUP
AHH
WOW, I DID IT!
YEAH, YEAH. LOOK INSIDE!
HM?
WHO THE HECK ARE YOU?!
OH GEEZ, I'M SORRY, MA'AM, I--
THUNK
BLARRGGH!
UGGGHHHH...

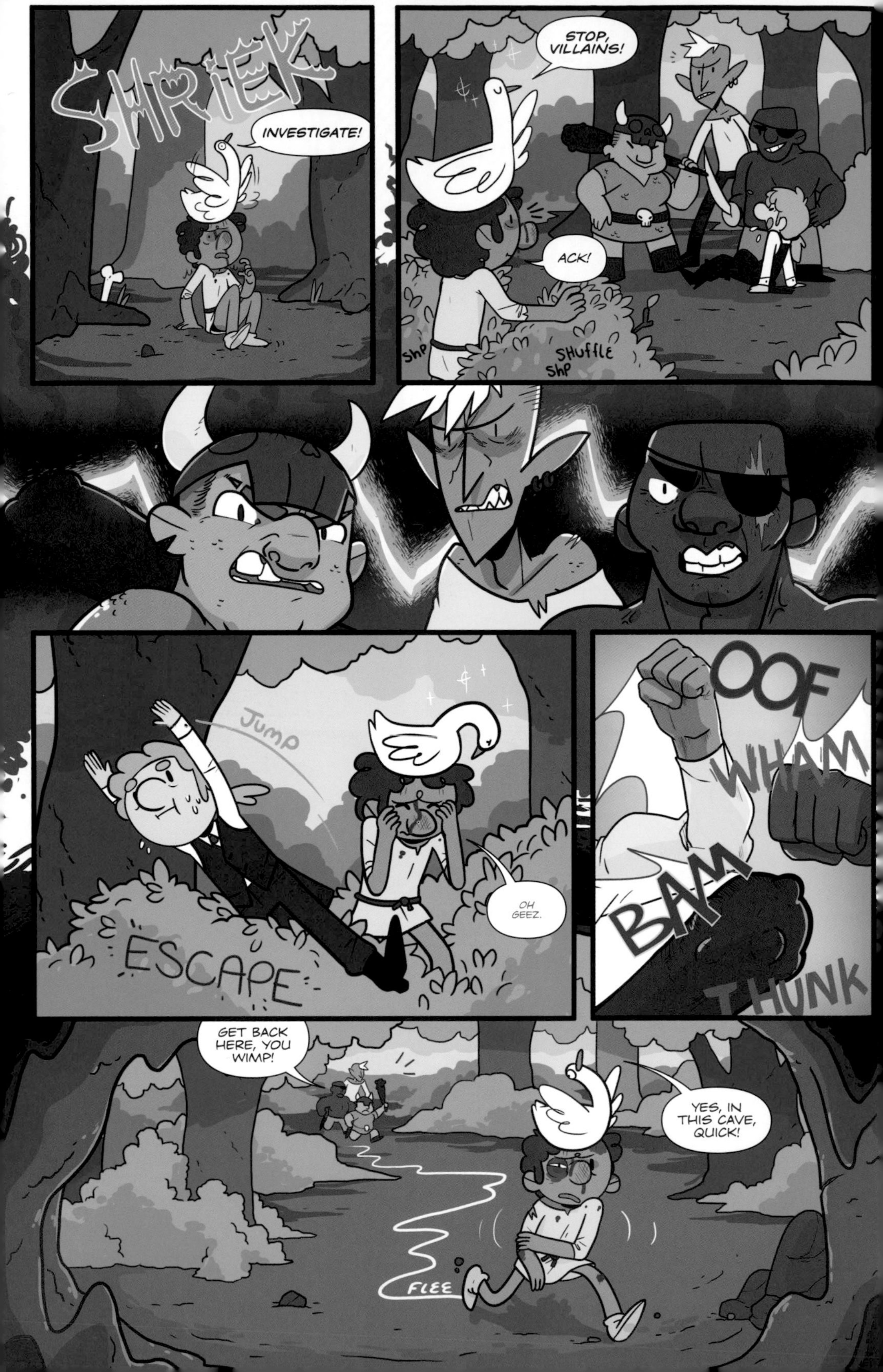
SHRIEK
INVESTIGATE!
STOP, VILLAINS!
ACK!
SHP
SHUFFLE
SHP
JUMP
ESCAPE
OH GEEZ.
OOF
WHAM
BAM
THUNK
GET BACK HERE, YOU WIMP!
YES, IN THIS CAVE, QUICK!
FLEE

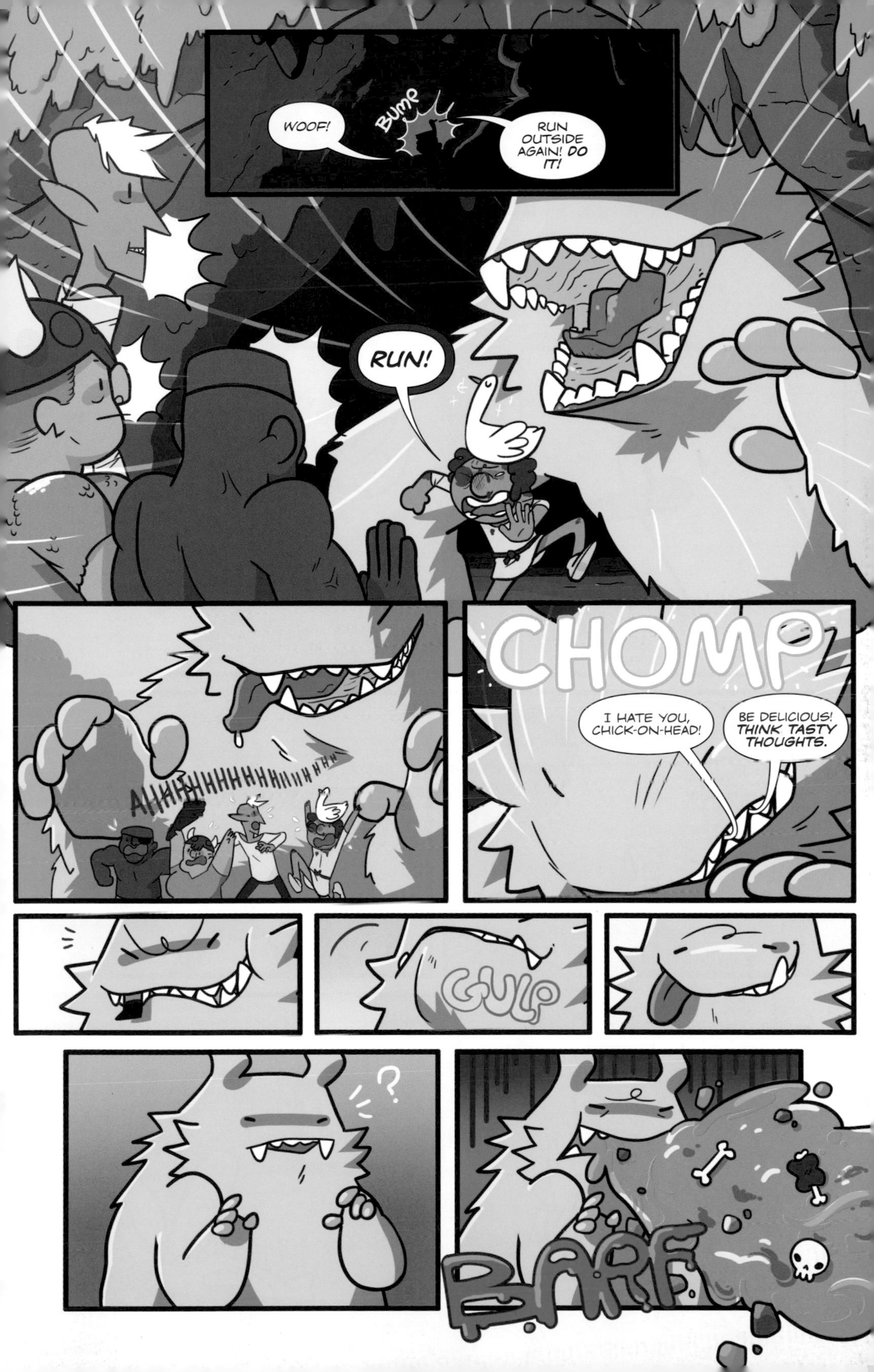
WOOF!
BUMP
RUN OUTSIDE AGAIN! *DO IT!*
RUN!
AHHHHHHHHHHHHHHHHHH
CHOMP
I HATE YOU, CHICK-ON-HEAD!
BE DELICIOUS! *THINK TASTY THOUGHTS.*
GULP
?
BARF

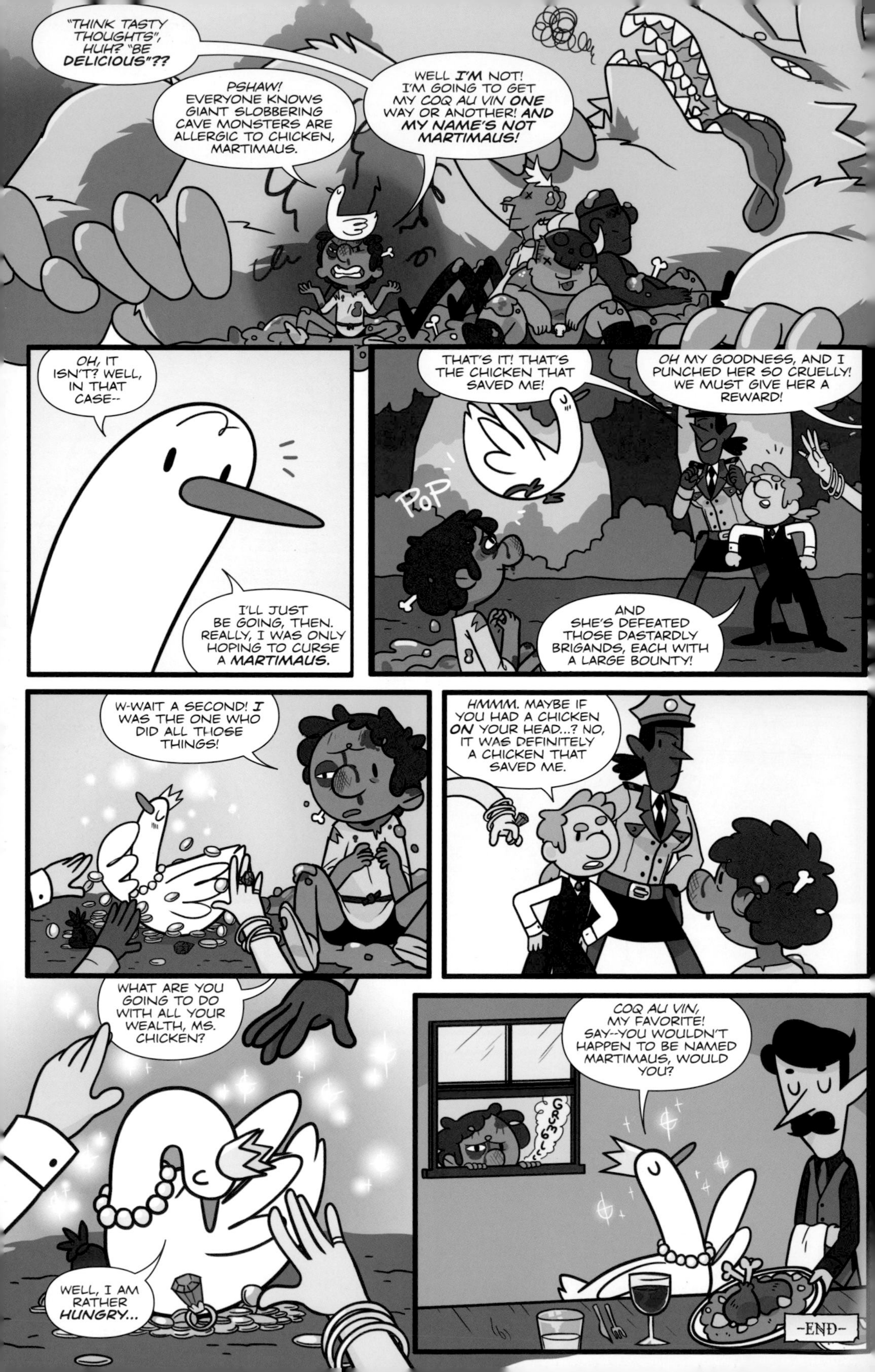

"THINK TASTY THOUGHTS", HUH? "BE DELICIOUS"??
PSHAW! EVERYONE KNOWS GIANT SLOBBERING CAVE MONSTERS ARE ALLERGIC TO CHICKEN, MARTIMAUS.
WELL I'M NOT! I'M GOING TO GET MY COQ AU VIN ONE WAY OR ANOTHER! AND MY NAME'S NOT MARTIMAUS!
OH, IT ISN'T? WELL, IN THAT CASE--
I'LL JUST BE GOING, THEN. REALLY, I WAS ONLY HOPING TO CURSE A MARTIMAUS.
POP
THAT'S IT! THAT'S THE CHICKEN THAT SAVED ME!
OH MY GOODNESS, AND I PUNCHED HER SO CRUELLY! WE MUST GIVE HER A REWARD!
AND SHE'S DEFEATED THOSE DASTARDLY BRIGANDS, EACH WITH A LARGE BOUNTY!
W-WAIT A SECOND! I WAS THE ONE WHO DID ALL THOSE THINGS!
HMMM. MAYBE IF YOU HAD A CHICKEN ON YOUR HEAD...? NO, IT WAS DEFINITELY A CHICKEN THAT SAVED ME.
WHAT ARE YOU GOING TO DO WITH ALL YOUR WEALTH, MS. CHICKEN?
WELL, I AM RATHER HUNGRY...
GRGGL
COQ AU VIN, MY FAVORITE! SAY--YOU WOULDN'T HAPPEN TO BE NAMED MARTIMAUS, WOULD YOU?
-END-

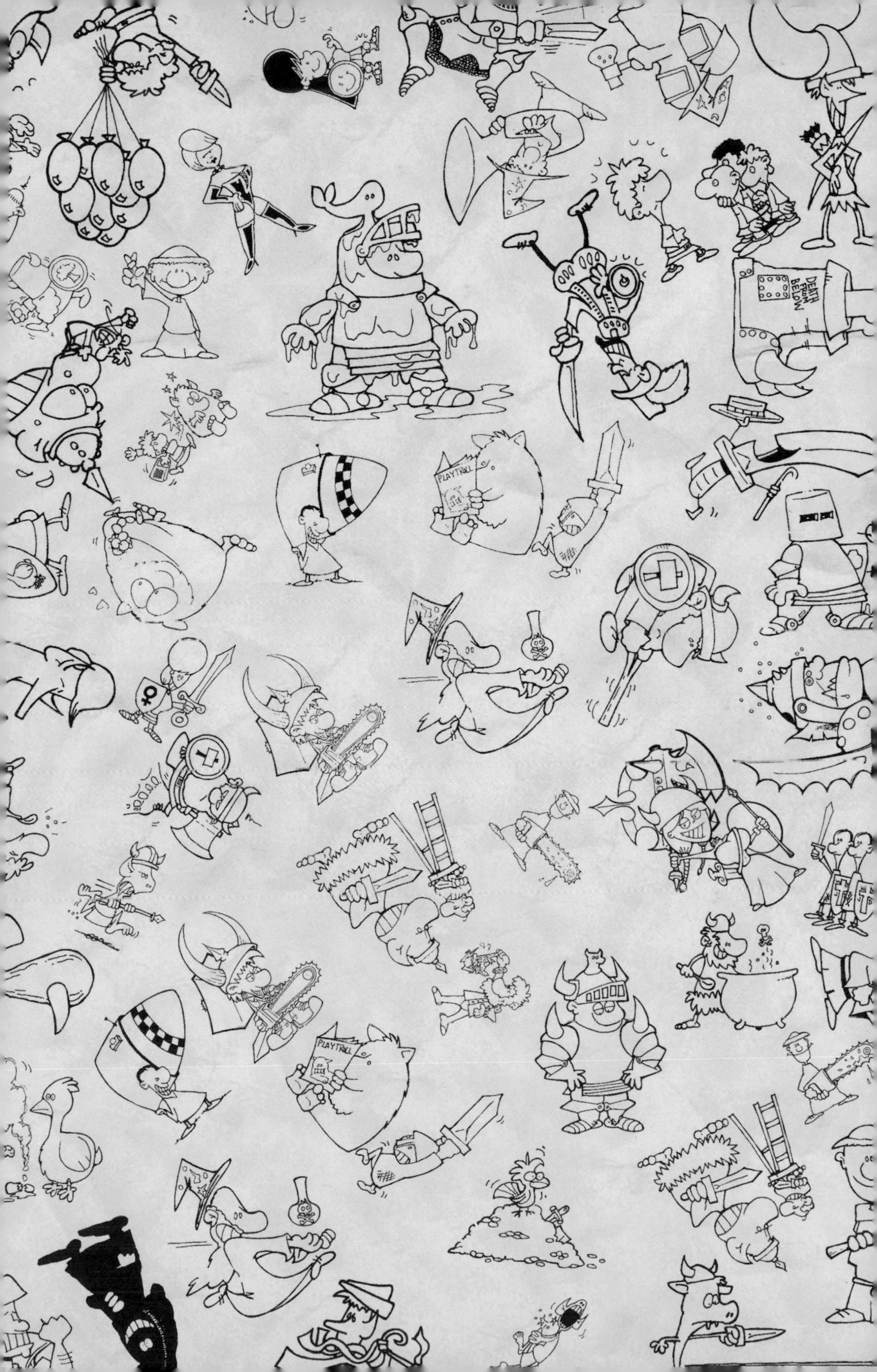
DEATH FROM BELOW
PLAYTROLL
PLAYTROLL

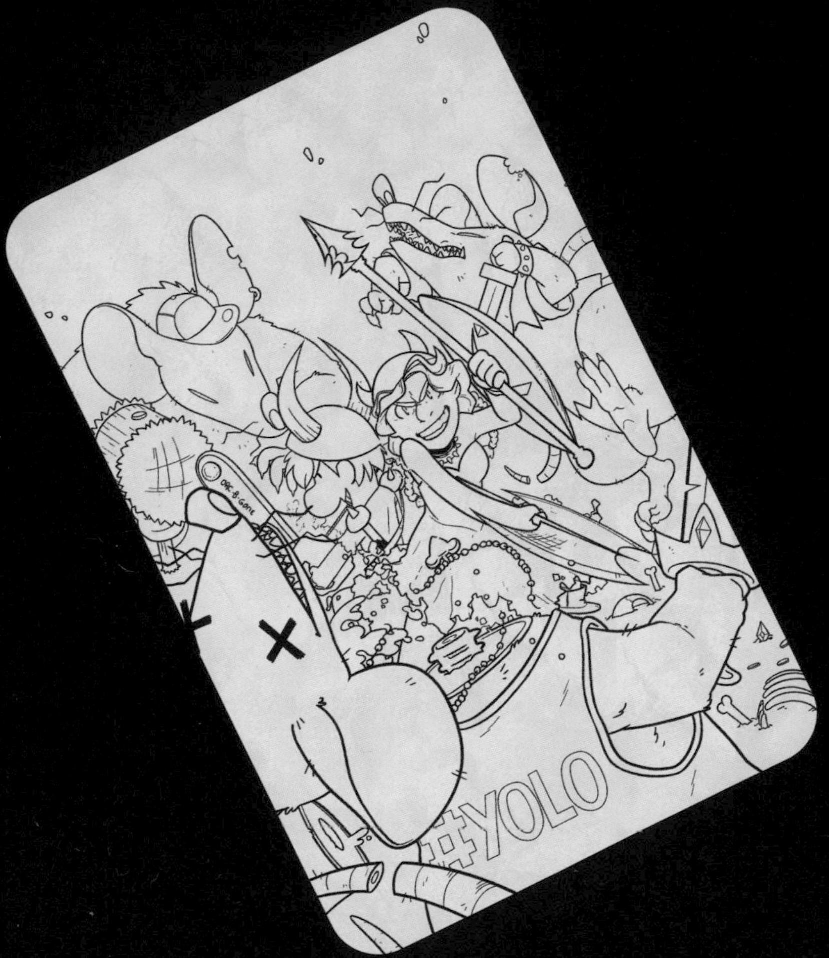
ORC-B-GONE
#YOLO

CHAPTER SIX

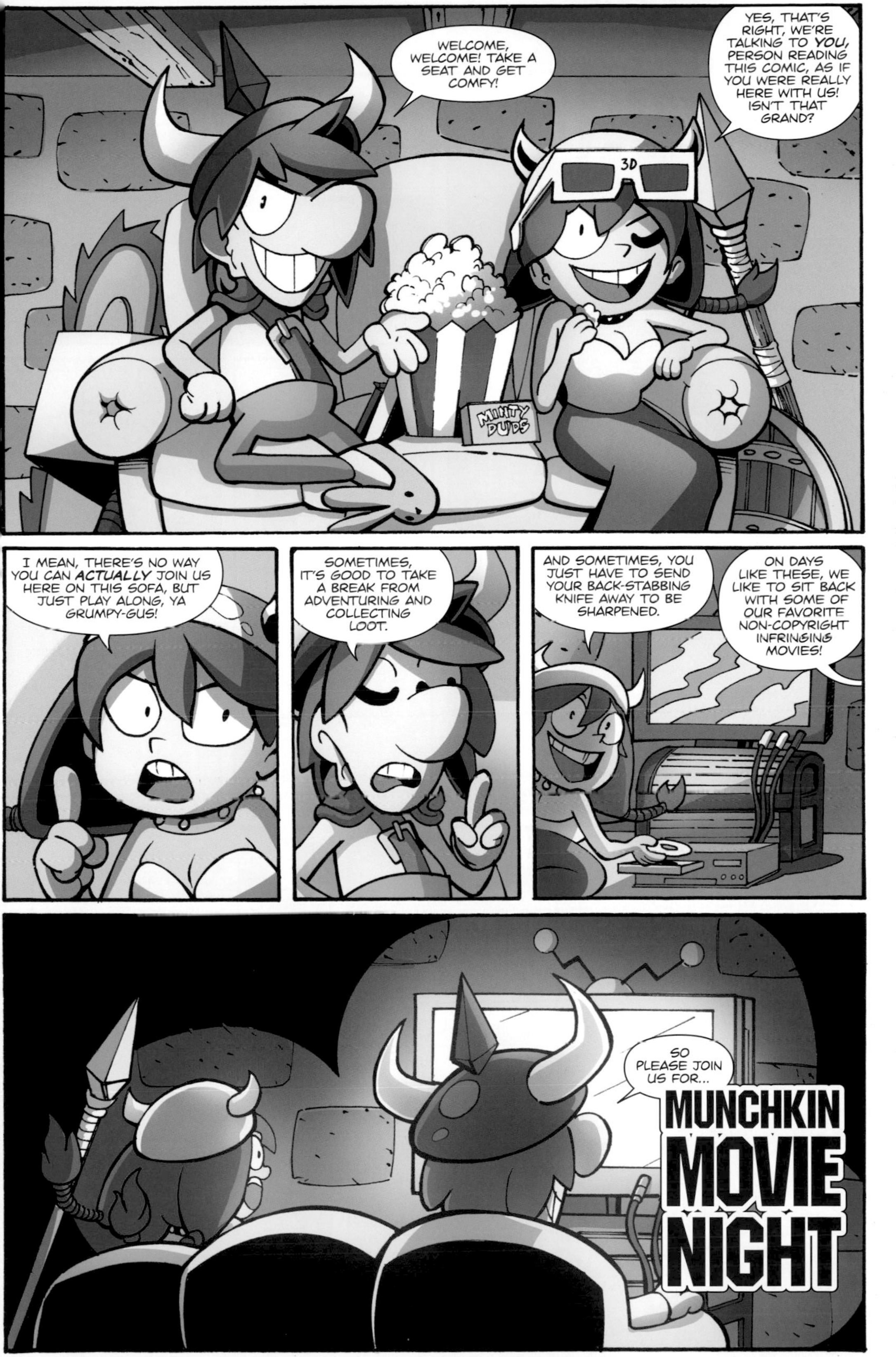
WELCOME, WELCOME! TAKE A SEAT AND GET COMFY!
YES, THAT'S RIGHT, WE'RE TALKING TO YOU, PERSON READING THIS COMIC, AS IF YOU WERE REALLY HERE WITH US! ISN'T THAT GRAND?
3D
MINTY DUDS
I MEAN, THERE'S NO WAY YOU CAN ACTUALLY JOIN US HERE ON THIS SOFA, BUT JUST PLAY ALONG, YA GRUMPY-GUS!
SOMETIMES, IT'S GOOD TO TAKE A BREAK FROM ADVENTURING AND COLLECTING LOOT.
AND SOMETIMES, YOU JUST HAVE TO SEND YOUR BACK-STABBING KNIFE AWAY TO BE SHARPENED.
ON DAYS LIKE THESE, WE LIKE TO SIT BACK WITH SOME OF OUR FAVORITE NON-COPYRIGHT INFRINGING MOVIES!
SO PLEASE JOIN US FOR...
MUNCHKIN MOVIE NIGHT

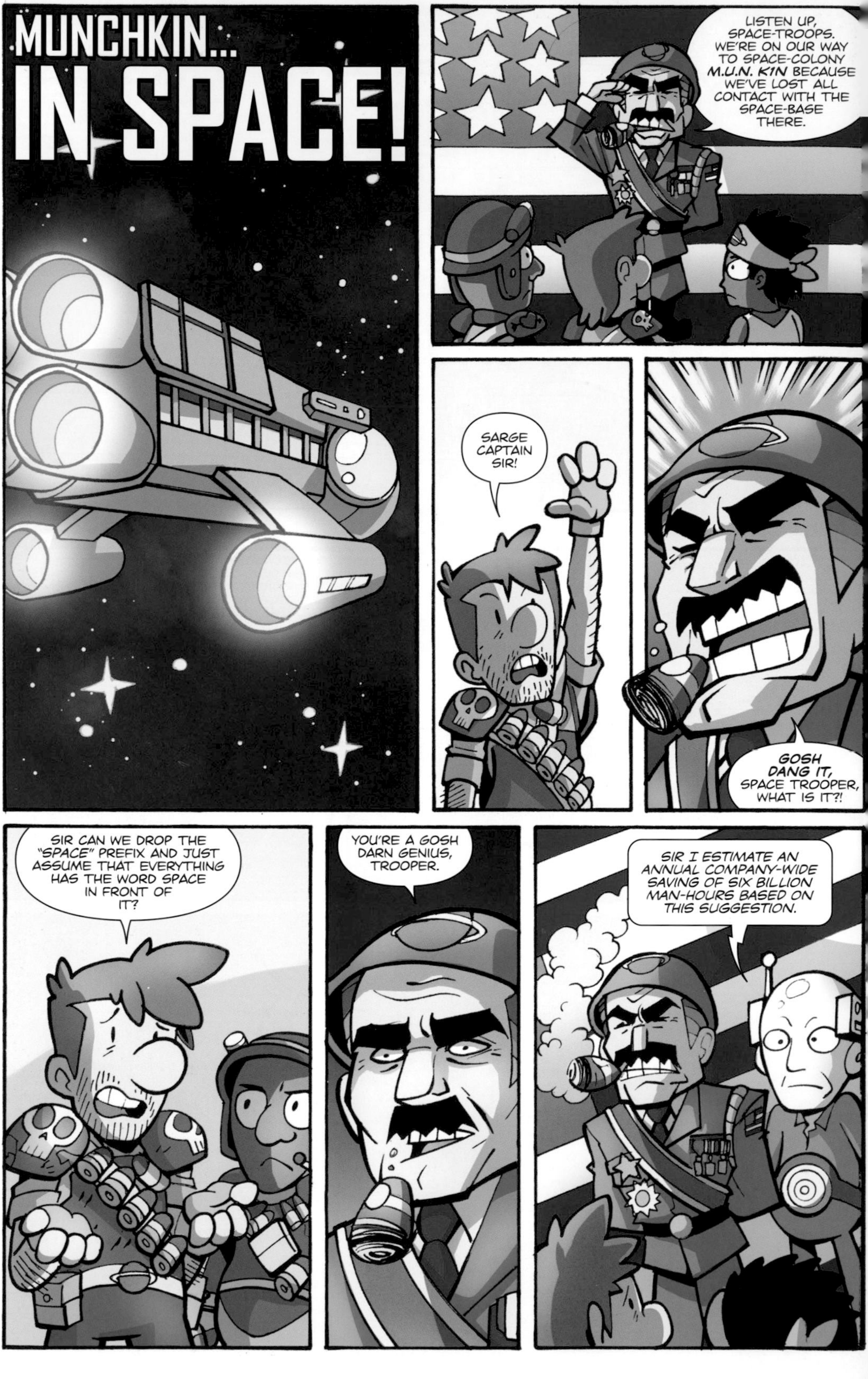
MUNCHKIN... IN SPACE!
LISTEN UP, SPACE-TROOPS. WE'RE ON OUR WAY TO SPACE-COLONY M.U.N. KIN BECAUSE WE'VE LOST ALL CONTACT WITH THE SPACE-BASE THERE.
SARGE CAPTAIN SIR!
GOSH DANG IT, SPACE TROOPER, WHAT IS IT?!
SIR CAN WE DROP THE "SPACE" PREFIX AND JUST ASSUME THAT EVERYTHING HAS THE WORD SPACE IN FRONT OF IT?
YOU'RE A GOSH DARN GENIUS, TROOPER.
SIR I ESTIMATE AN ANNUAL COMPANY-WIDE SAVING OF SIX BILLION MAN-HOURS BASED ON THIS SUGGESTION.

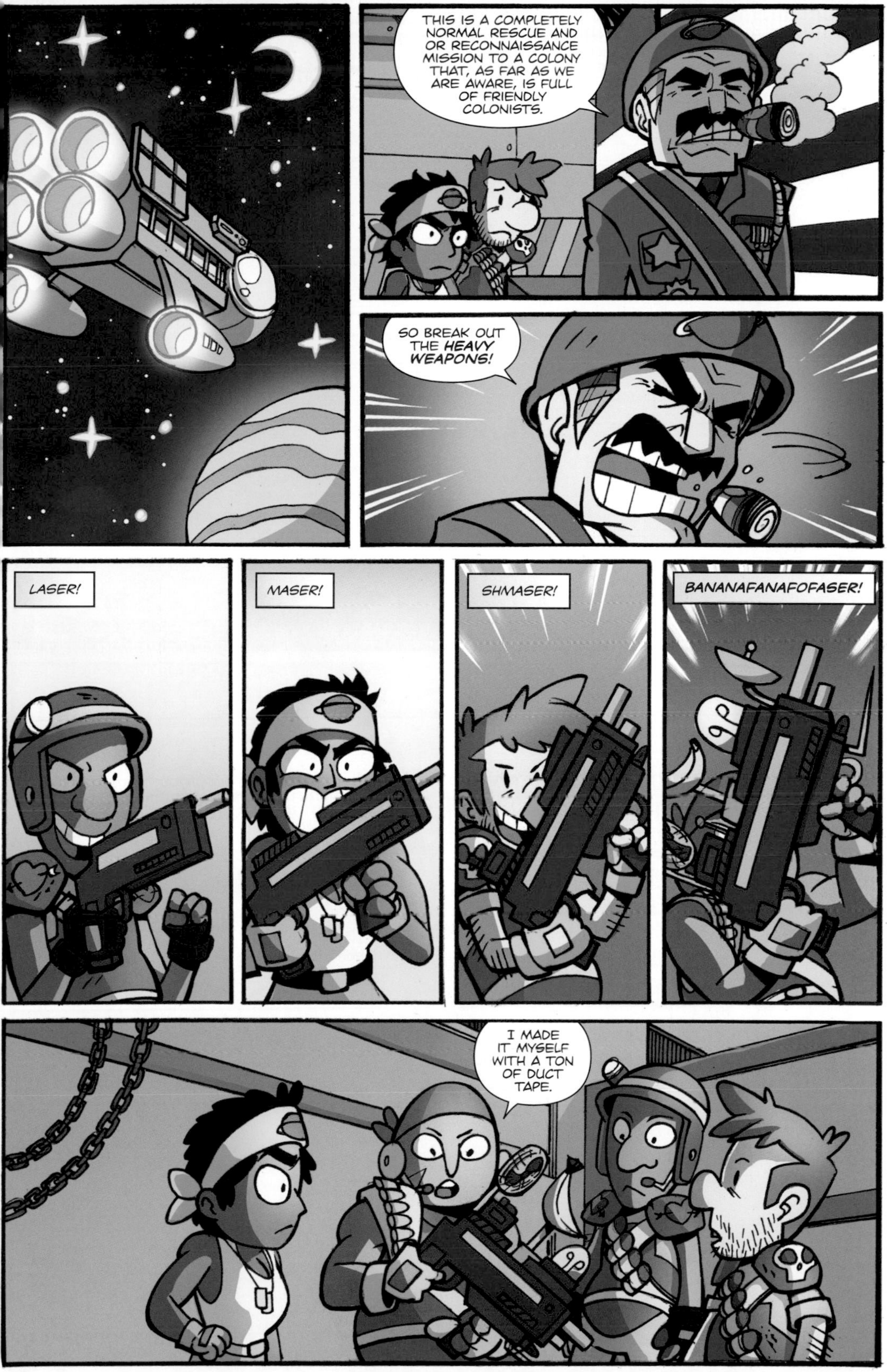
THIS IS A COMPLETELY NORMAL RESCUE AND OR RECONNAISSANCE MISSION TO A COLONY THAT, AS FAR AS WE ARE AWARE, IS FULL OF FRIENDLY COLONISTS.
SO BREAK OUT THE HEAVY WEAPONS!
LASER!
MASER!
SHMASER!
BANANAFANAFOFASER!
I MADE IT MYSELF WITH A TON OF DUCT TAPE.

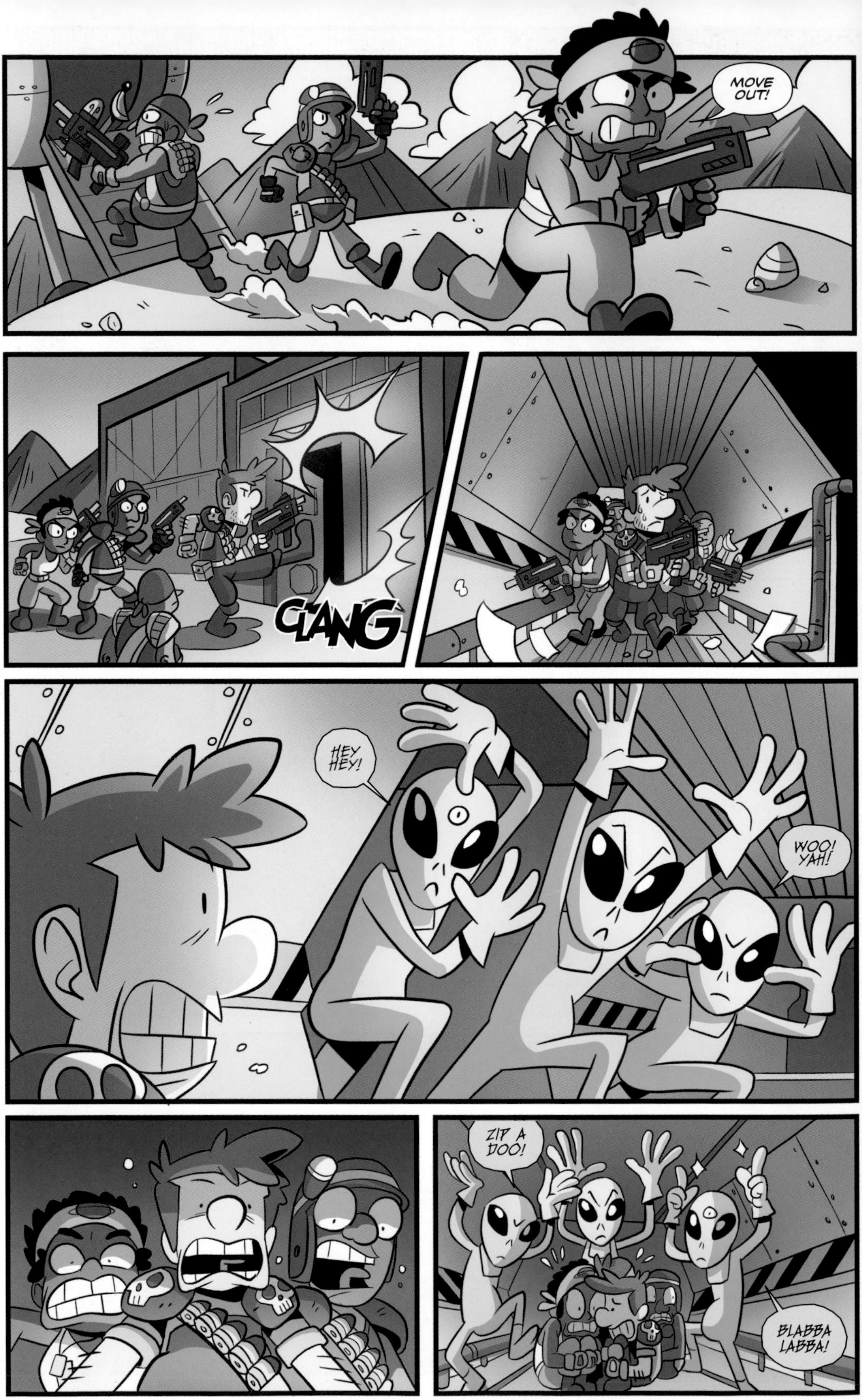
MOVE OUT!
CLANG
HEY HEY!
WOO! YAH!
ZIP A DOO!
BLABBA LABBA!

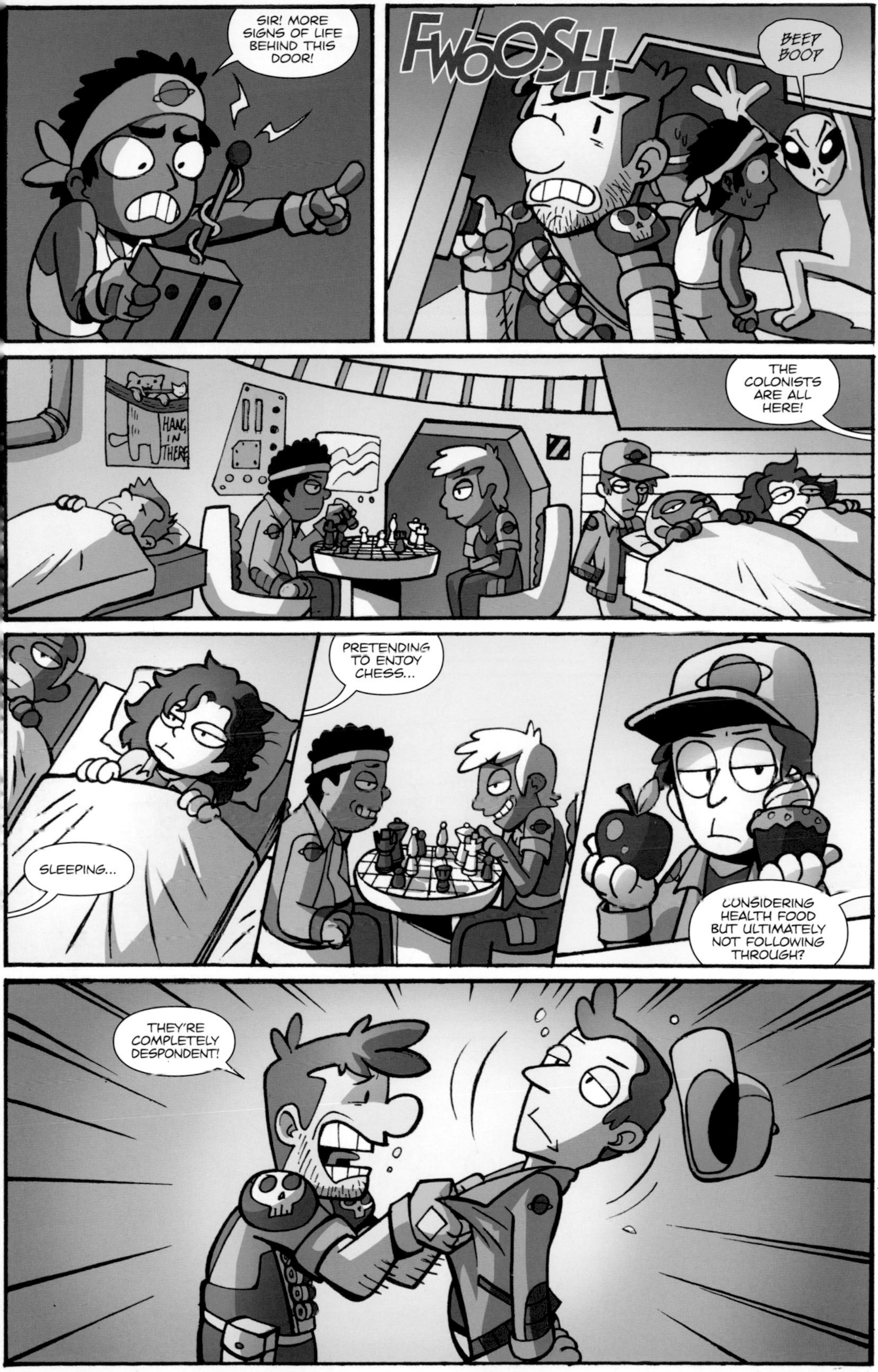
SIR! MORE SIGNS OF LIFE BEHIND THIS DOOR!
FWOOSH
BEEP BOOP
HANG IN THERE
THE COLONISTS ARE ALL HERE!
SLEEPING...
PRETENDING TO ENJOY CHESS...
CONSIDERING HEALTH FOOD BUT ULTIMATELY NOT FOLLOWING THROUGH?
THEY'RE COMPLETELY DESPONDENT!

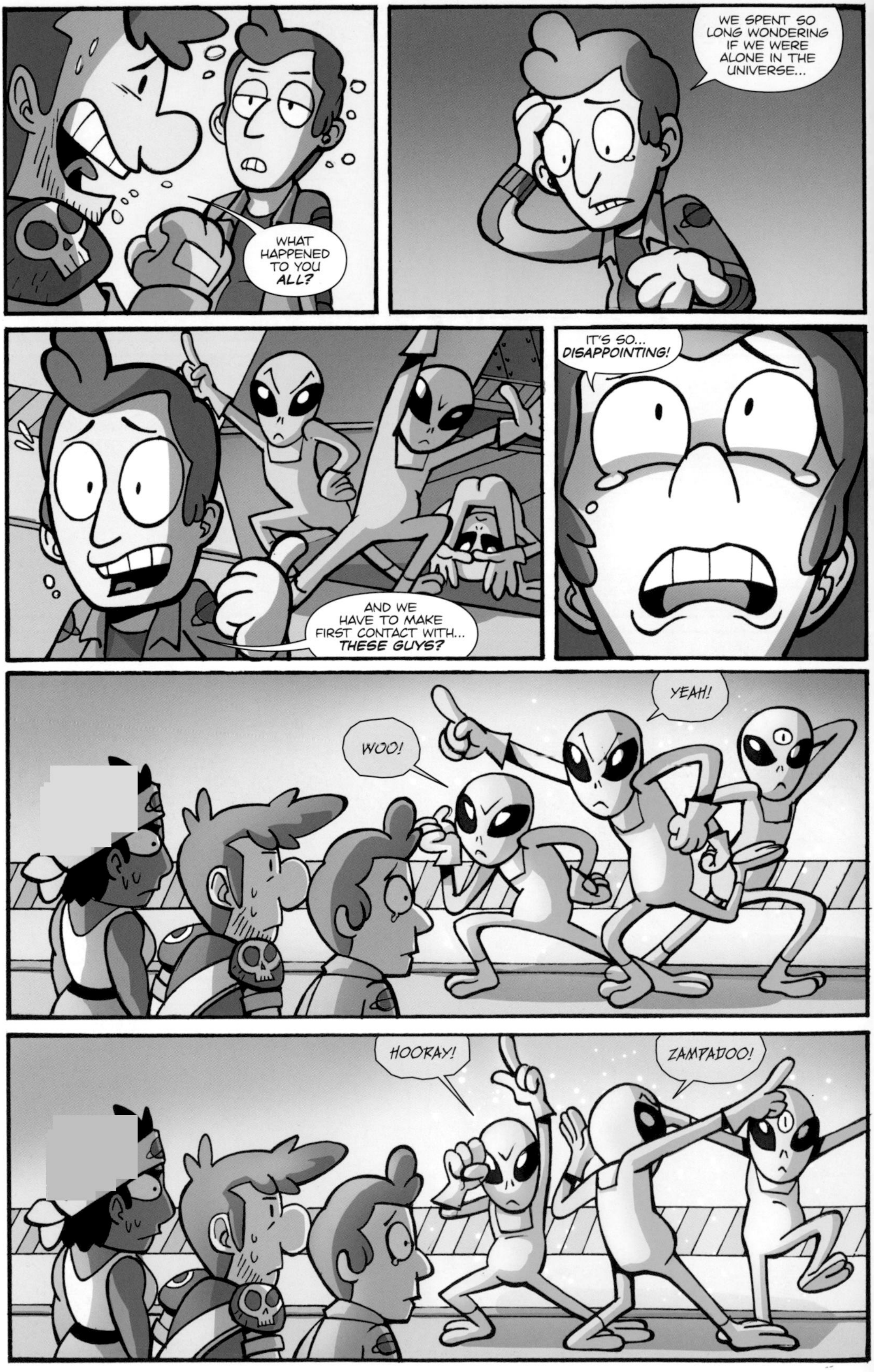
WHAT HAPPENED TO YOU ALL?
WE SPENT SO LONG WONDERING IF WE WERE ALONE IN THE UNIVERSE...
AND WE HAVE TO MAKE FIRST CONTACT WITH... THESE GUYS?
IT'S SO... DISAPPOINTING!
WOO!
YEAH!
HOORAY!
ZAMPADOO!

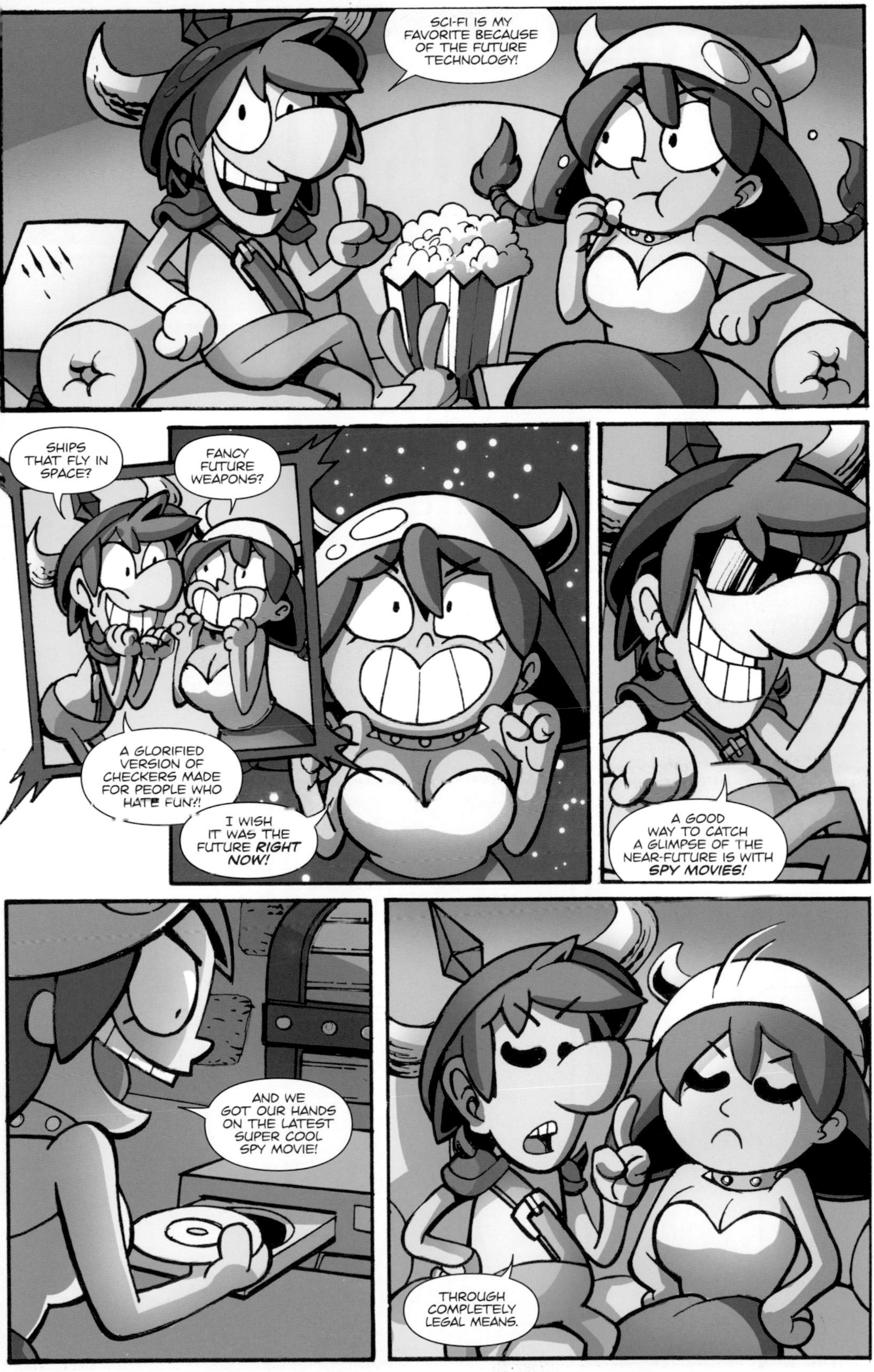
SCI-FI IS MY FAVORITE BECAUSE OF THE FUTURE TECHNOLOGY!
SHIPS THAT FLY IN SPACE?
FANCY FUTURE WEAPONS?
A GLORIFIED VERSION OF CHECKERS MADE FOR PEOPLE WHO HATE FUN?!
I WISH IT WAS THE FUTURE RIGHT NOW!
A GOOD WAY TO CATCH A GLIMPSE OF THE NEAR-FUTURE IS WITH SPY MOVIES!
AND WE GOT OUR HANDS ON THE LATEST SUPER COOL SPY MOVIE!
THROUGH COMPLETELY LEGAL MEANS.

MUNCHKIN: IMPOSSIBLER

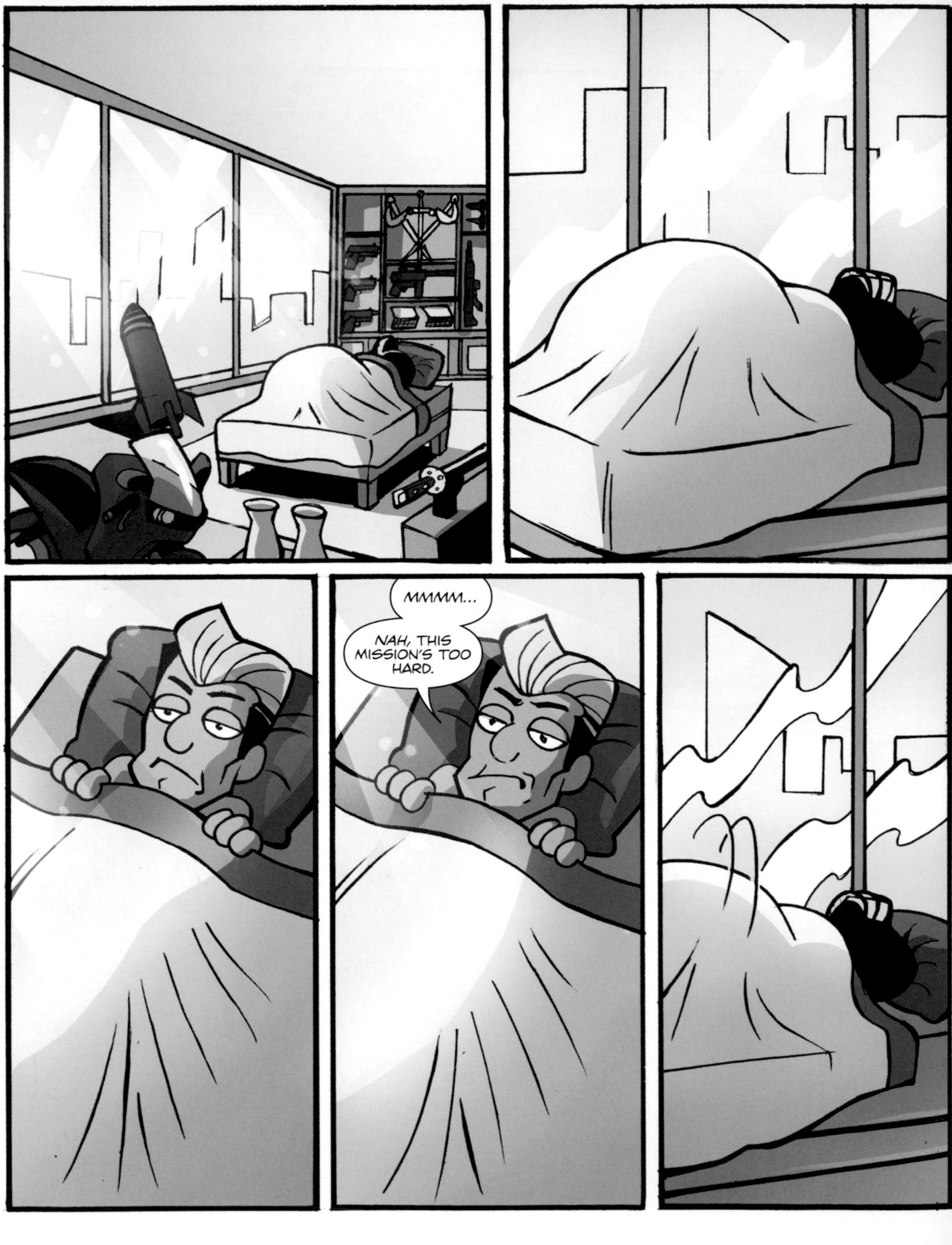
MMMM...
NAH, THIS MISSION'S TOO HARD.

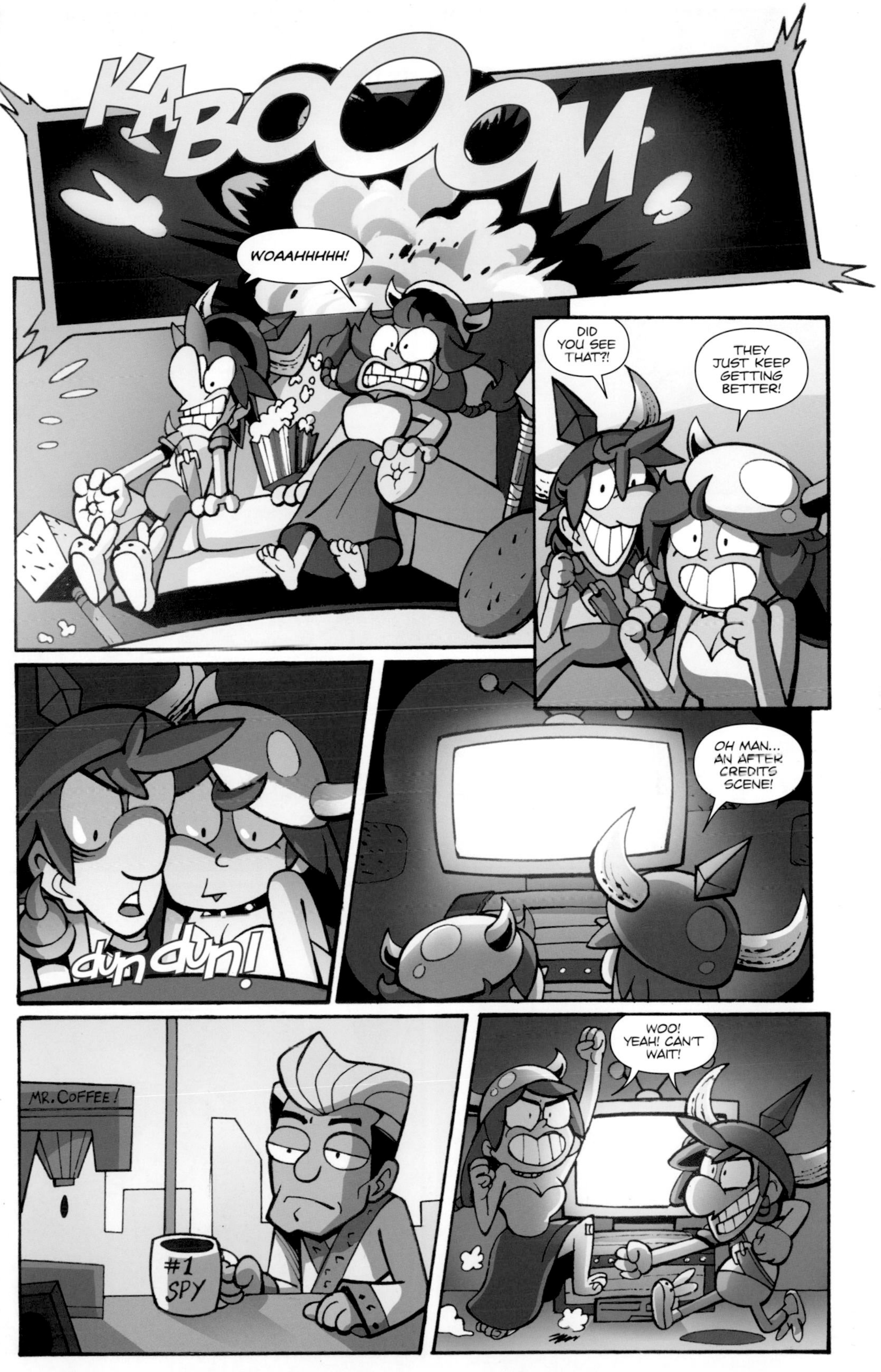
KABOOOM
WOAAHHHHH!
DID YOU SEE THAT?!
THEY JUST KEEP GETTING BETTER!
dun dun!
OH MAN... AN AFTER CREDITS SCENE!
MR. COFFEE!
#1 SPY
WOO! YEAH! CAN'T WAIT!

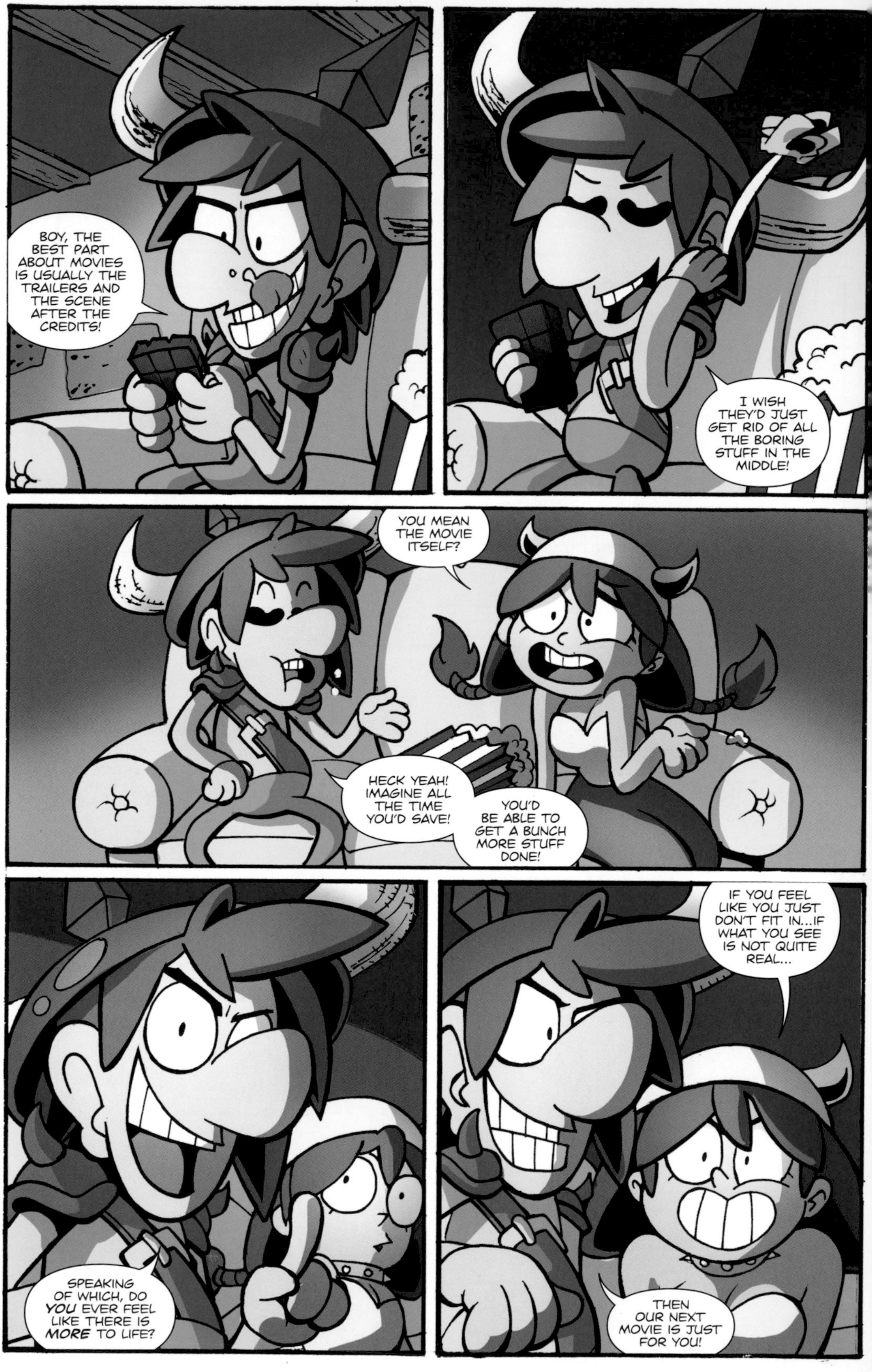
BOY, THE BEST PART ABOUT MOVIES IS USUALLY THE TRAILERS AND THE SCENE AFTER THE CREDITS!
I WISH THEY'D JUST GET RID OF ALL THE BORING STUFF IN THE MIDDLE!
YOU MEAN THE MOVIE ITSELF?
HECK YEAH! IMAGINE ALL THE TIME YOU'D SAVE!
YOU'D BE ABLE TO GET A BUNCH MORE STUFF DONE!
SPEAKING OF WHICH, DO *YOU* EVER FEEL LIKE THERE IS *MORE* TO LIFE?
IF YOU FEEL LIKE YOU JUST DON'T FIT IN...IF WHAT YOU SEE IS NOT QUITE REAL...
THEN OUR NEXT MOVIE IS JUST FOR YOU!

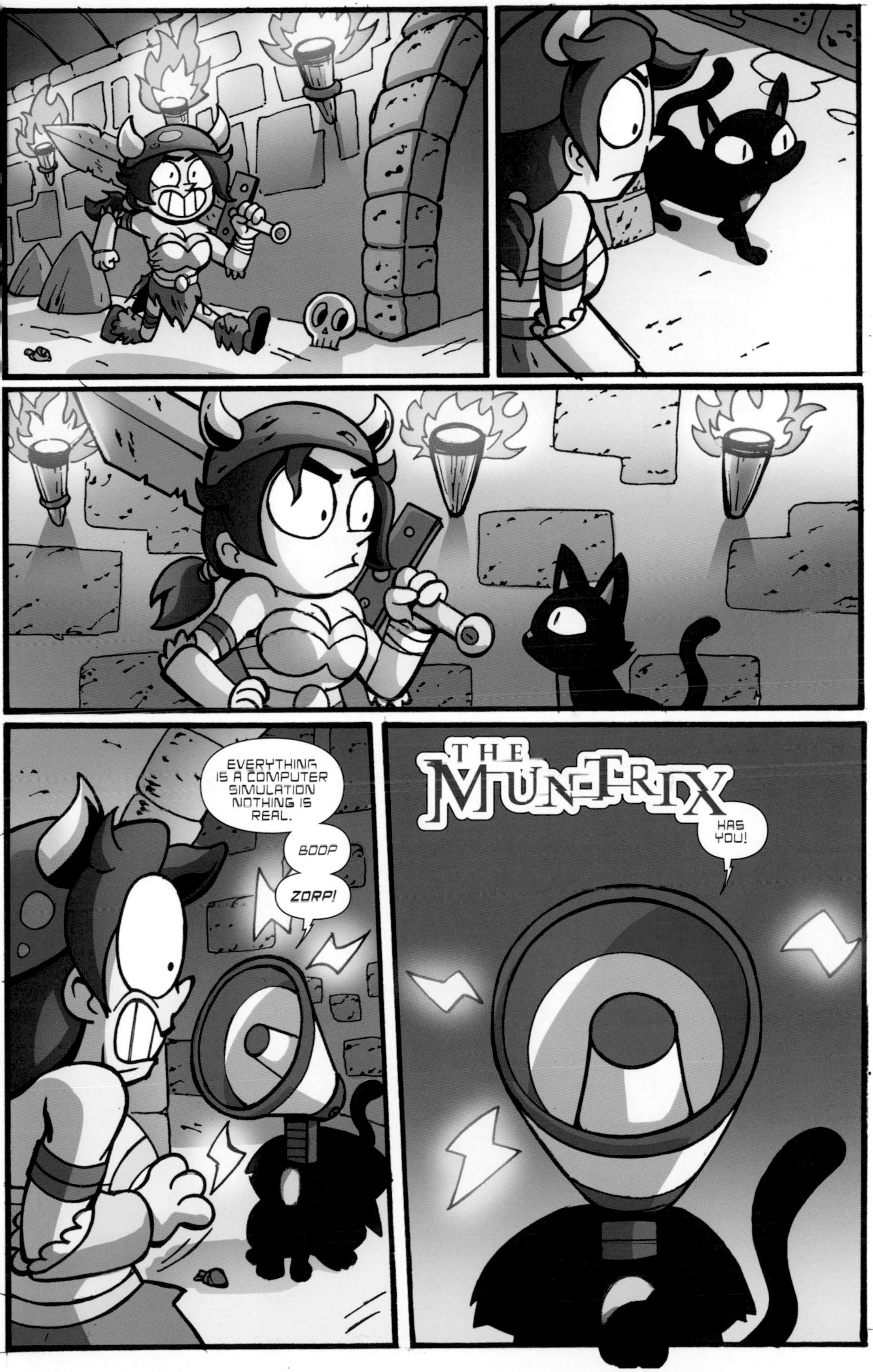
EVERYTHING IS A COMPUTER SIMULATION NOTHING IS REAL.
BOOP
ZORP!
THE MUNTRIX
HAS YOU!

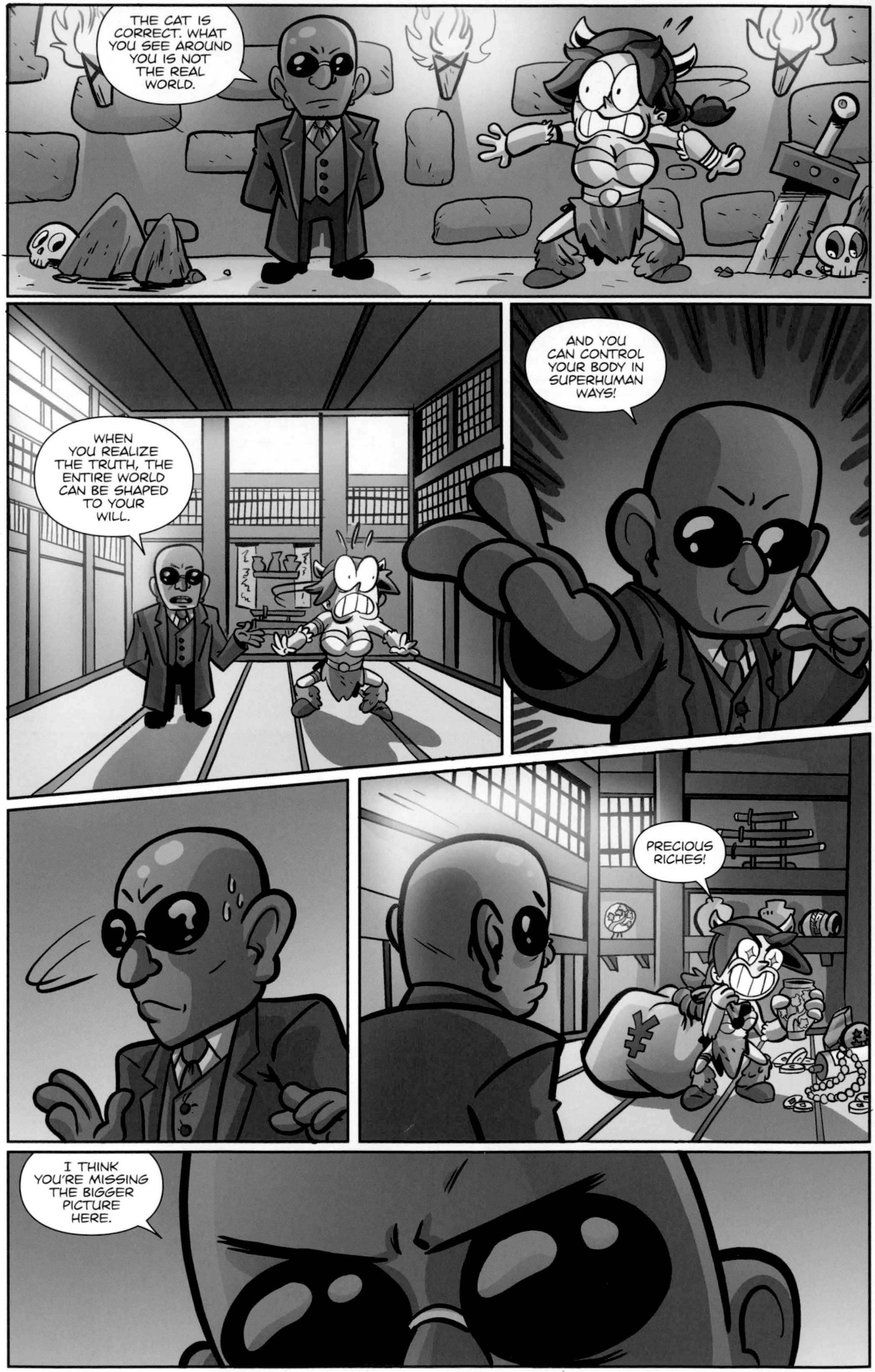
THE CAT IS CORRECT. WHAT YOU SEE AROUND YOU IS NOT THE REAL WORLD.
WHEN YOU REALIZE THE TRUTH, THE ENTIRE WORLD CAN BE SHAPED TO YOUR WILL.
AND YOU CAN CONTROL YOUR BODY IN SUPERHUMAN WAYS!
PRECIOUS RICHES!
I THINK YOU'RE MISSING THE BIGGER PICTURE HERE.

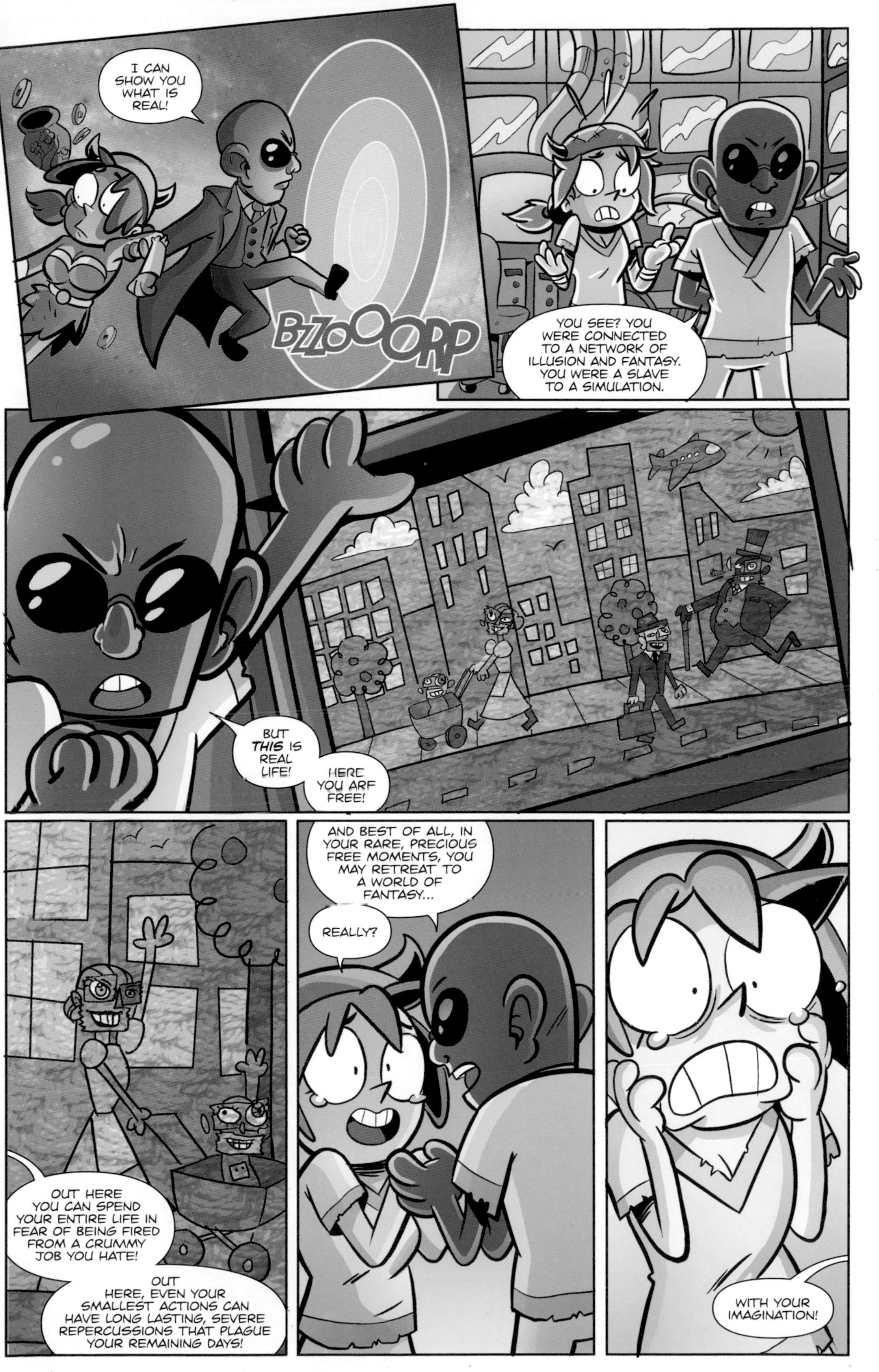
I CAN SHOW YOU WHAT IS REAL!
BZZOOOORP
YOU SEE? YOU WERE CONNECTED TO A NETWORK OF ILLUSION AND FANTASY. YOU WERE A SLAVE TO A SIMULATION.
BUT THIS IS REAL LIFE!
HERE YOU ARE FREE!
OUT HERE YOU CAN SPEND YOUR ENTIRE LIFE IN FEAR OF BEING FIRED FROM A CRUMMY JOB YOU HATE!
OUT HERE, EVEN YOUR SMALLEST ACTIONS CAN HAVE LONG LASTING, SEVERE REPERCUSSIONS THAT PLAGUE YOUR REMAINING DAYS!
AND BEST OF ALL, IN YOUR RARE, PRECIOUS FREE MOMENTS, YOU MAY RETREAT TO A WORLD OF FANTASY...
REALLY?
WITH YOUR IMAGINATION!

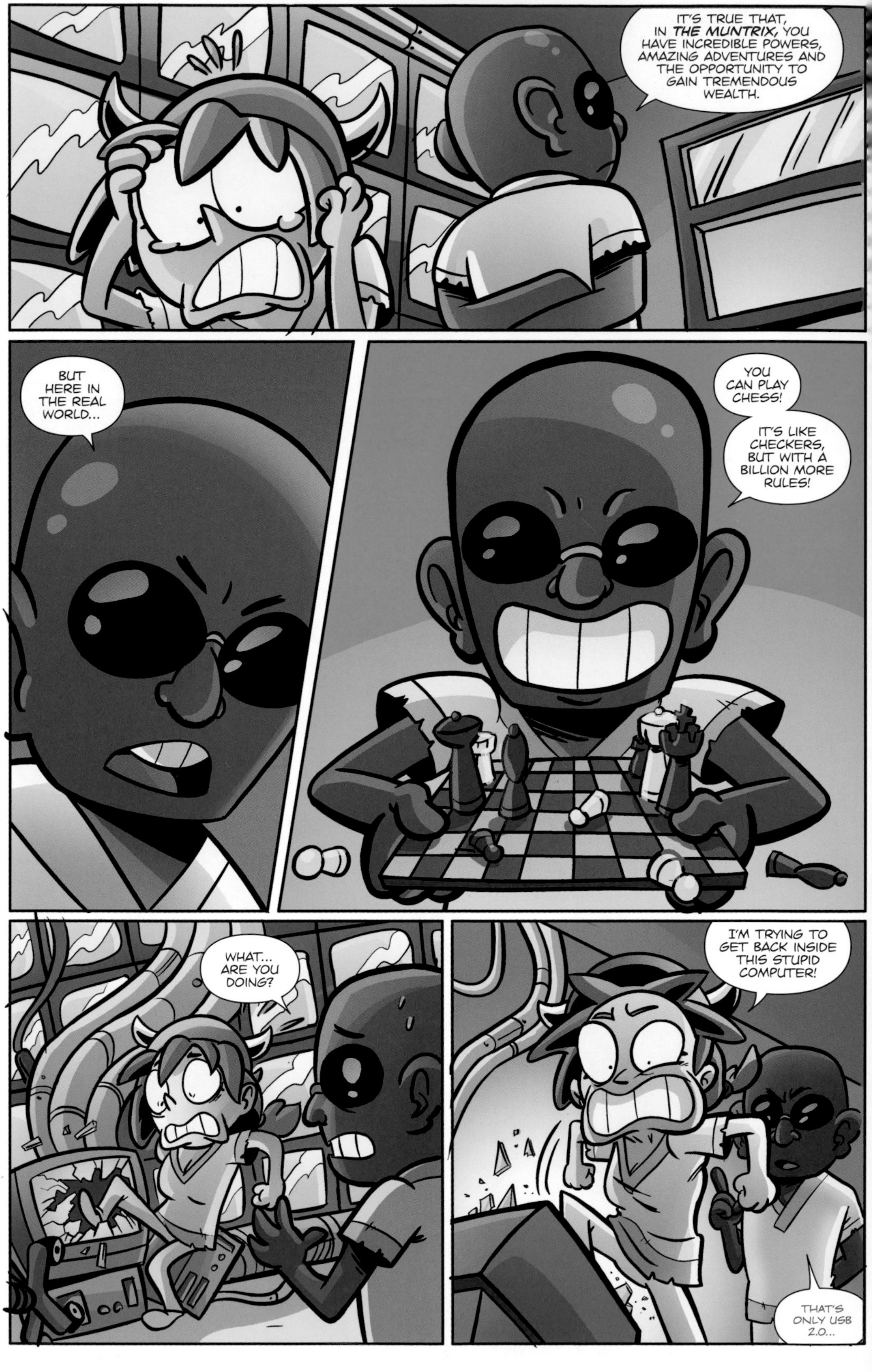
IT'S TRUE THAT, IN THE MUNTRIX, YOU HAVE INCREDIBLE POWERS, AMAZING ADVENTURES AND THE OPPORTUNITY TO GAIN TREMENDOUS WEALTH.
BUT HERE IN THE REAL WORLD...
YOU CAN PLAY CHESS!
IT'S LIKE CHECKERS, BUT WITH A BILLION MORE RULES!
WHAT... ARE YOU DOING?
I'M TRYING TO GET BACK INSIDE THIS STUPID COMPUTER!
THAT'S ONLY USB 2.0...

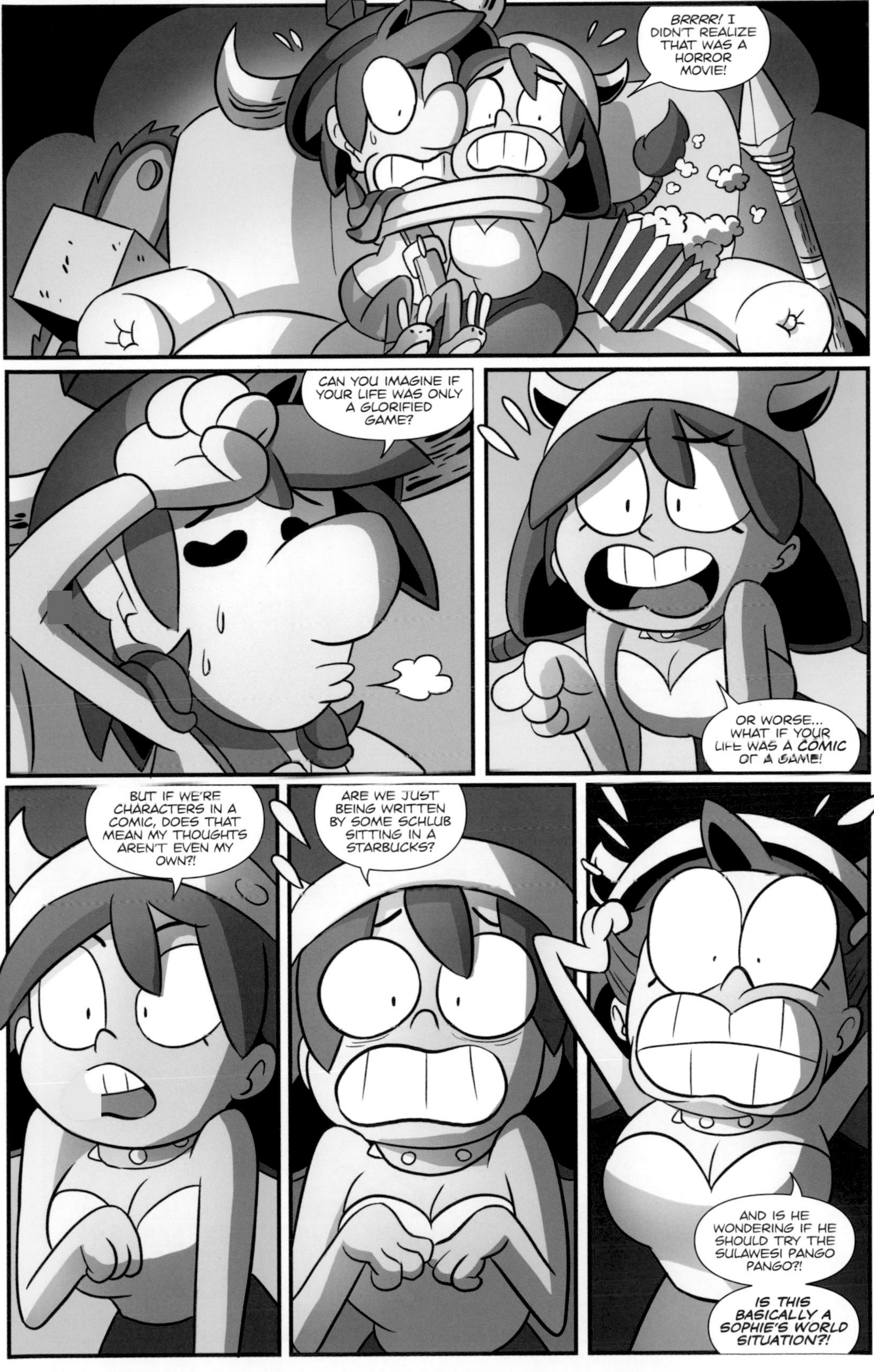
BRRRR! I DIDN'T REALIZE THAT WAS A HORROR MOVIE!
CAN YOU IMAGINE IF YOUR LIFE WAS ONLY A GLORIFIED GAME?
OR WORSE... WHAT IF YOUR LIFE WAS A COMIC OF A GAME!
BUT IF WE'RE CHARACTERS IN A COMIC, DOES THAT MEAN MY THOUGHTS AREN'T EVEN MY OWN?!
ARE WE JUST BEING WRITTEN BY SOME SCHLUB SITTING IN A STARBUCKS?
AND IS HE WONDERING IF HE SHOULD TRY THE SULAWESI PANGO PANGO?!
IS THIS BASICALLY A SOPHIE'S WORLD SITUATION?!

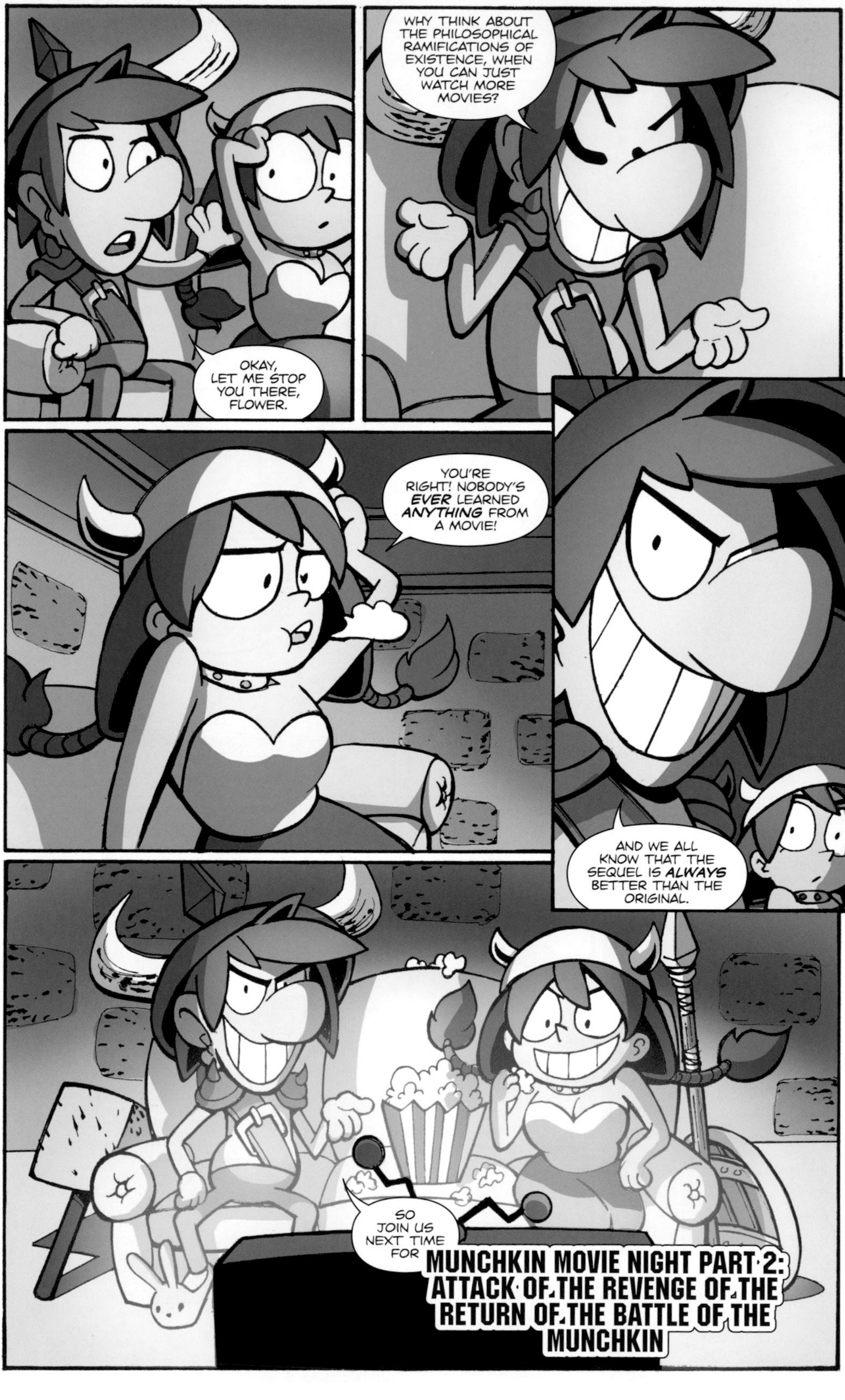
OKAY, LET ME STOP YOU THERE, FLOWER.
WHY THINK ABOUT THE PHILOSOPHICAL RAMIFICATIONS OF EXISTENCE, WHEN YOU CAN JUST WATCH MORE MOVIES?
YOU'RE RIGHT! NOBODY'S EVER LEARNED ANYTHING FROM A MOVIE!
AND WE ALL KNOW THAT THE SEQUEL IS ALWAYS BETTER THAN THE ORIGINAL.
SO JOIN US NEXT TIME FOR
MUNCHKIN MOVIE NIGHT PART 2: ATTACK OF THE REVENGE OF THE RETURN OF THE BATTLE OF THE MUNCHKIN

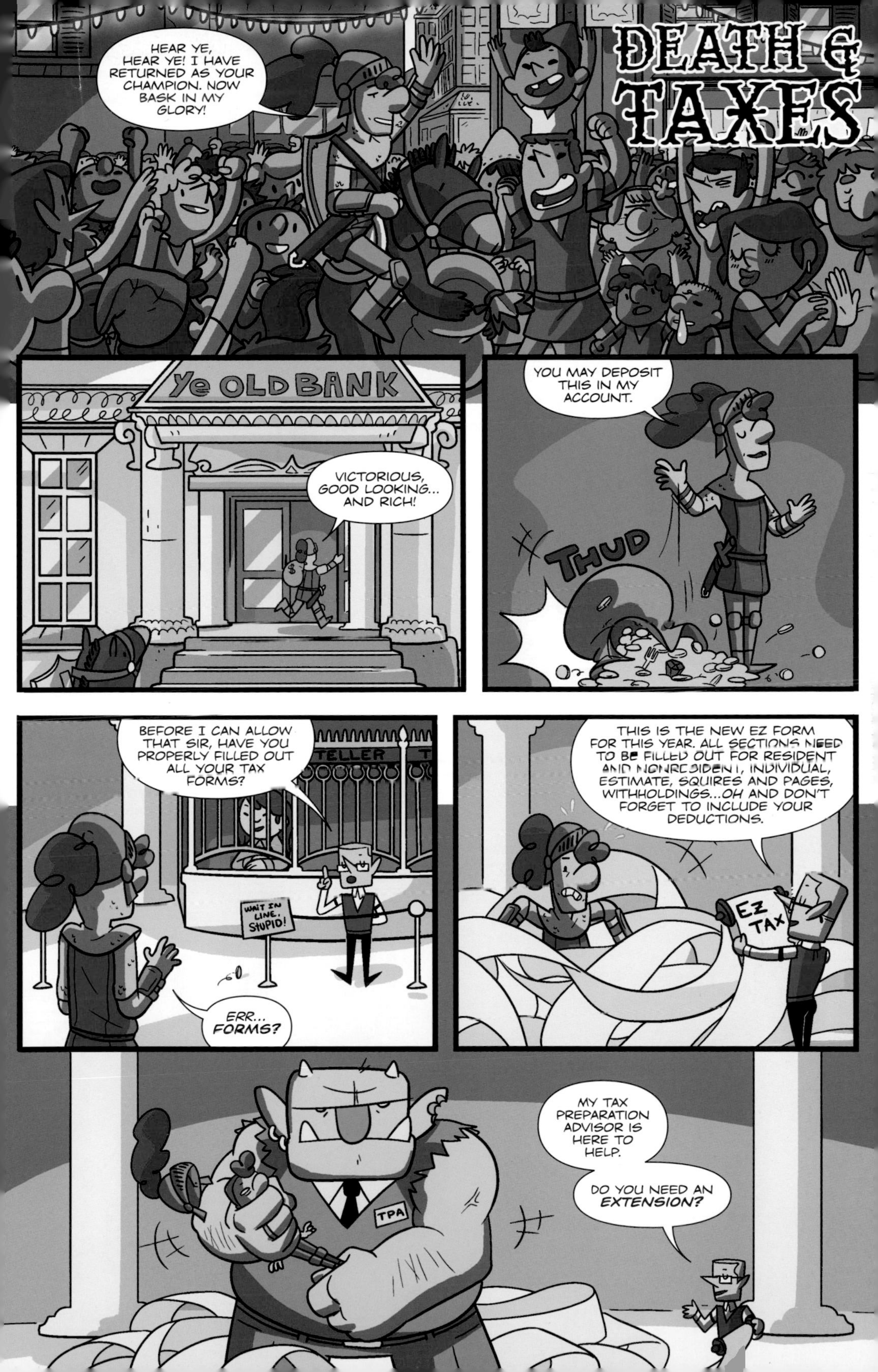
DEATH & TAXES
HEAR YE, HEAR YE! I HAVE RETURNED AS YOUR CHAMPION. NOW BASK IN MY GLORY!
Ye OLD BANK
VICTORIOUS, GOOD LOOKING... AND RICH!
YOU MAY DEPOSIT THIS IN MY ACCOUNT.
THUD
BEFORE I CAN ALLOW THAT SIR, HAVE YOU PROPERLY FILLED OUT ALL YOUR TAX FORMS?
TELLER
WAIT IN LINE, STUPID!
ERR... *FORMS?*
THIS IS THE NEW EZ FORM FOR THIS YEAR. ALL SECTIONS NEED TO BE FILLED OUT FOR RESIDENT AND NONRESIDENT, INDIVIDUAL, ESTIMATE, SQUIRES AND PAGES, WITHHOLDINGS...*OH* AND DON'T FORGET TO INCLUDE YOUR DEDUCTIONS.
EZ TAX
TPA
MY TAX PREPARATION ADVISOR IS HERE TO HELP.
DO YOU NEED AN *EXTENSION?*

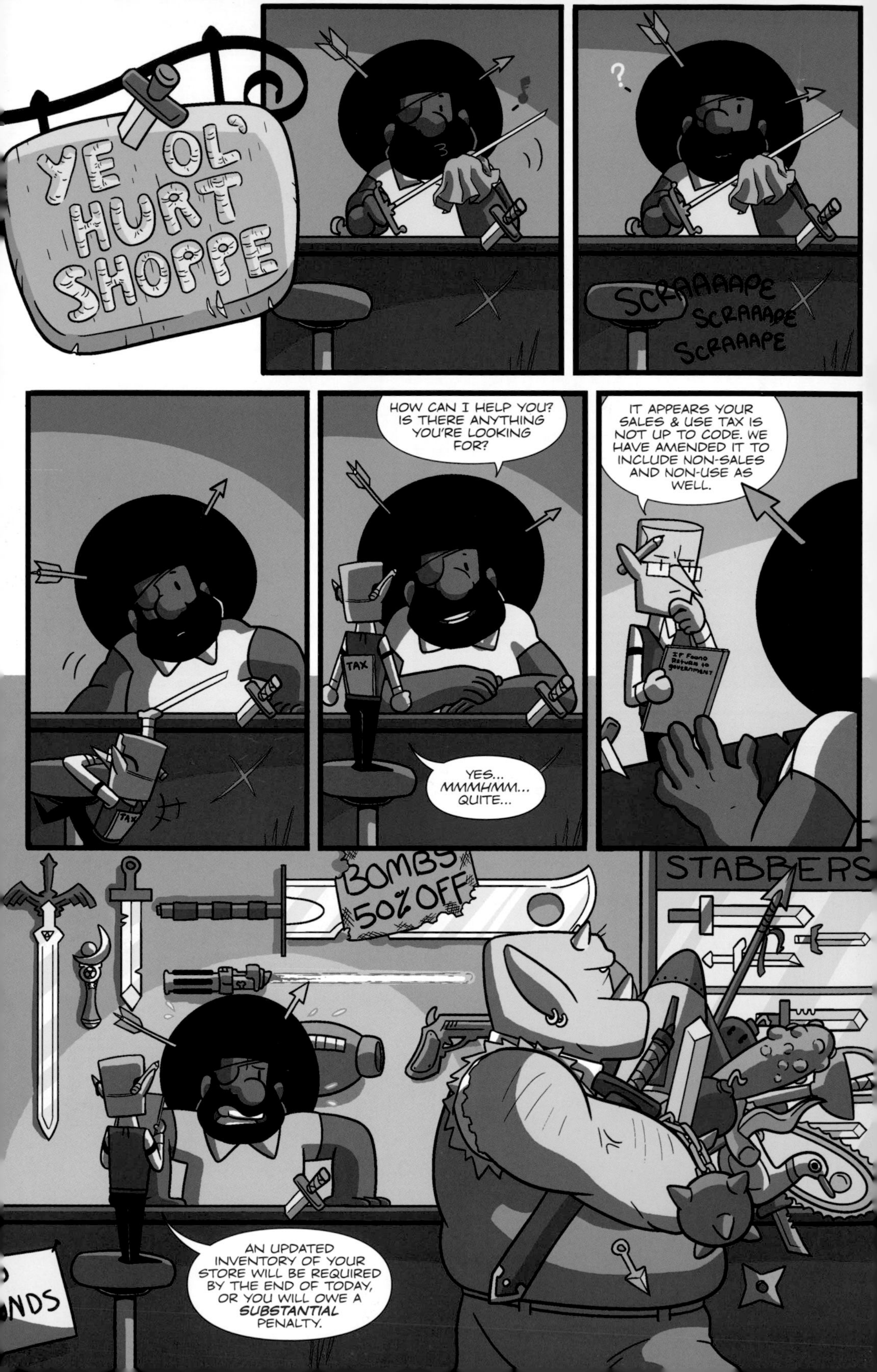
YE OL' HURT SHOPPE
SCRAAAAPE SCRAAAPE SCRAAAPE
HOW CAN I HELP YOU? IS THERE ANYTHING YOU'RE LOOKING FOR?
TAX
YES... MMMHMM... QUITE...
IT APPEARS YOUR SALES & USE TAX IS NOT UP TO CODE. WE HAVE AMENDED IT TO INCLUDE NON-SALES AND NON-USE AS WELL.
IF FOUND RETURN TO GOVERNMENT
BOMBS 50% OFF
STABBERS
AN UPDATED INVENTORY OF YOUR STORE WILL BE REQUIRED BY THE END OF TODAY, OR YOU WILL OWE A ***SUBSTANTIAL*** PENALTY.

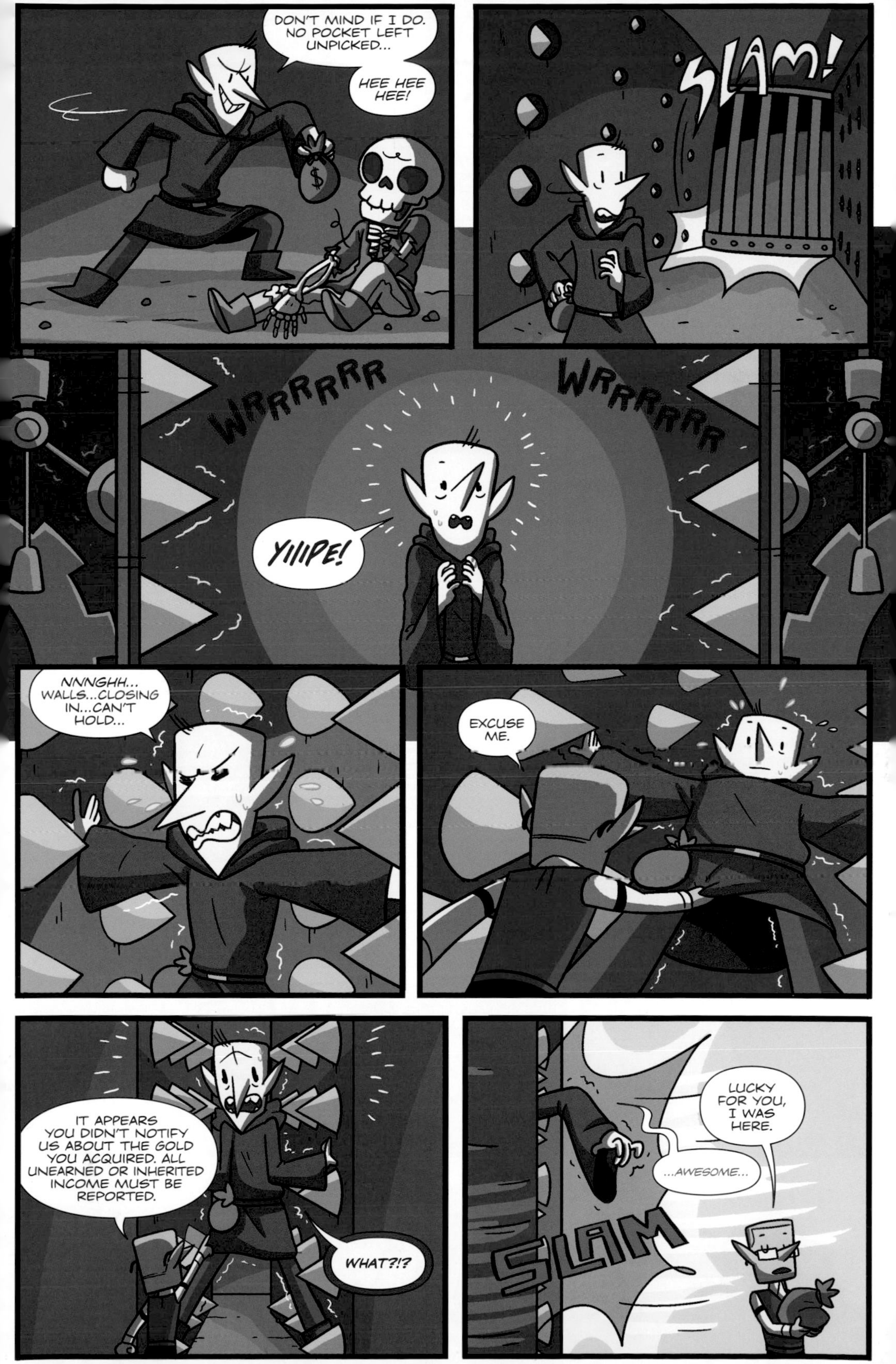
DON'T MIND IF I DO. NO POCKET LEFT UNPICKED...
HEE HEE HEE!
SLAM!
WRRRRRR
WRRRRRRR
YIIIPE!
NNNGHH... WALLS...CLOSING IN...CAN'T HOLD...
EXCUSE ME.
IT APPEARS YOU DIDN'T NOTIFY US ABOUT THE GOLD YOU ACQUIRED. ALL UNEARNED OR INHERITED INCOME MUST BE REPORTED.
WHAT?!?
LUCKY FOR YOU, I WAS HERE.
...AWESOME...
SLAM

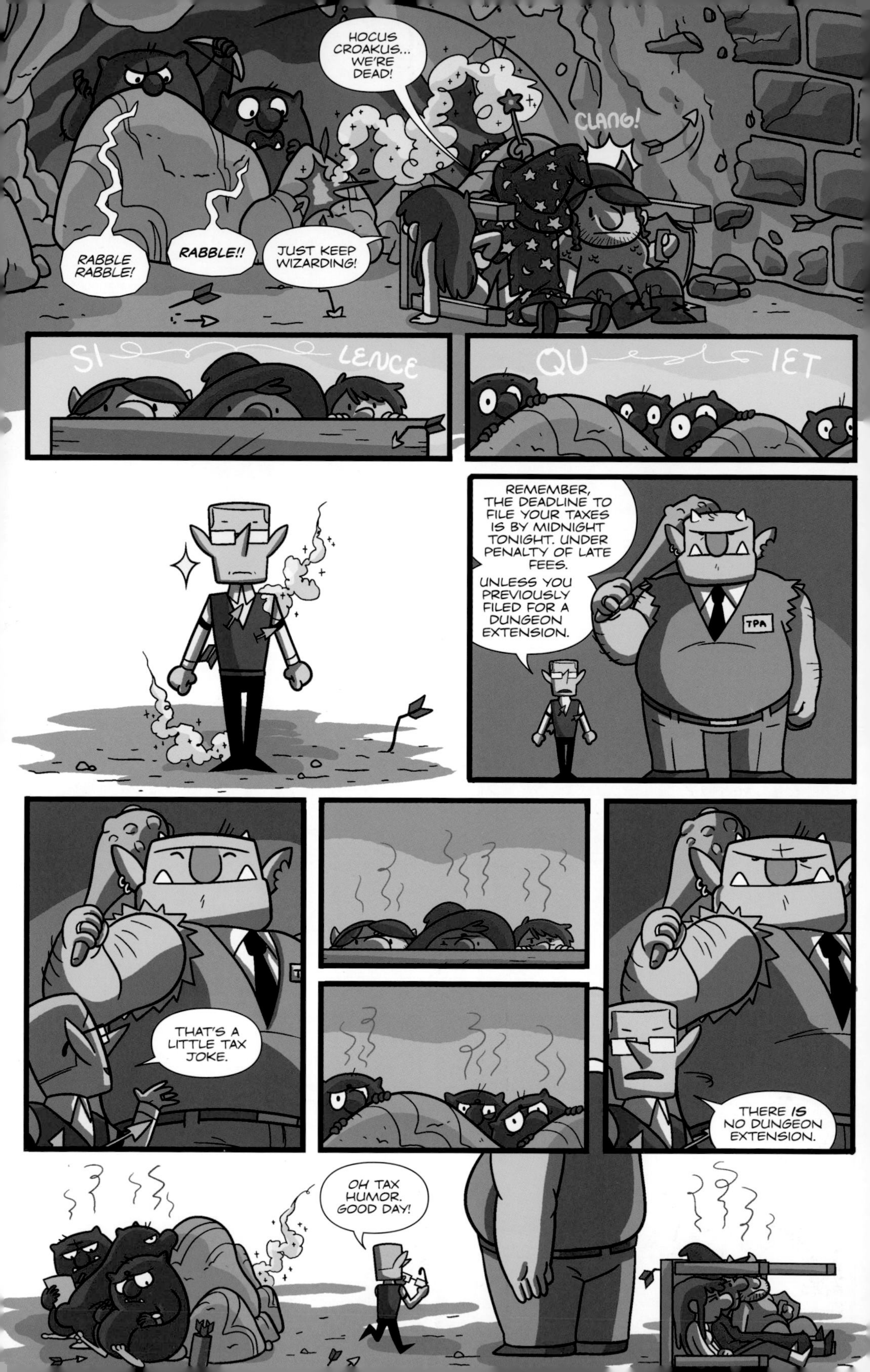
HOCUS CROAKUS... WE'RE DEAD!
CLANG!
RABBLE RABBLE!
RABBLE!!
JUST KEEP WIZARDING!
SI LENCE
QU IET
REMEMBER, THE DEADLINE TO FILE YOUR TAXES IS BY MIDNIGHT TONIGHT. UNDER PENALTY OF LATE FEES.
UNLESS YOU PREVIOUSLY FILED FOR A DUNGEON EXTENSION.
TPA
THAT'S A LITTLE TAX JOKE.
THERE IS NO DUNGEON EXTENSION.
OH TAX HUMOR. GOOD DAY!

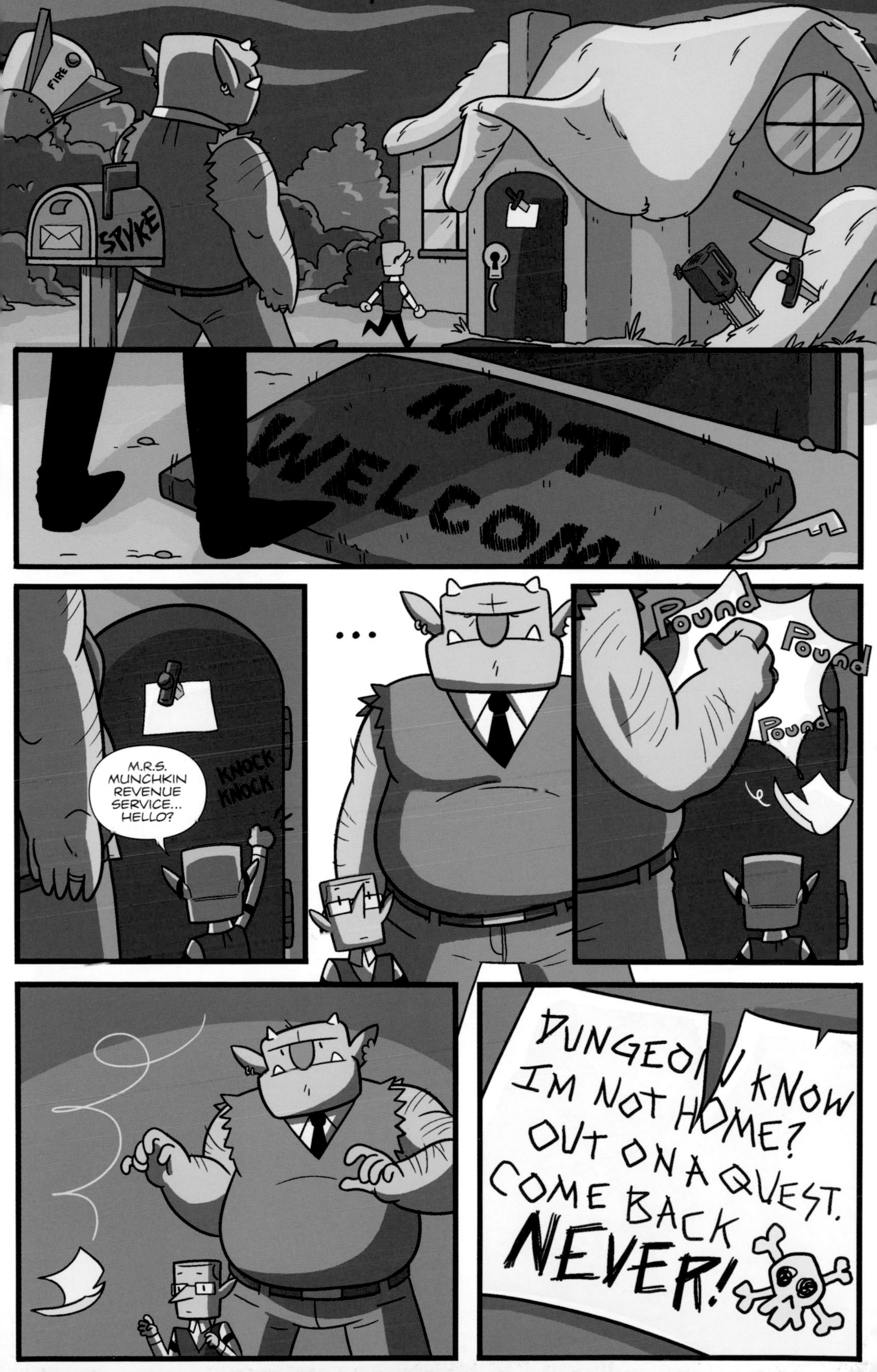
FIRE
SPYKE
NOT WELCOM
M.R.S. MUNCHKIN REVENUE SERVICE... HELLO?
KNOCK KNOCK
...
Pound
Pound
Pound
DUNGEON I KNOW I'M NOT HOME? OUT ON A QUEST. COME BACK NEVER!

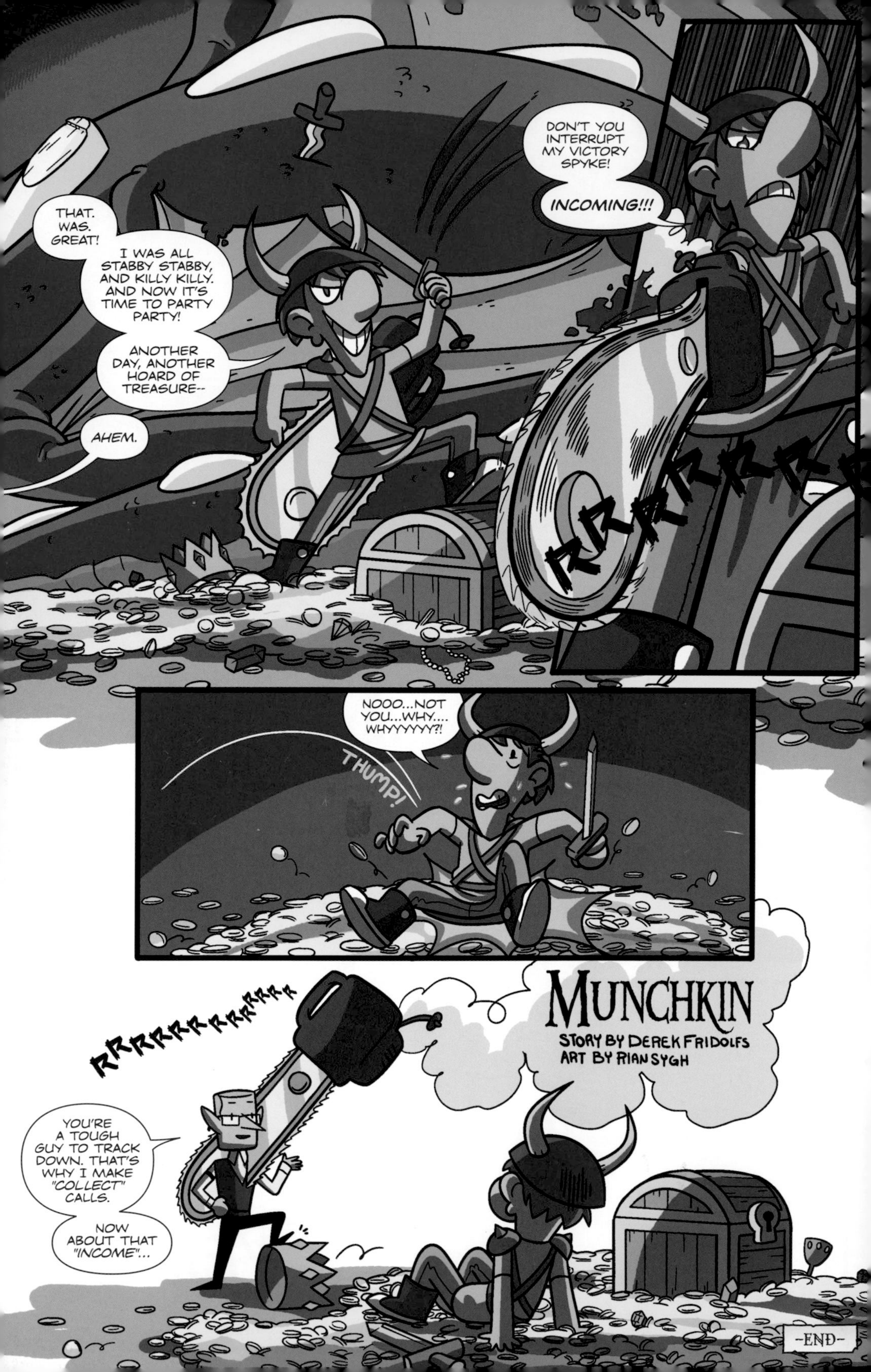
THAT. WAS. GREAT!
I WAS ALL STABBY STABBY, AND KILLY KILLY. AND NOW IT'S TIME TO PARTY PARTY!
ANOTHER DAY, ANOTHER HOARD OF TREASURE--
AHEM.
DON'T YOU INTERRUPT MY VICTORY SPYKE!
INCOMING!!!
RRRRRRRR
NOOO...NOT YOU...WHY.... WHYYYYYY?!
THUMP!
RRRRRRRRRRRRRR
MUNCHKIN
STORY BY DEREK FRIDOLFS
ART BY RIAN SYGH
YOU'RE A TOUGH GUY TO TRACK DOWN. THAT'S WHY I MAKE "COLLECT" CALLS.
NOW ABOUT THAT "INCOME"...
-END-

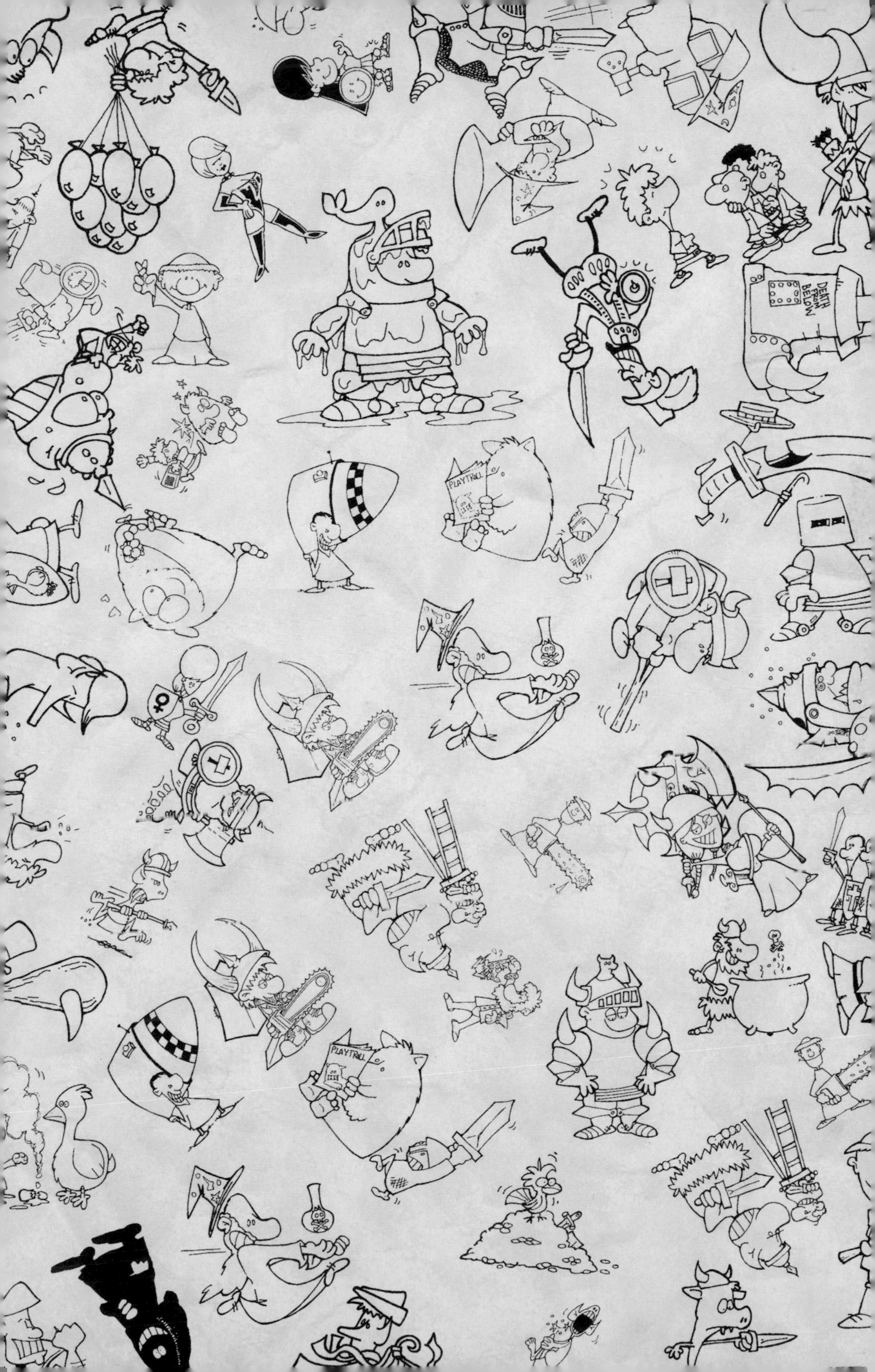
DEATH FROM BELOW
PLAYTROLL
PLAYTROLL

CHAPTER
SEVEN

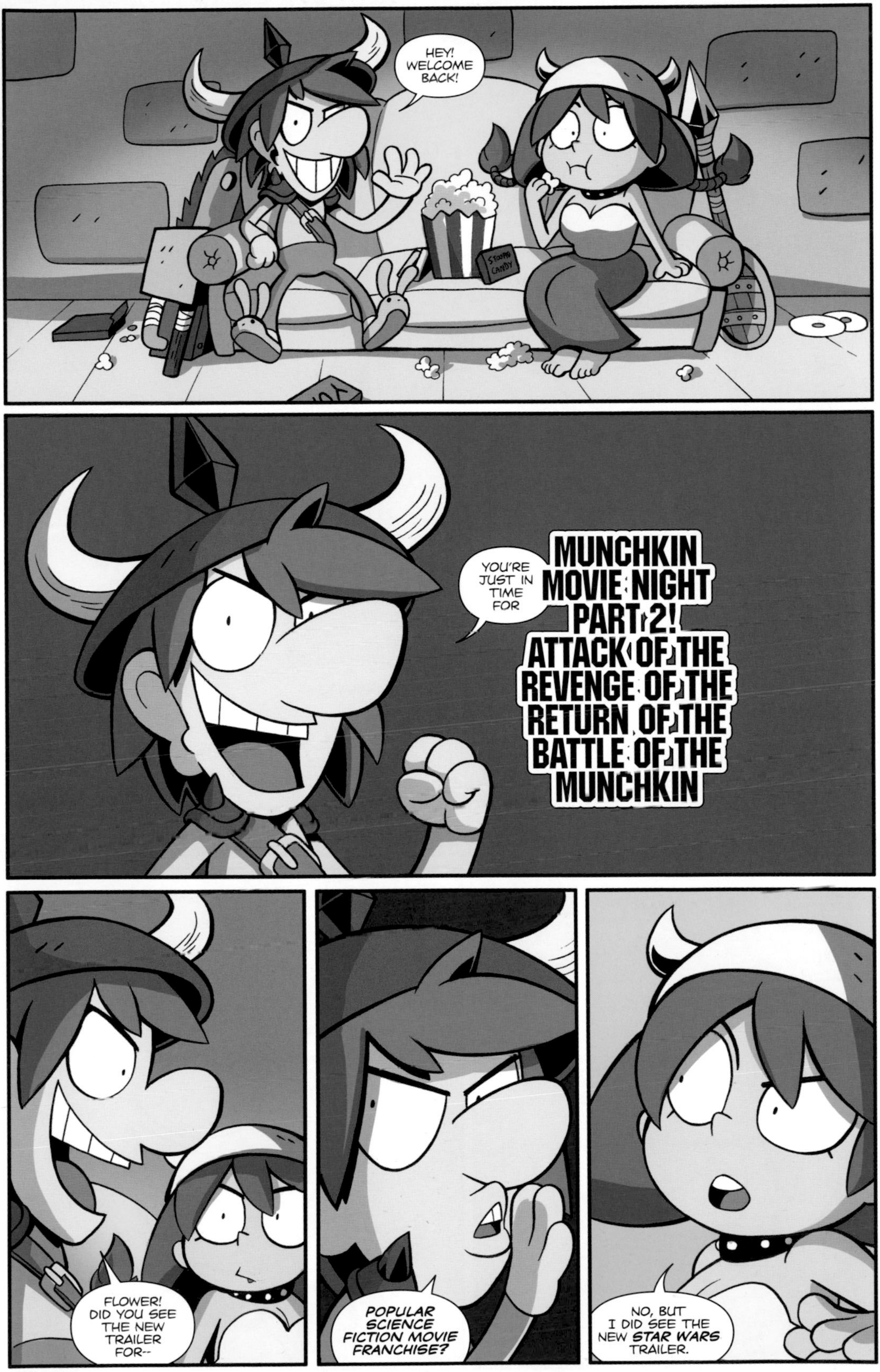
HEY! WELCOME BACK!
STOOPID CANDY
YOU'RE JUST IN TIME FOR
MUNCHKIN MOVIE NIGHT PART 2! ATTACK OF THE REVENGE OF THE RETURN OF THE BATTLE OF THE MUNCHKIN
FLOWER! DID YOU SEE THE NEW TRAILER FOR--
POPULAR SCIENCE FICTION MOVIE FRANCHISE?
NO, BUT I DID SEE THE NEW STAR WARS TRAILER.

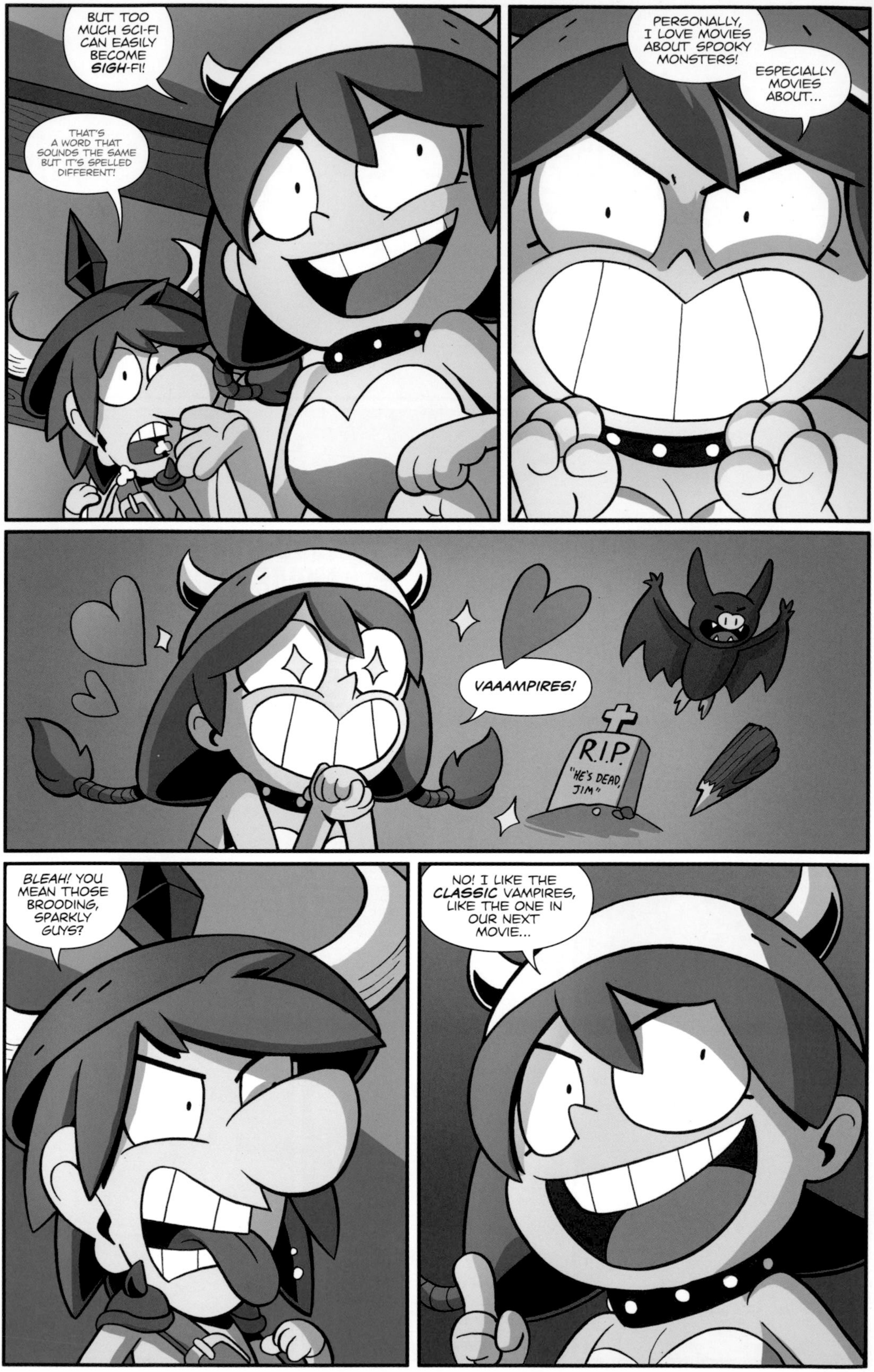
BUT TOO MUCH SCI-FI CAN EASILY BECOME SIGH-FI!
THAT'S A WORD THAT SOUNDS THE SAME BUT IT'S SPELLED DIFFERENT!
PERSONALLY, I LOVE MOVIES ABOUT SPOOKY MONSTERS!
ESPECIALLY MOVIES ABOUT...
VAAAMPIRES!
R.I.P.
"HE'S DEAD, JIM"
BLEAH! YOU MEAN THOSE BROODING, SPARKLY GUYS?
NO! I LIKE THE CLASSIC VAMPIRES, LIKE THE ONE IN OUR NEXT MOVIE...

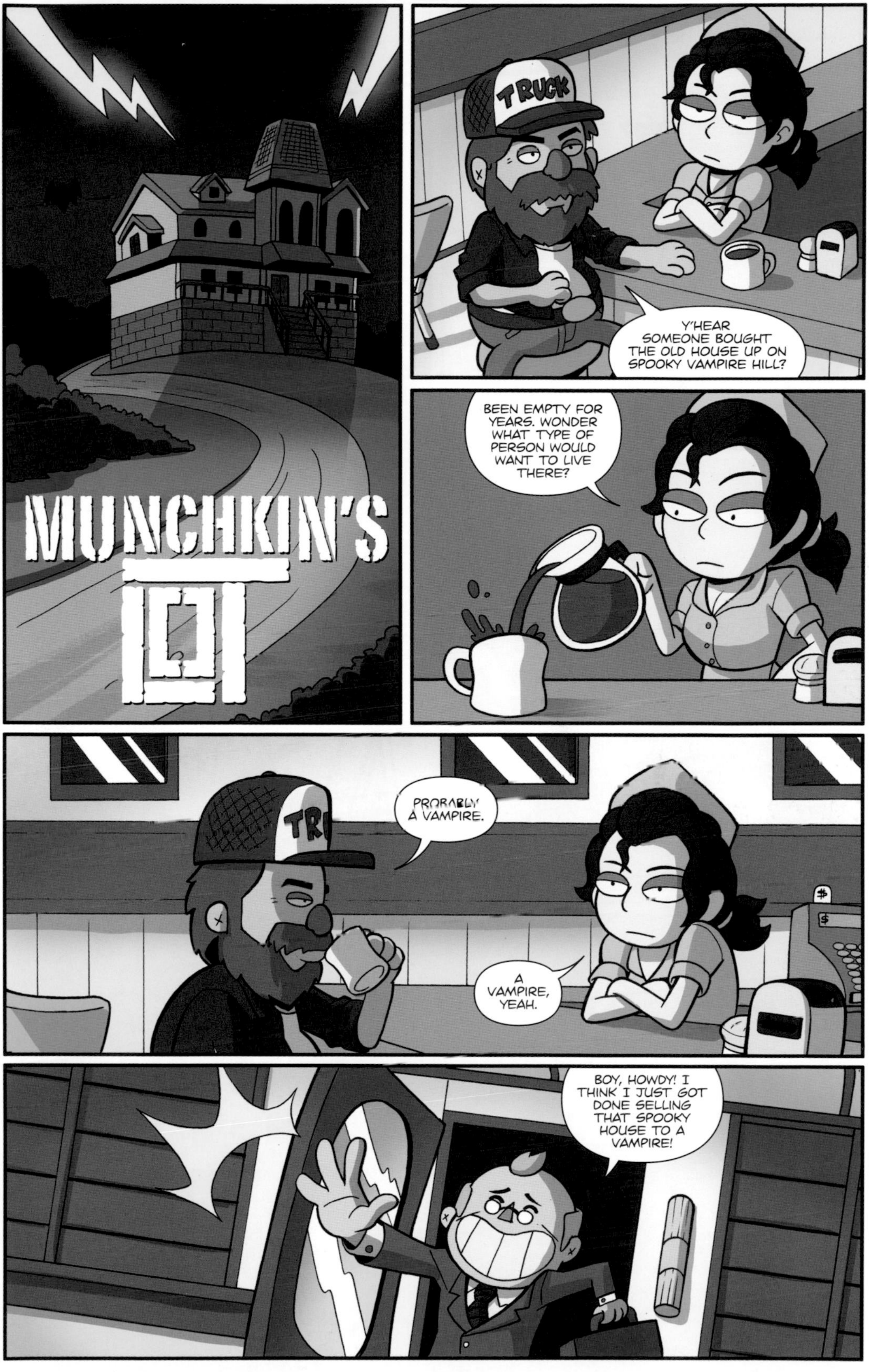
MUNCHKIN'S
TRUCK
Y'HEAR SOMEONE BOUGHT THE OLD HOUSE UP ON SPOOKY VAMPIRE HILL?
BEEN EMPTY FOR YEARS. WONDER WHAT TYPE OF PERSON WOULD WANT TO LIVE THERE?
PROBABLY A VAMPIRE.
A VAMPIRE, YEAH.
BOY, HOWDY! I THINK I JUST GOT DONE SELLING THAT SPOOKY HOUSE TO A VAMPIRE!

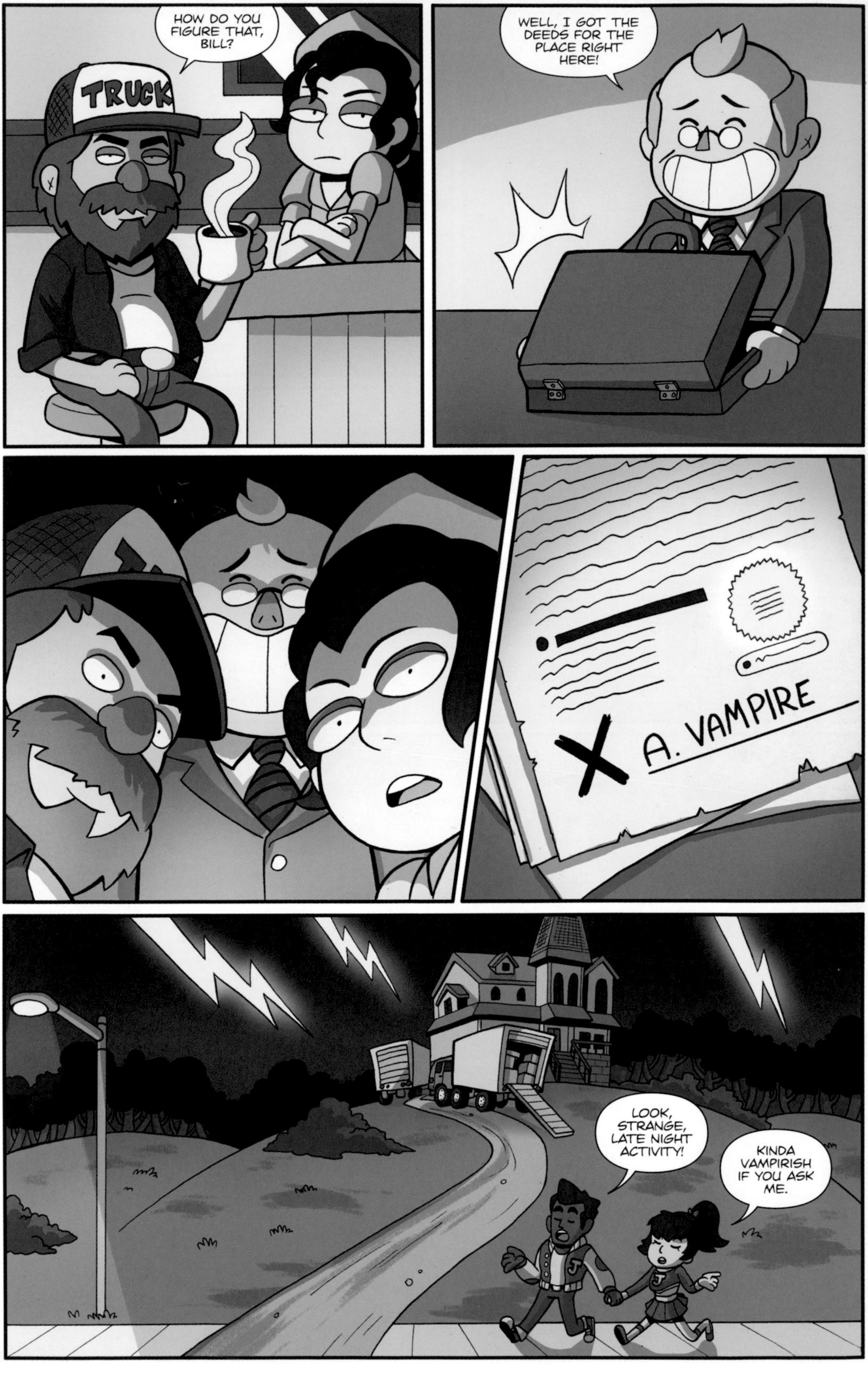
HOW DO YOU FIGURE THAT, BILL?
TRUCK
WELL, I GOT THE DEEDS FOR THE PLACE RIGHT HERE!
A. VAMPIRE
LOOK, STRANGE, LATE NIGHT ACTIVITY!
KINDA VAMPIRISH IF YOU ASK ME.

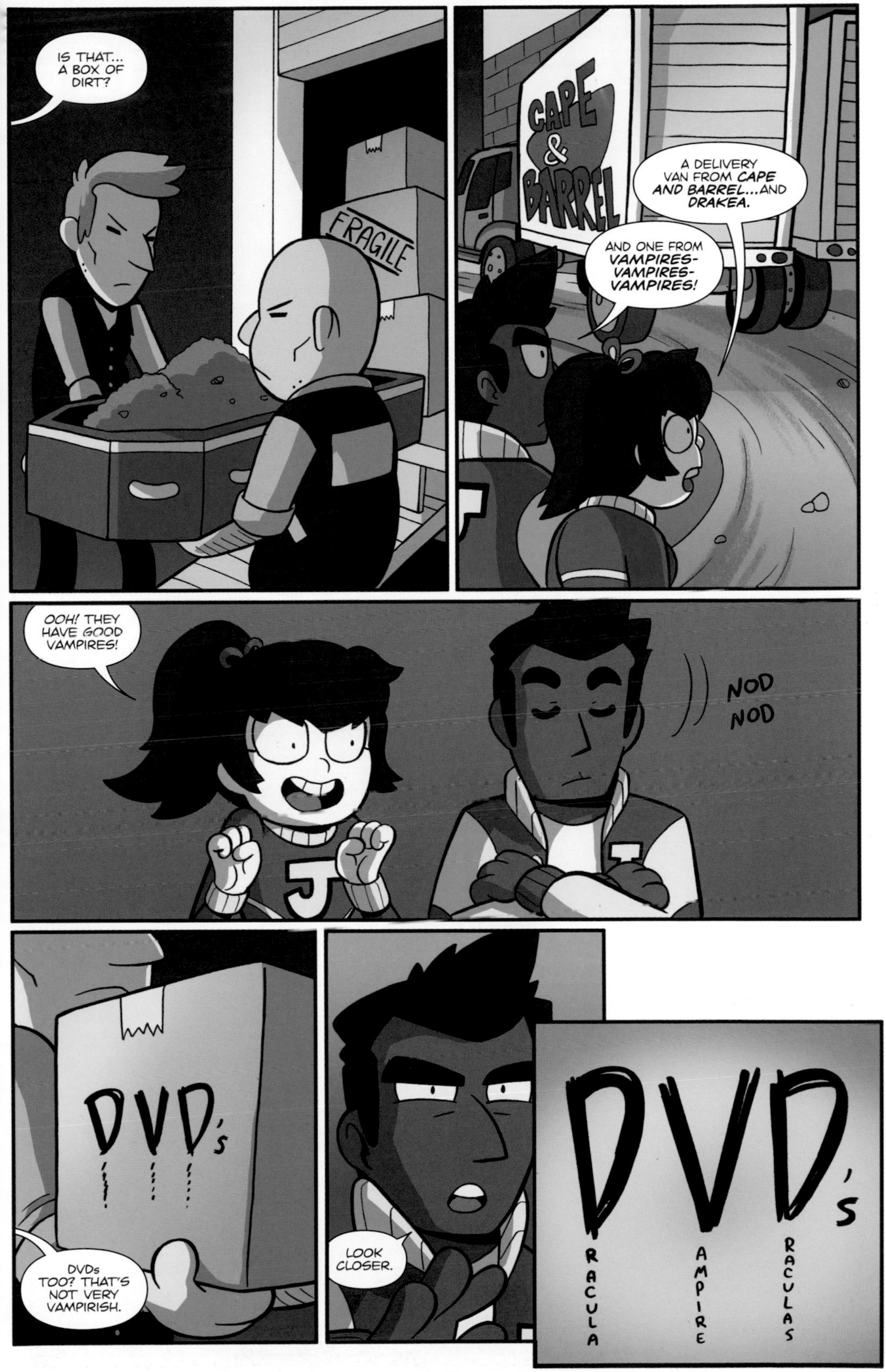
IS THAT... A BOX OF DIRT?
FRAGILE
CAPE & BARREL
A DELIVERY VAN FROM CAPE AND BARREL...AND DRAKEA.
AND ONE FROM VAMPIRES-VAMPIRES-VAMPIRES!
OOH! THEY HAVE GOOD VAMPIRES!
NOD NOD
DVD's
DVDs TOO? THAT'S NOT VERY VAMPIRISH.
LOOK CLOSER.
DVD's
RACULA
AMPIRE
RACULAS

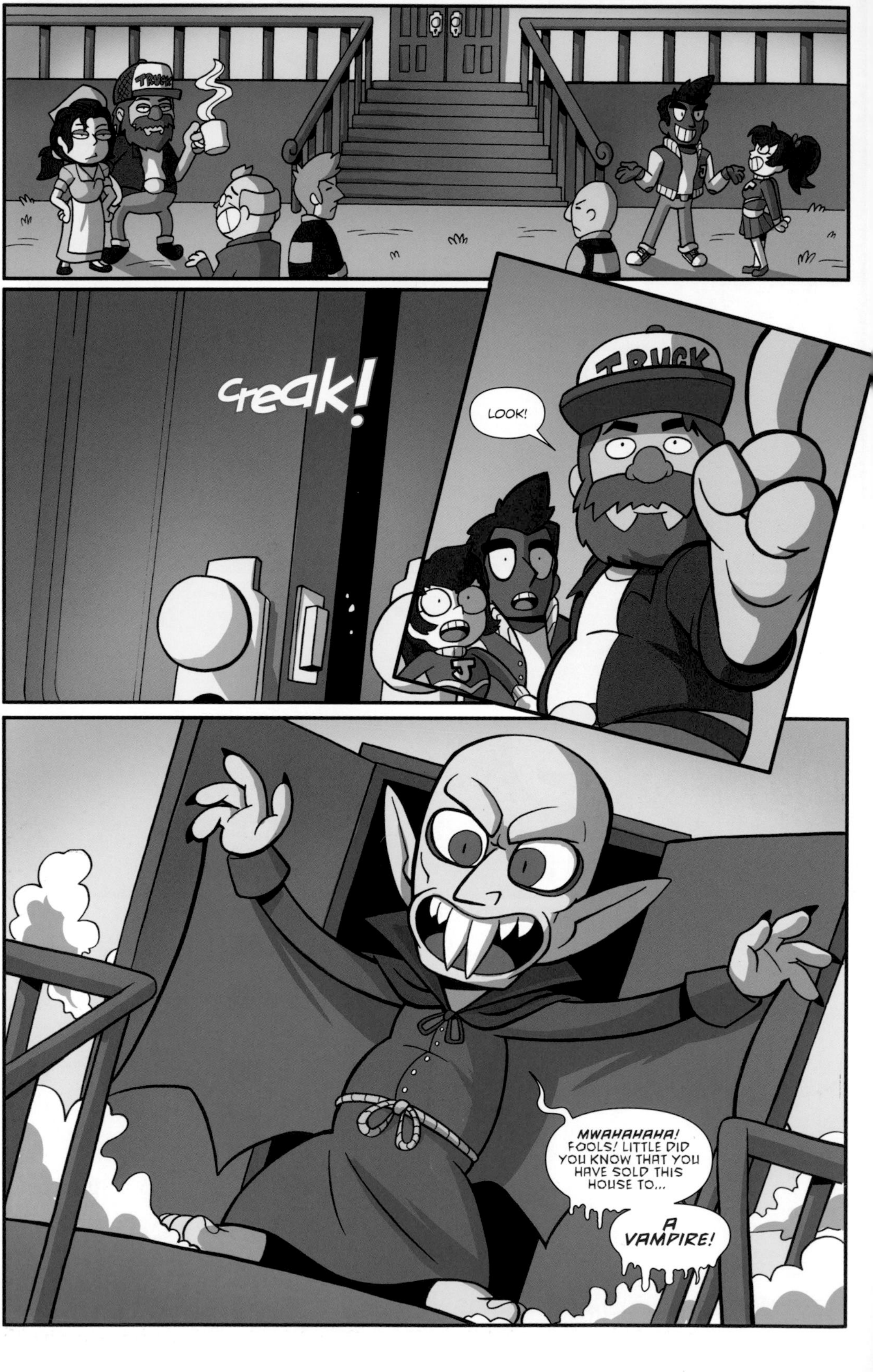
TRUCK
CREAK!
TRUCK
LOOK!
MWAHAHAHA! FOOLS! LITTLE DID YOU KNOW THAT YOU HAVE SOLD THIS HOUSE TO...
A VAMPIRE!

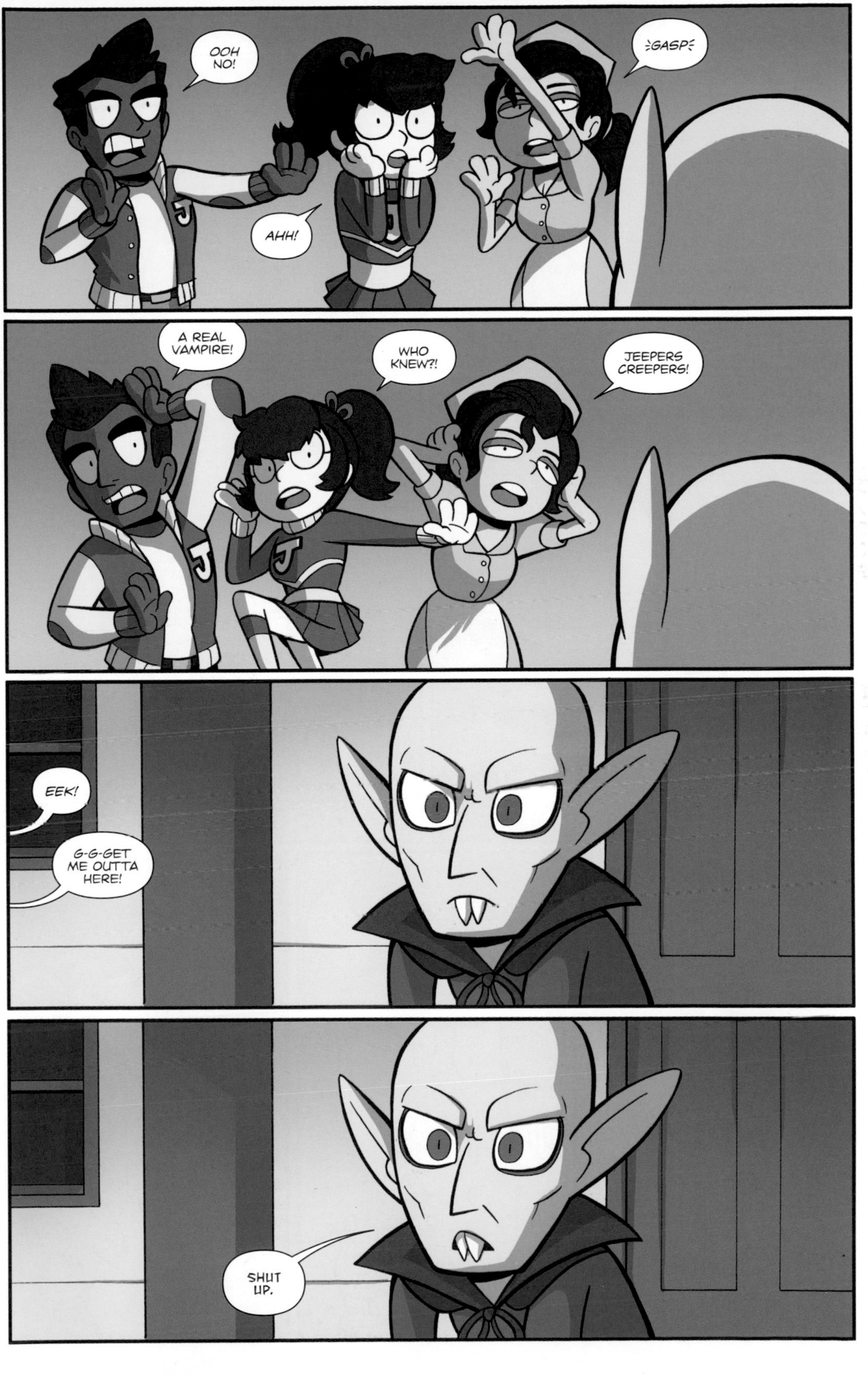
OOH NO!
AHH!
⁝GASP⁝
A REAL VAMPIRE!
WHO KNEW?!
JEEPERS CREEPERS!
EEK!
G-G-GET ME OUTTA HERE!
SHUT UP.

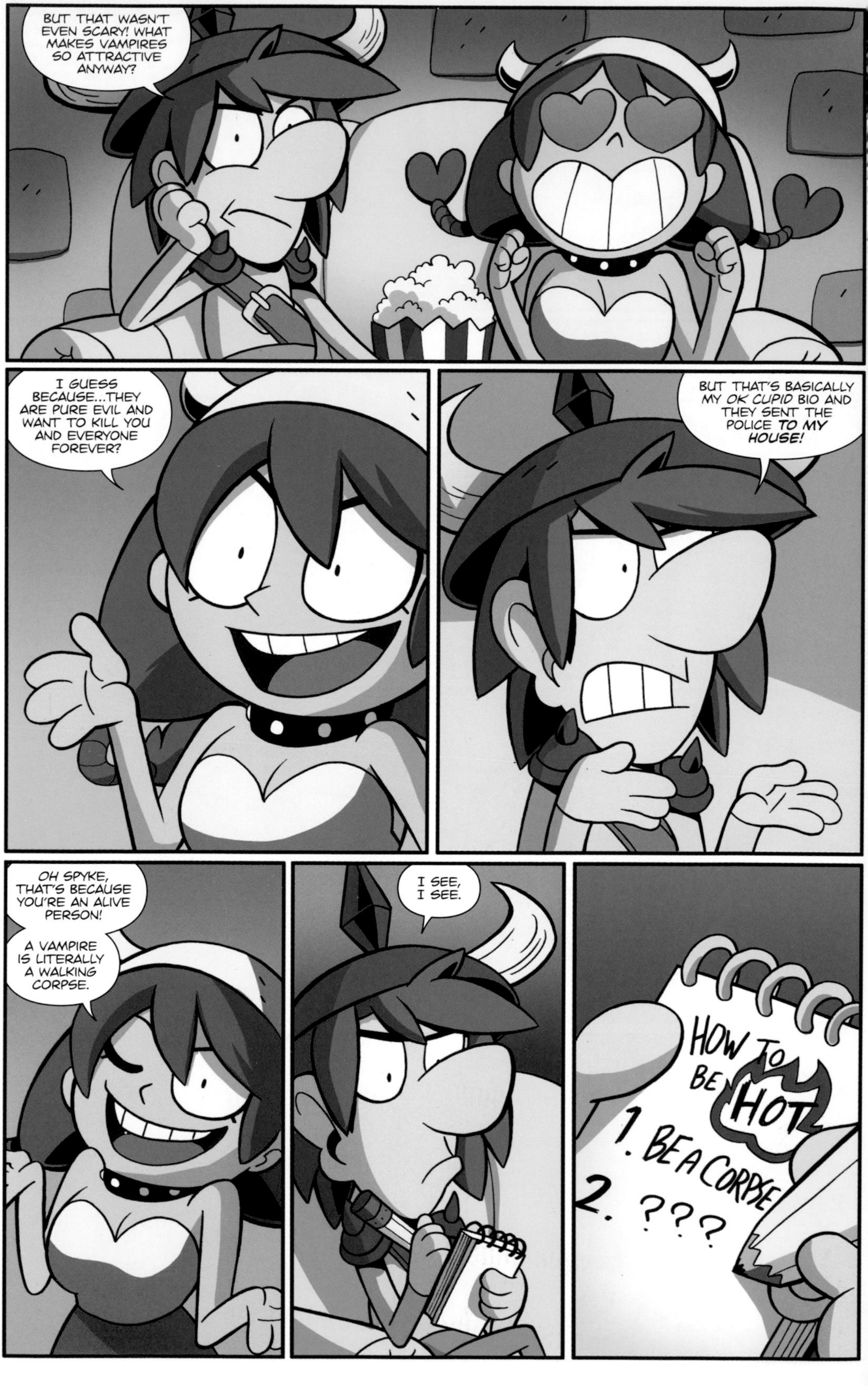
BUT THAT WASN'T EVEN SCARY! WHAT MAKES VAMPIRES SO ATTRACTIVE ANYWAY?
I GUESS BECAUSE...THEY ARE PURE EVIL AND WANT TO KILL YOU AND EVERYONE FOREVER?
BUT THAT'S BASICALLY MY *OK CUPID* BIO AND THEY SENT THE POLICE **TO MY HOUSE!**
OH SPYKE, THAT'S BECAUSE YOU'RE AN ALIVE PERSON!
A VAMPIRE IS LITERALLY A WALKING CORPSE.
I SEE, I SEE.
HOW TO BE HOT
1. BE A CORPSE
2. ???

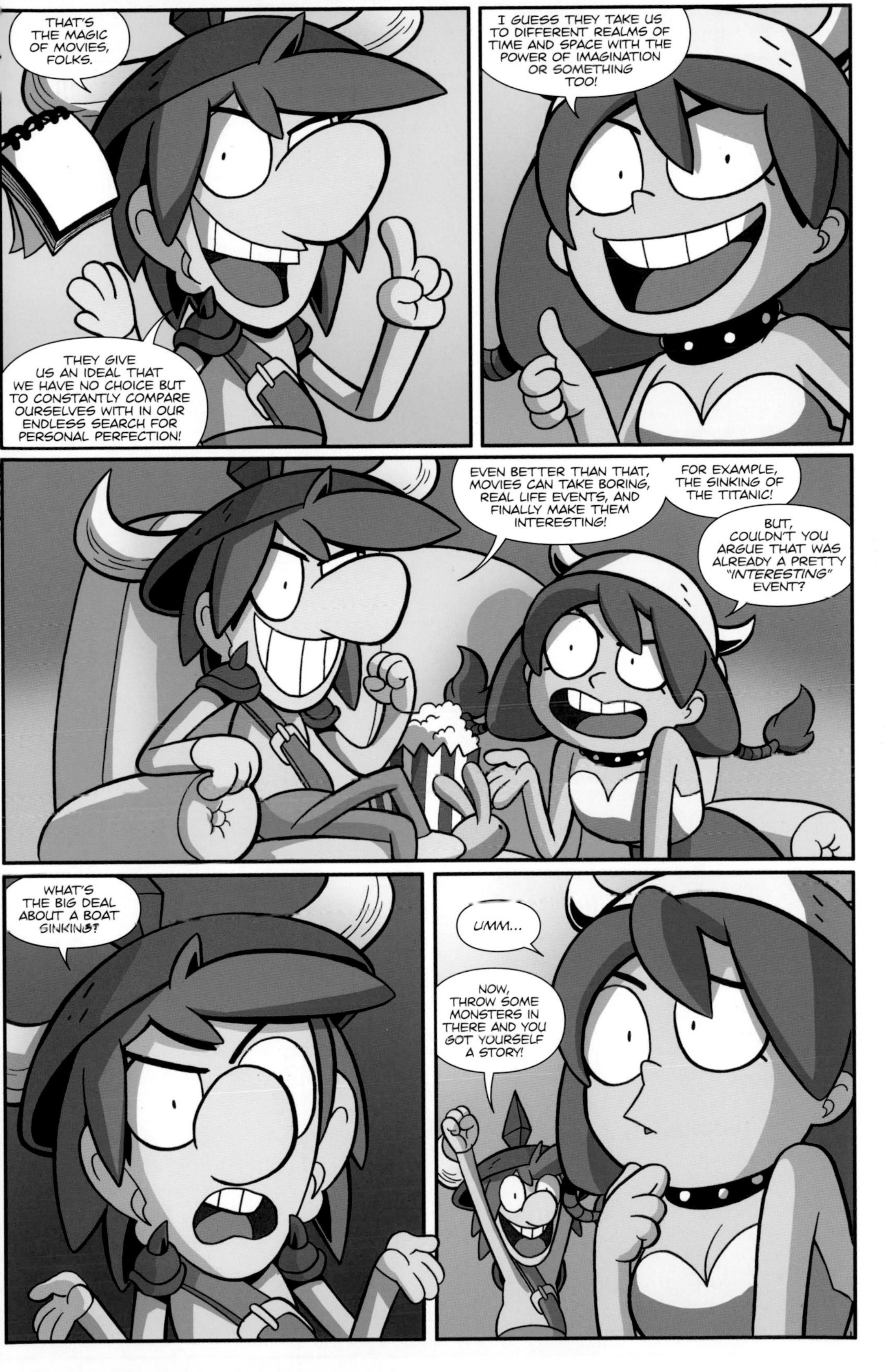
THAT'S THE MAGIC OF MOVIES, FOLKS.
THEY GIVE US AN IDEAL THAT WE HAVE NO CHOICE BUT TO CONSTANTLY COMPARE OURSELVES WITH IN OUR ENDLESS SEARCH FOR PERSONAL PERFECTION!
I GUESS THEY TAKE US TO DIFFERENT REALMS OF TIME AND SPACE WITH THE POWER OF IMAGINATION OR SOMETHING TOO!
EVEN BETTER THAN THAT, MOVIES CAN TAKE BORING, REAL LIFE EVENTS, AND FINALLY MAKE THEM INTERESTING!
FOR EXAMPLE, THE SINKING OF THE TITANIC!
BUT, COULDN'T YOU ARGUE THAT WAS ALREADY A PRETTY "INTERESTING" EVENT?
WHAT'S THE BIG DEAL ABOUT A BOAT SINKING?
UMM...
NOW, THROW SOME MONSTERS IN THERE AND YOU GOT YOURSELF A STORY!

TITANIC (MONSTERS)

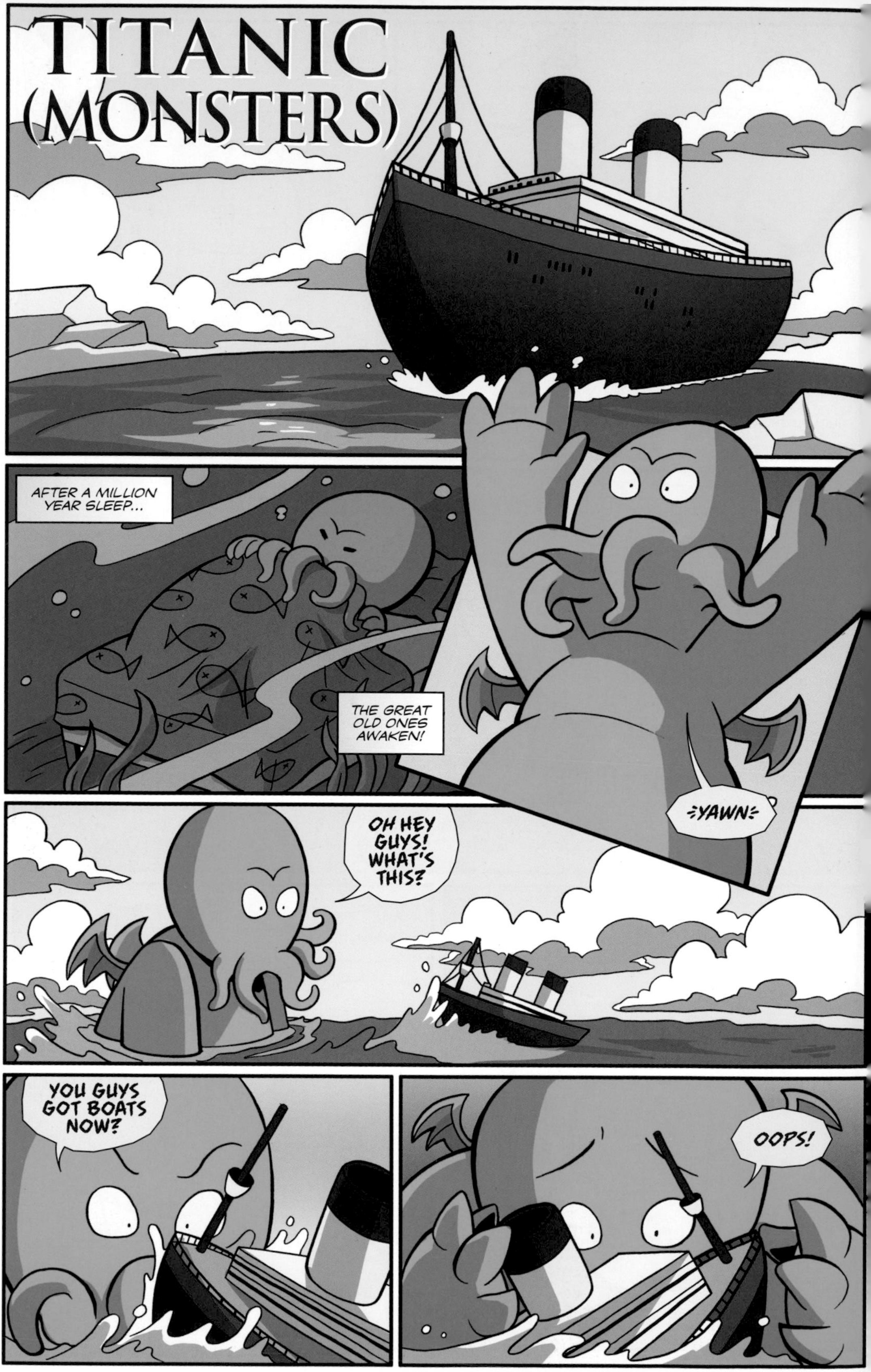
AFTER A MILLION YEAR SLEEP...
THE GREAT OLD ONES AWAKEN!
YAWN
OH HEY GUYS! WHAT'S THIS?
YOU GUYS GOT BOATS NOW?
OOPS!

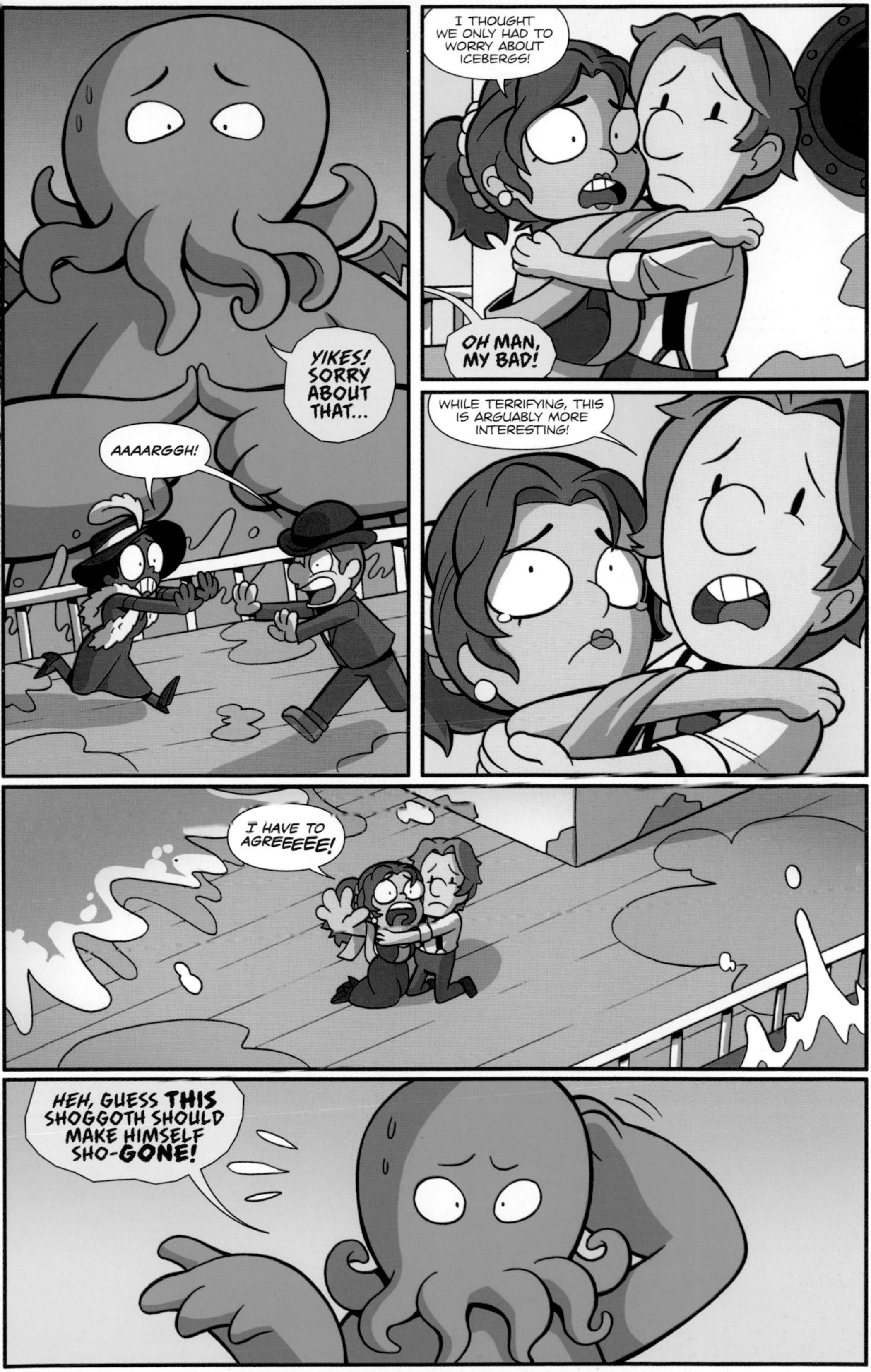
I THOUGHT WE ONLY HAD TO WORRY ABOUT ICEBERGS!
OH MAN, MY BAD!
YIKES! SORRY ABOUT THAT...
AAAARGGH!
WHILE TERRIFYING, THIS IS ARGUABLY MORE INTERESTING!
I HAVE TO AGREEEEEE!
HEH, GUESS THIS SHOGGOTH SHOULD MAKE HIMSELF SHO-GONE!

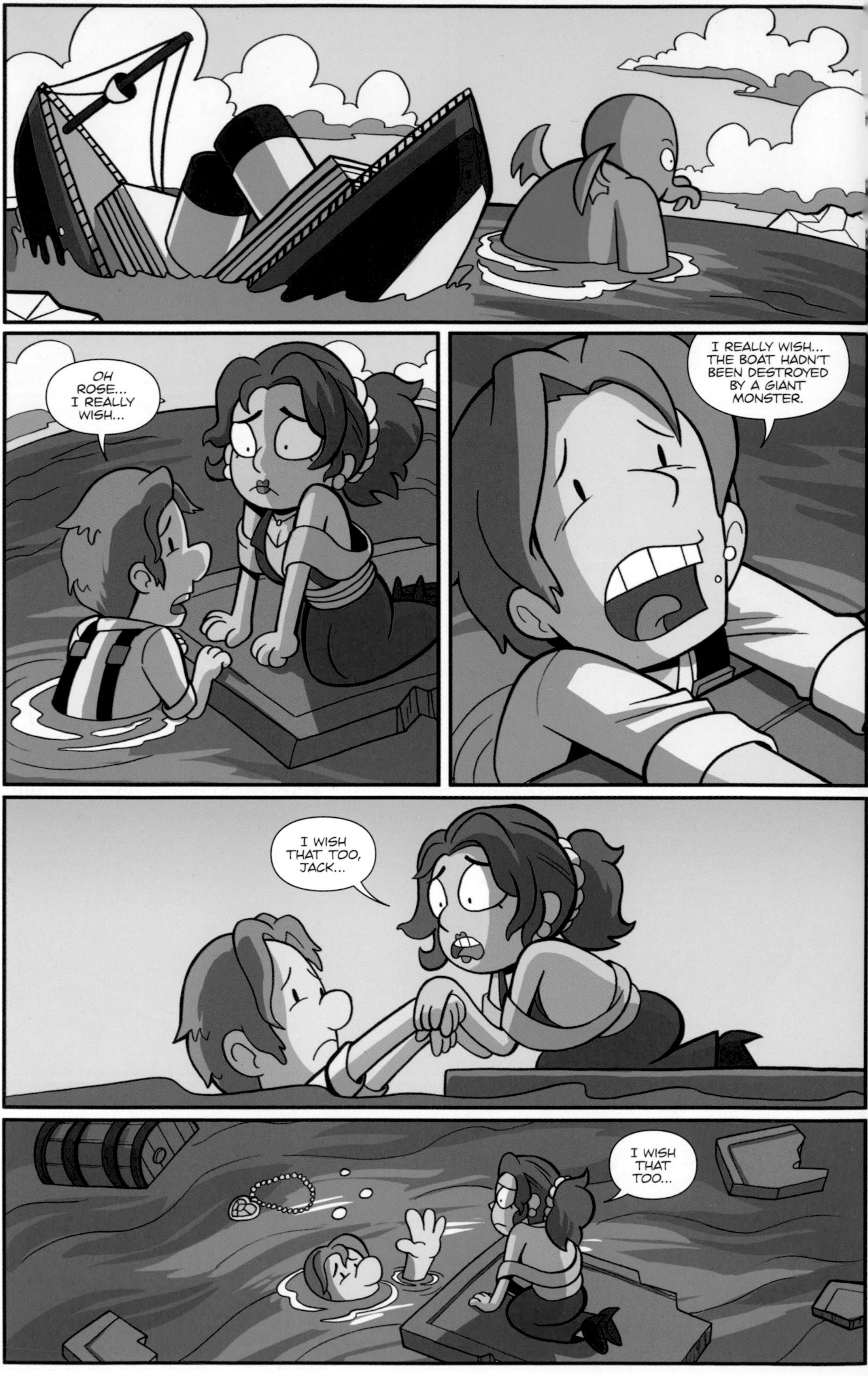
OH ROSE... I REALLY WISH...
I REALLY WISH... THE BOAT HADN'T BEEN DESTROYED BY A GIANT MONSTER.
I WISH THAT TOO, JACK...
I WISH THAT TOO...

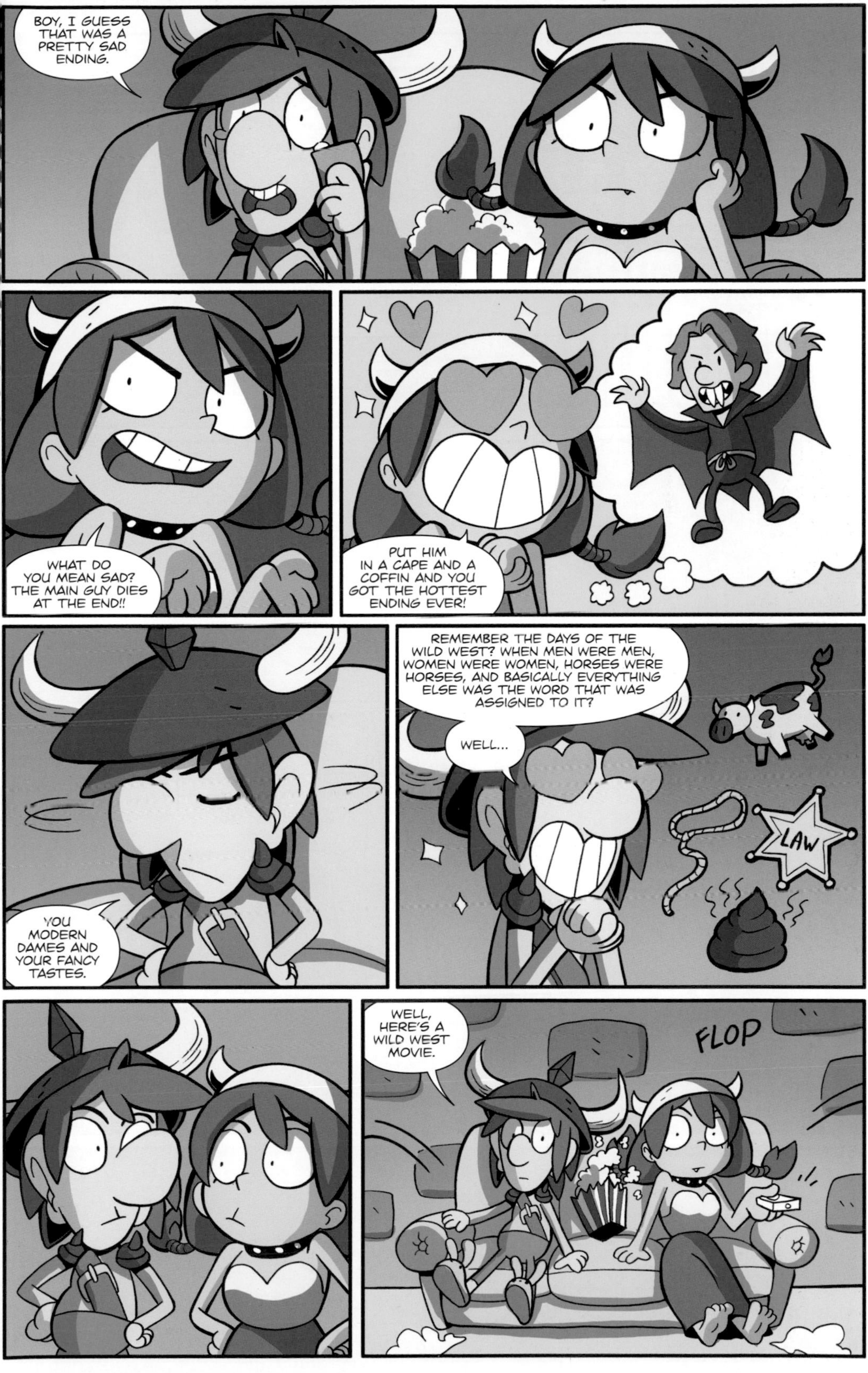
BOY, I GUESS THAT WAS A PRETTY SAD ENDING.
WHAT DO YOU MEAN SAD? THE MAIN GUY DIES AT THE END!!
PUT HIM IN A CAPE AND A COFFIN AND YOU GOT THE HOTTEST ENDING EVER!
YOU MODERN DAMES AND YOUR FANCY TASTES.
REMEMBER THE DAYS OF THE WILD WEST? WHEN MEN WERE MEN, WOMEN WERE WOMEN, HORSES WERE HORSES, AND BASICALLY EVERYTHING ELSE WAS THE WORD THAT WAS ASSIGNED TO IT?
WELL...
LAW
WELL, HERE'S A WILD WEST MOVIE.
FLOP

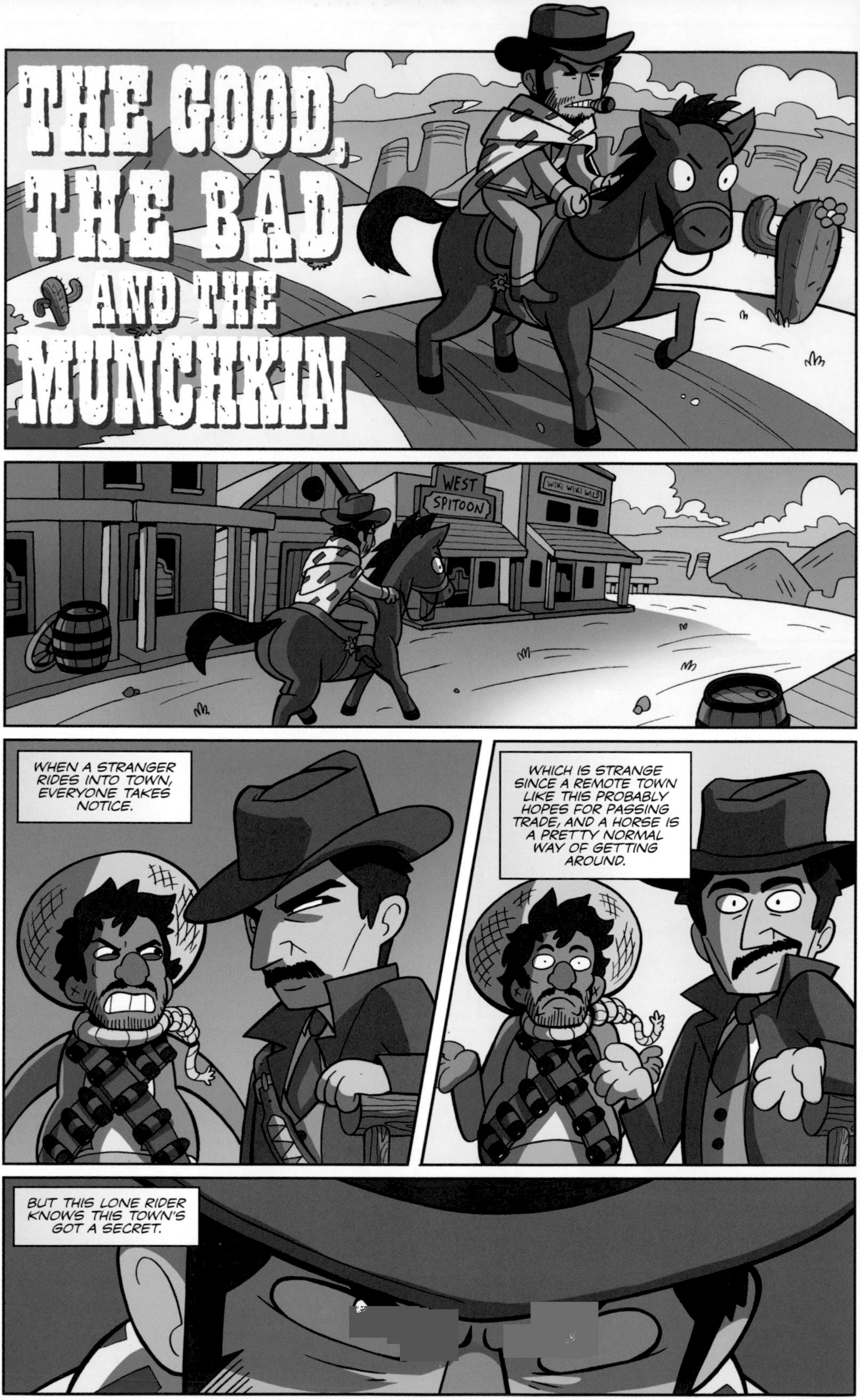
THE GOOD, THE BAD AND THE MUNCHKIN
WEST SPITOON
WIKI WIKI WILD
WHEN A STRANGER RIDES INTO TOWN, EVERYONE TAKES NOTICE.
WHICH IS STRANGE SINCE A REMOTE TOWN LIKE THIS PROBABLY HOPES FOR PASSING TRADE, AND A HORSE IS A PRETTY NORMAL WAY OF GETTING AROUND.
BUT THIS LONE RIDER KNOWS THIS TOWN'S GOT A SECRET.

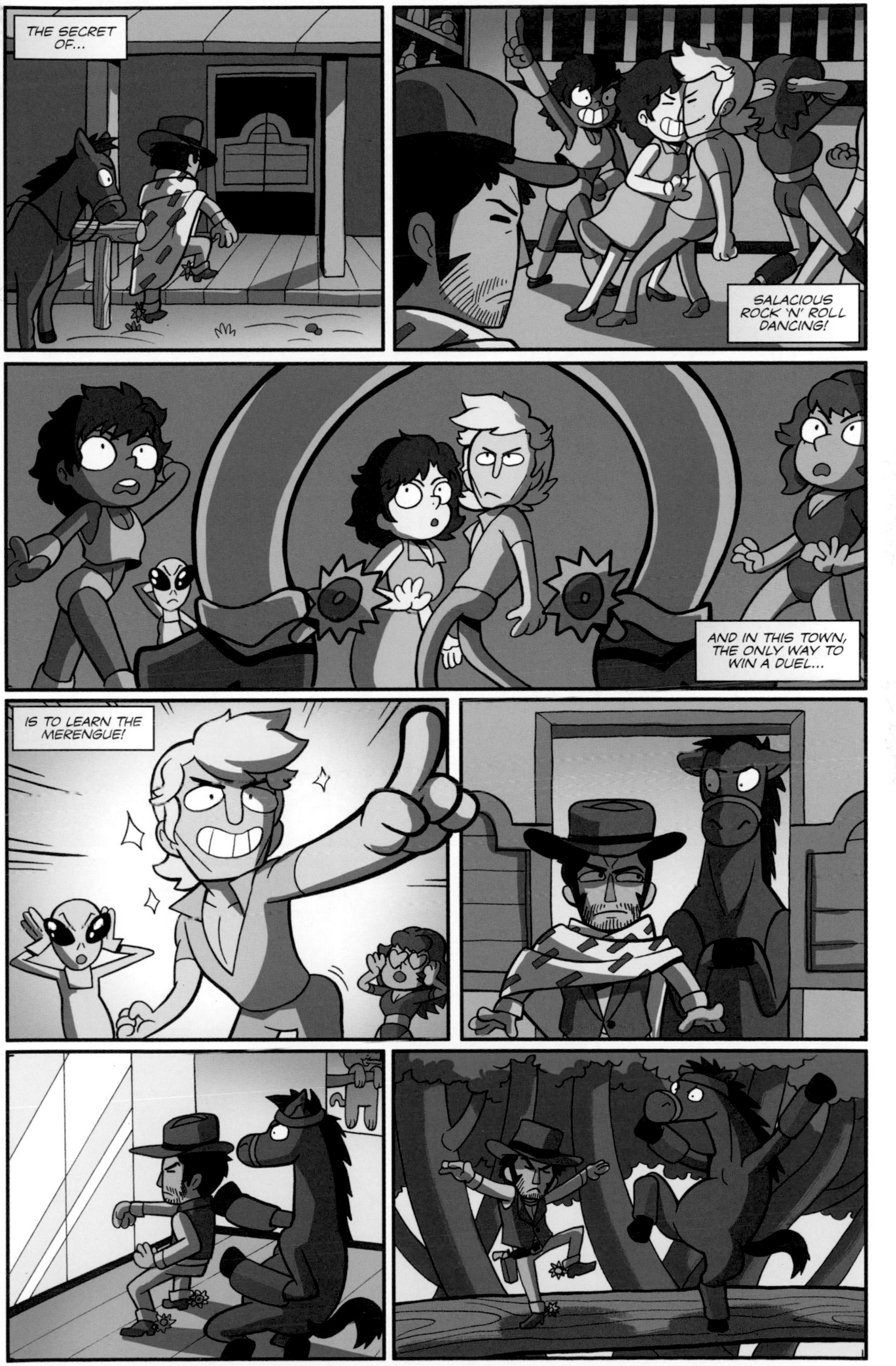
THE SECRET OF...
SALACIOUS ROCK 'N' ROLL DANCING!
AND IN THIS TOWN, THE ONLY WAY TO WIN A DUEL...
IS TO LEARN THE MERENGUE!

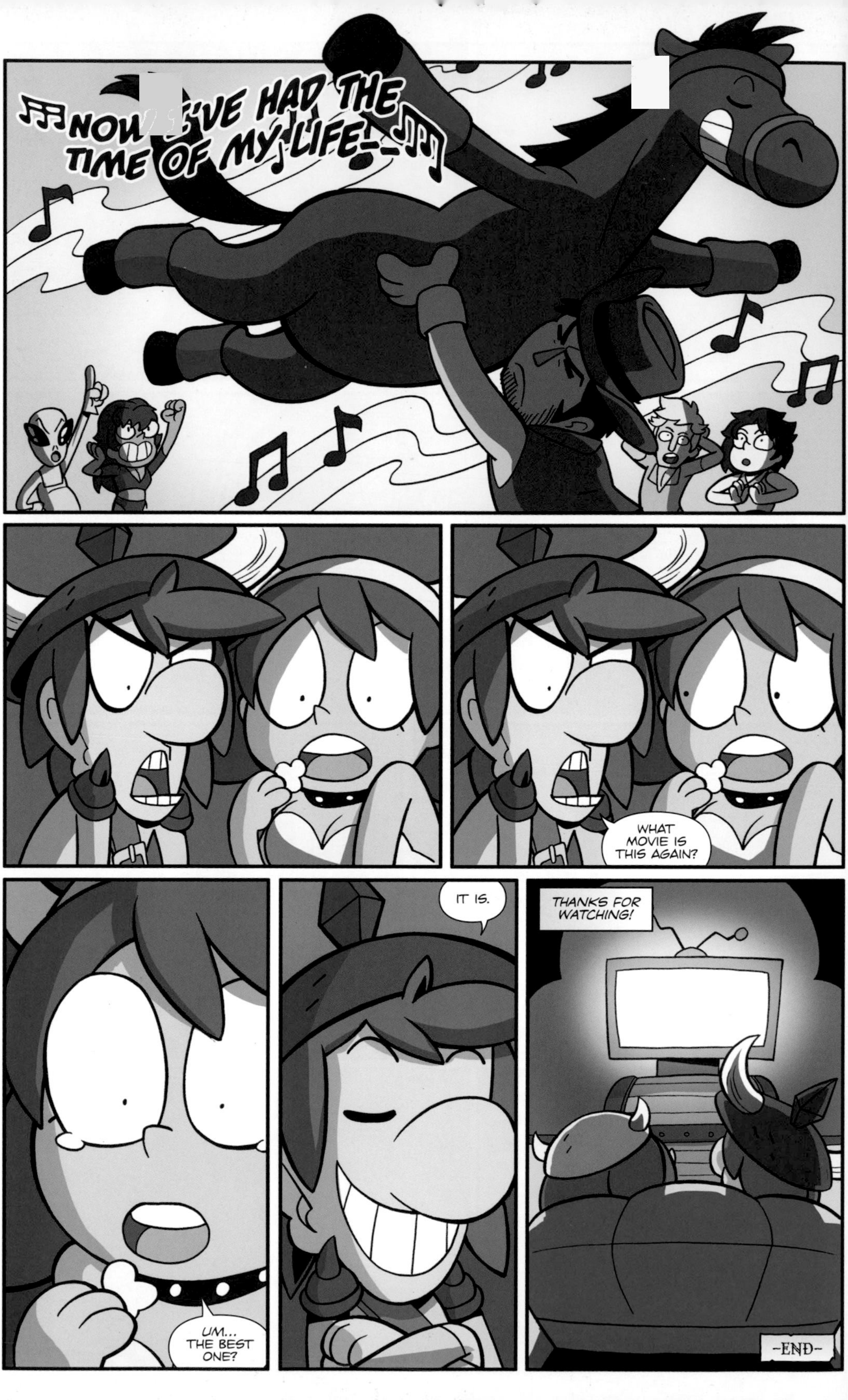
NOW I'VE HAD THE TIME OF MY LIFE!
WHAT MOVIE IS THIS AGAIN?
UM... THE BEST ONE?
IT IS.
THANKS FOR WATCHING!
-END-

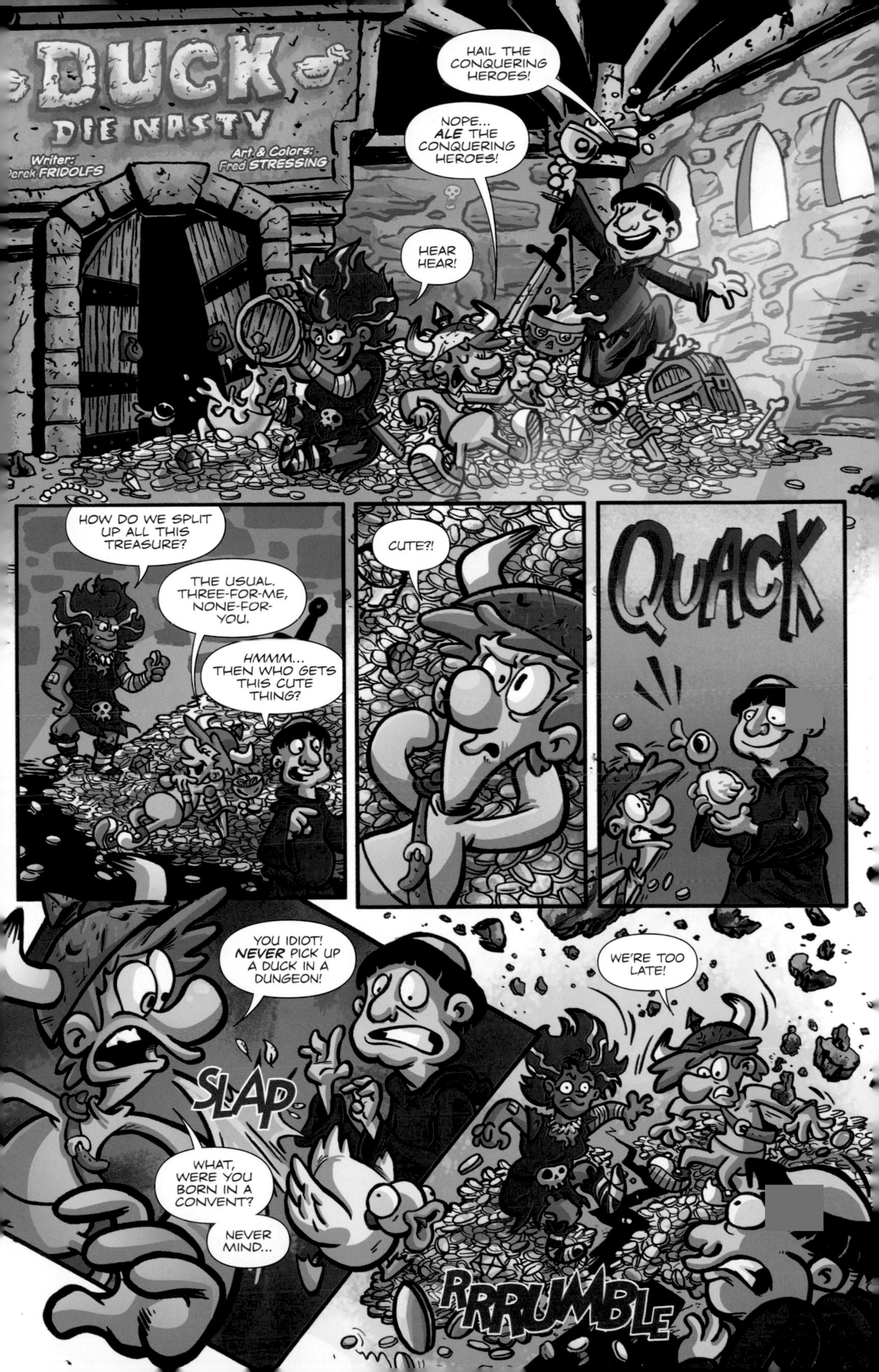
DUCK DIE NASTY
Writer: Derek FRIDOLFS
Art & Colors: Fred STRESSING
HAIL THE CONQUERING HEROES!
NOPE... ALE THE CONQUERING HEROES!
HEAR HEAR!
HOW DO WE SPLIT UP ALL THIS TREASURE?
THE USUAL. THREE-FOR-ME, NONE-FOR-YOU.
HMMM... THEN WHO GETS THIS CUTE THING?
CUTE?!
QUACK
YOU IDIOT! NEVER PICK UP A DUCK IN A DUNGEON!
SLAP
WHAT, WERE YOU BORN IN A CONVENT?
NEVER MIND...
WE'RE TOO LATE!
RRRUMBLE

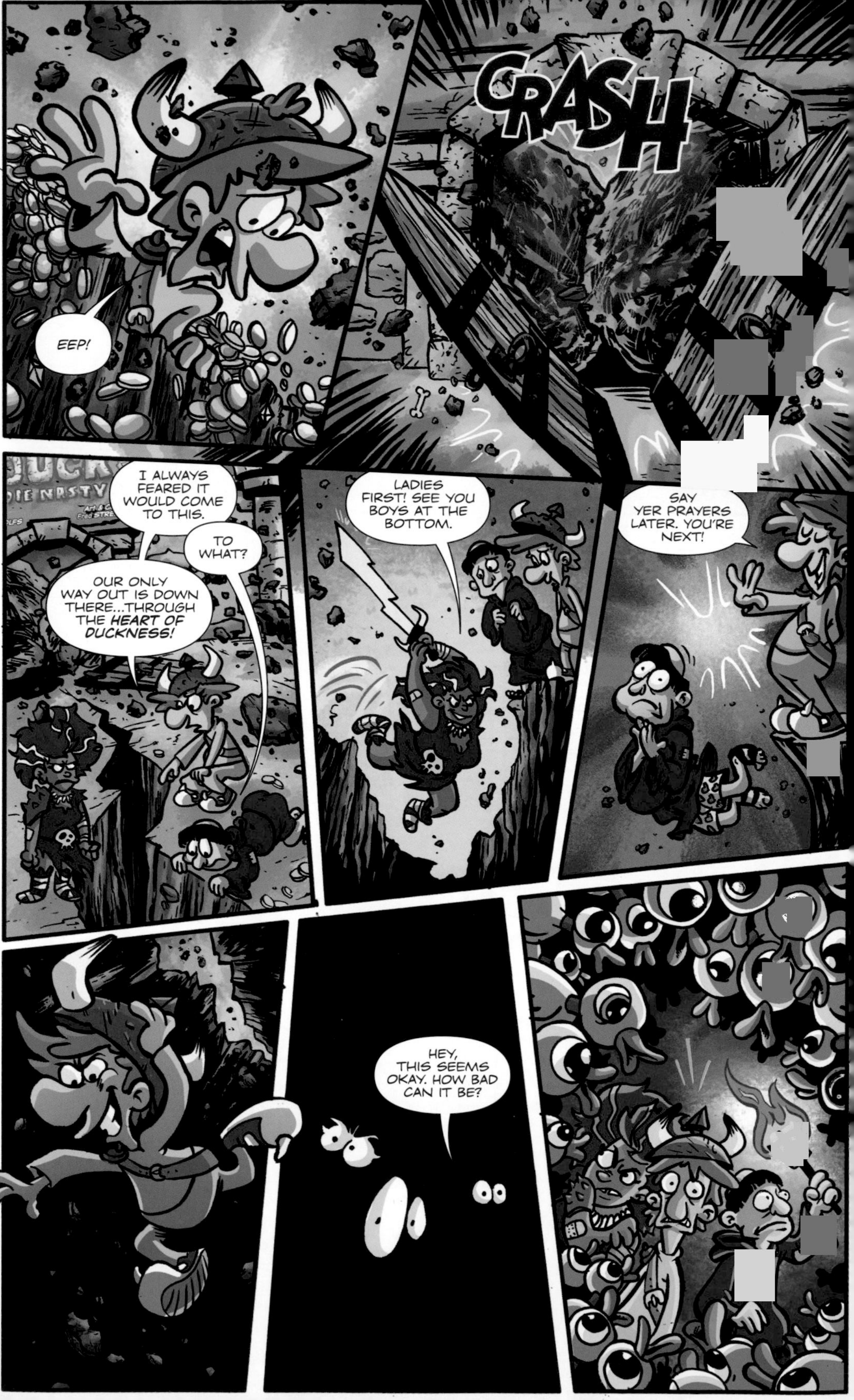
EEP!
CRASH
I ALWAYS FEARED IT WOULD COME TO THIS.
TO WHAT?
OUR ONLY WAY OUT IS DOWN THERE...THROUGH THE HEART OF DUCKNESS!
LADIES FIRST! SEE YOU BOYS AT THE BOTTOM.
SAY YER PRAYERS LATER. YOU'RE NEXT!
HEY, THIS SEEMS OKAY. HOW BAD CAN IT BE?

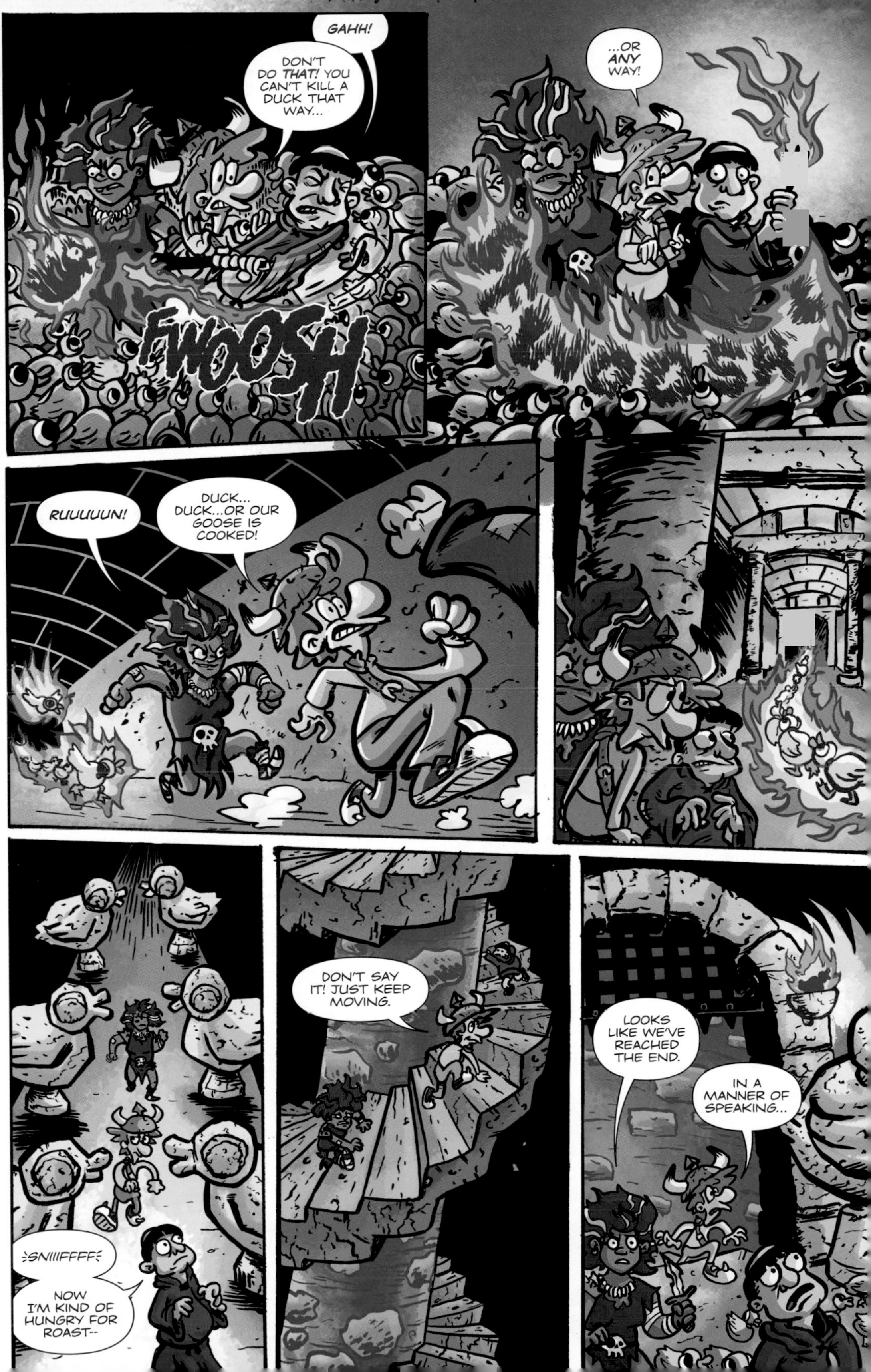
GAHH!
DON'T DO THAT! YOU CAN'T KILL A DUCK THAT WAY...
FWOOSH
...OR ANY WAY!
FWOOSH
RUUUUUN!
DUCK... DUCK...OR OUR GOOSE IS COOKED!
SNIIIFFFF
NOW I'M KIND OF HUNGRY FOR ROAST--
DON'T SAY IT! JUST KEEP MOVING.
LOOKS LIKE WE'VE REACHED THE END.
IN A MANNER OF SPEAKING...

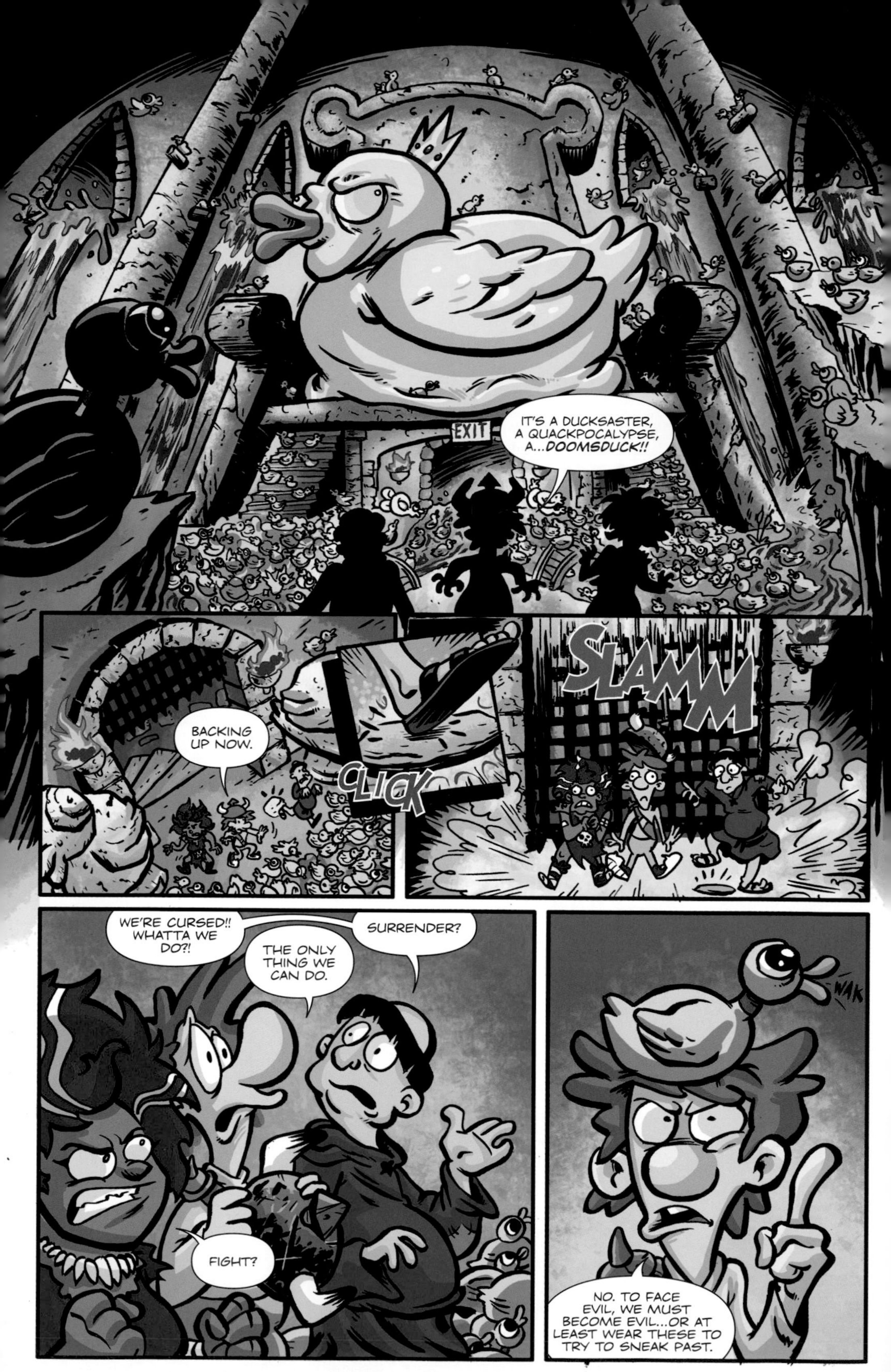
IT'S A DUCKSASTER, A QUACKPOCALYPSE, A...DOOMSDUCK!!
EXIT
BACKING UP NOW.
CLICK
SLAMM
WE'RE CURSED!! WHATTA WE DO?!
SURRENDER?
THE ONLY THING WE CAN DO.
FIGHT?
WAK
NO. TO FACE EVIL, WE MUST BECOME EVIL...OR AT LEAST WEAR THESE TO TRY TO SNEAK PAST.

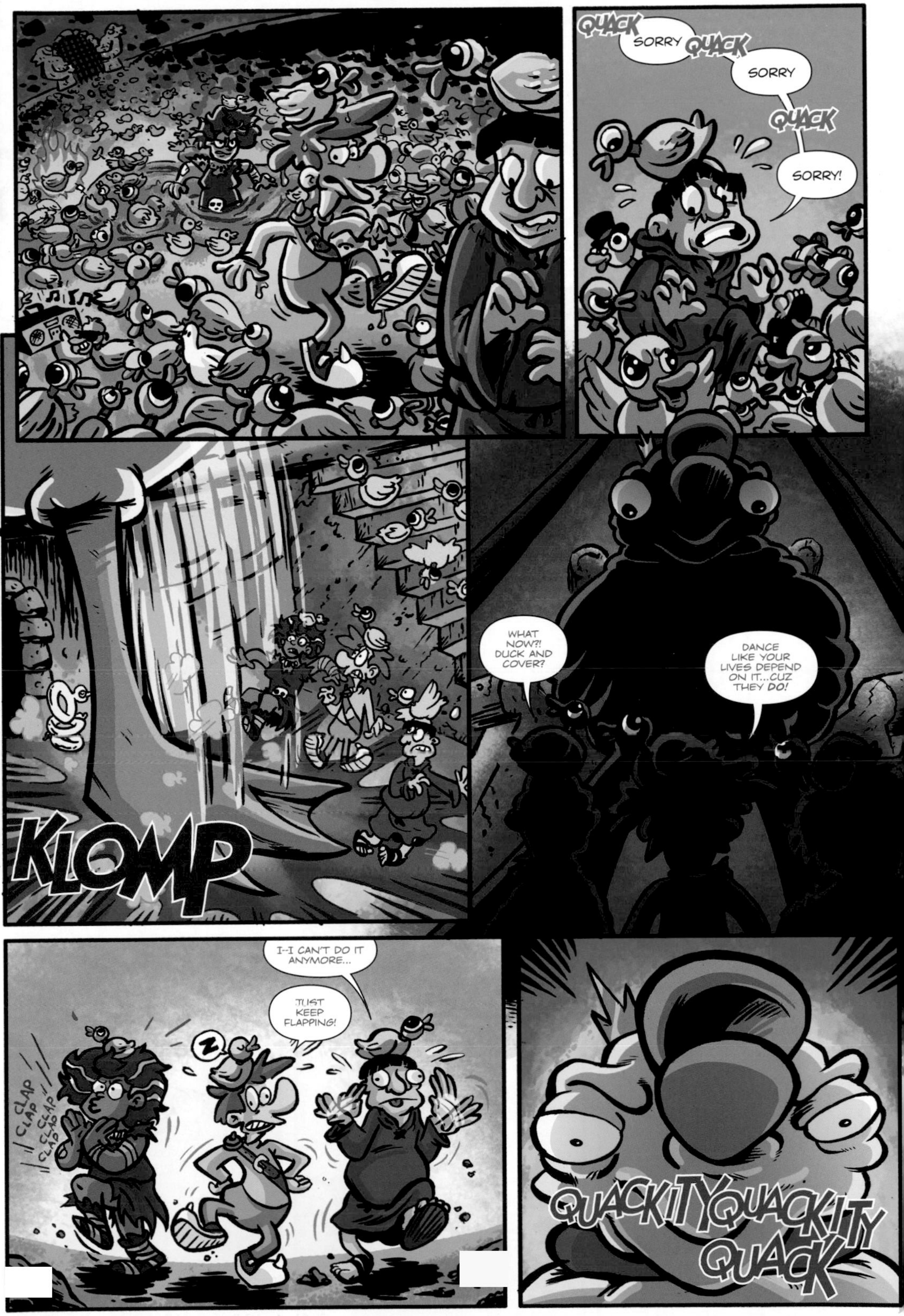
QUACK
SORRY
QUACK
SORRY
QUACK
SORRY!
KLOMP
WHAT NOW?! DUCK AND COVER?
DANCE LIKE YOUR LIVES DEPEND ON IT...CUZ THEY DO!
I--I CAN'T DO IT ANYMORE...
JUST KEEP FLAPPING!
CLAP CLAP CLAP CLAP
QUACKITYQUACKITY QUACK

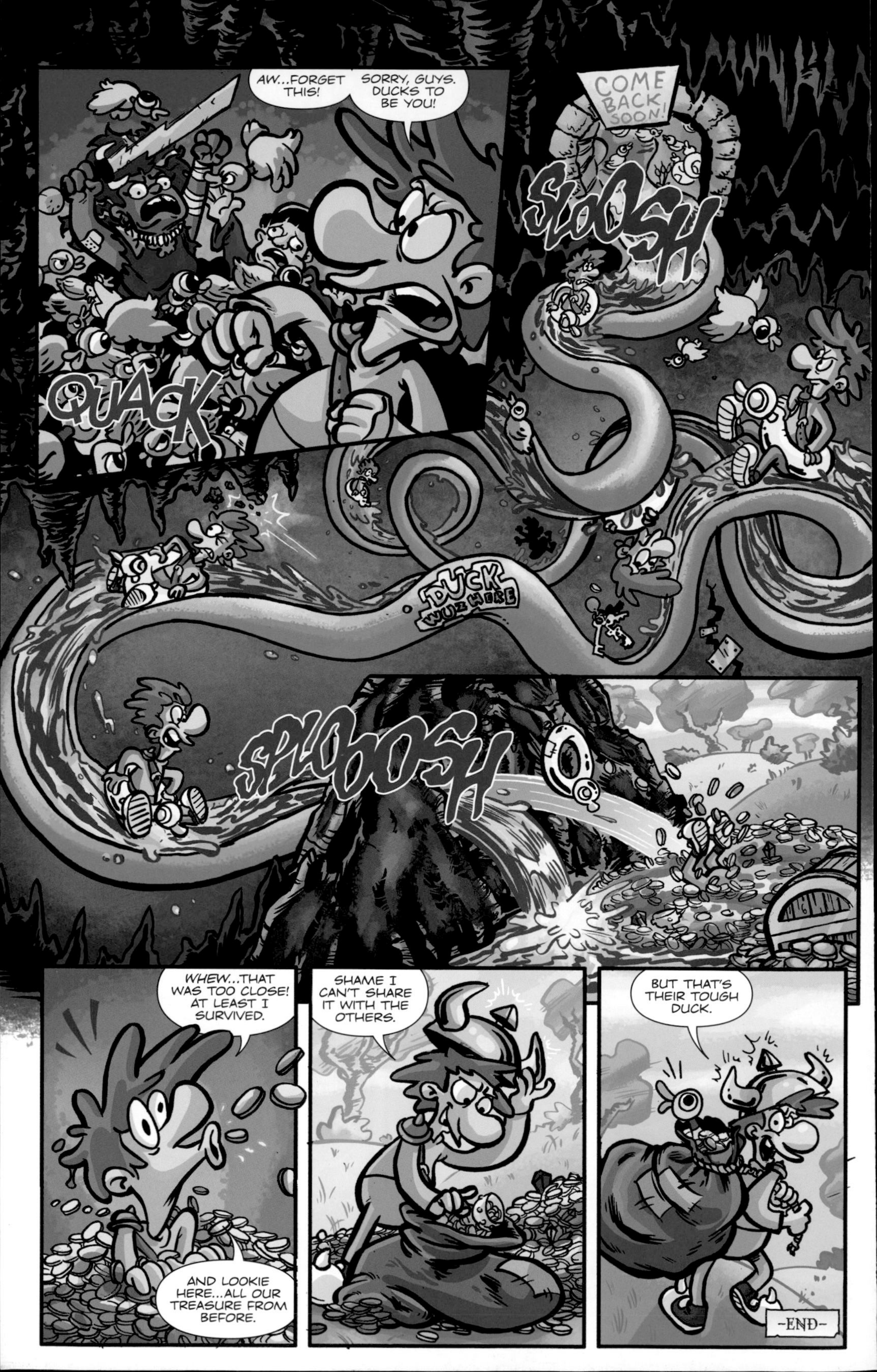
AW...FORGET THIS!
SORRY, GUYS. DUCKS TO BE YOU!
QUACK
COME BACK SOON!
SLOOSH
DUCK WUZ HERE
SPLOOSH
WHEW...THAT WAS TOO CLOSE! AT LEAST I SURVIVED.
AND LOOKIE HERE...ALL OUR TREASURE FROM BEFORE.
SHAME I CAN'T SHARE IT WITH THE OTHERS.
BUT THAT'S THEIR TOUGH DUCK.
-END-

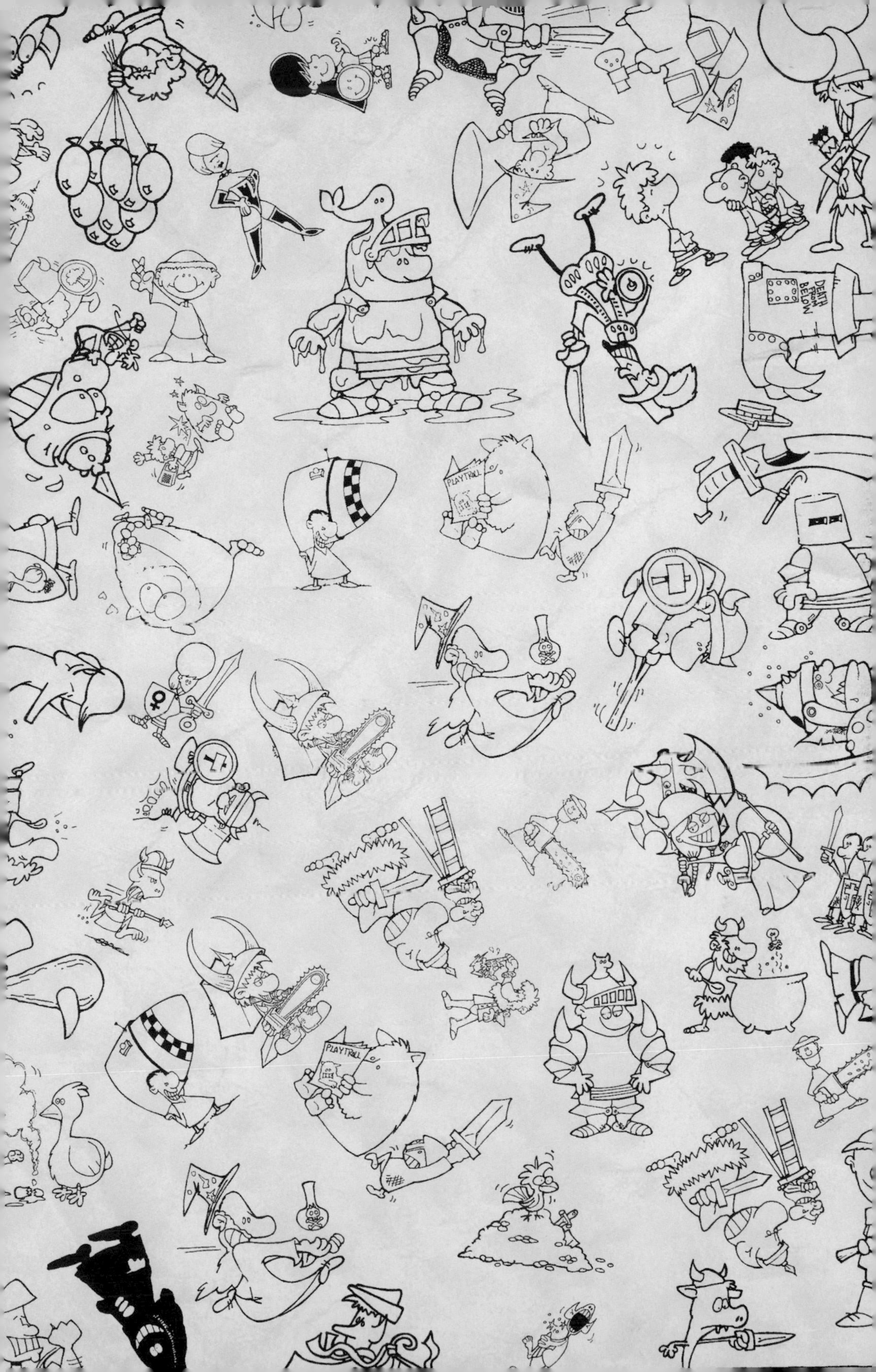
DEATH FROM BELOW
PLAYTROLL
PLAYTROLL

CHAPTER EIGHT

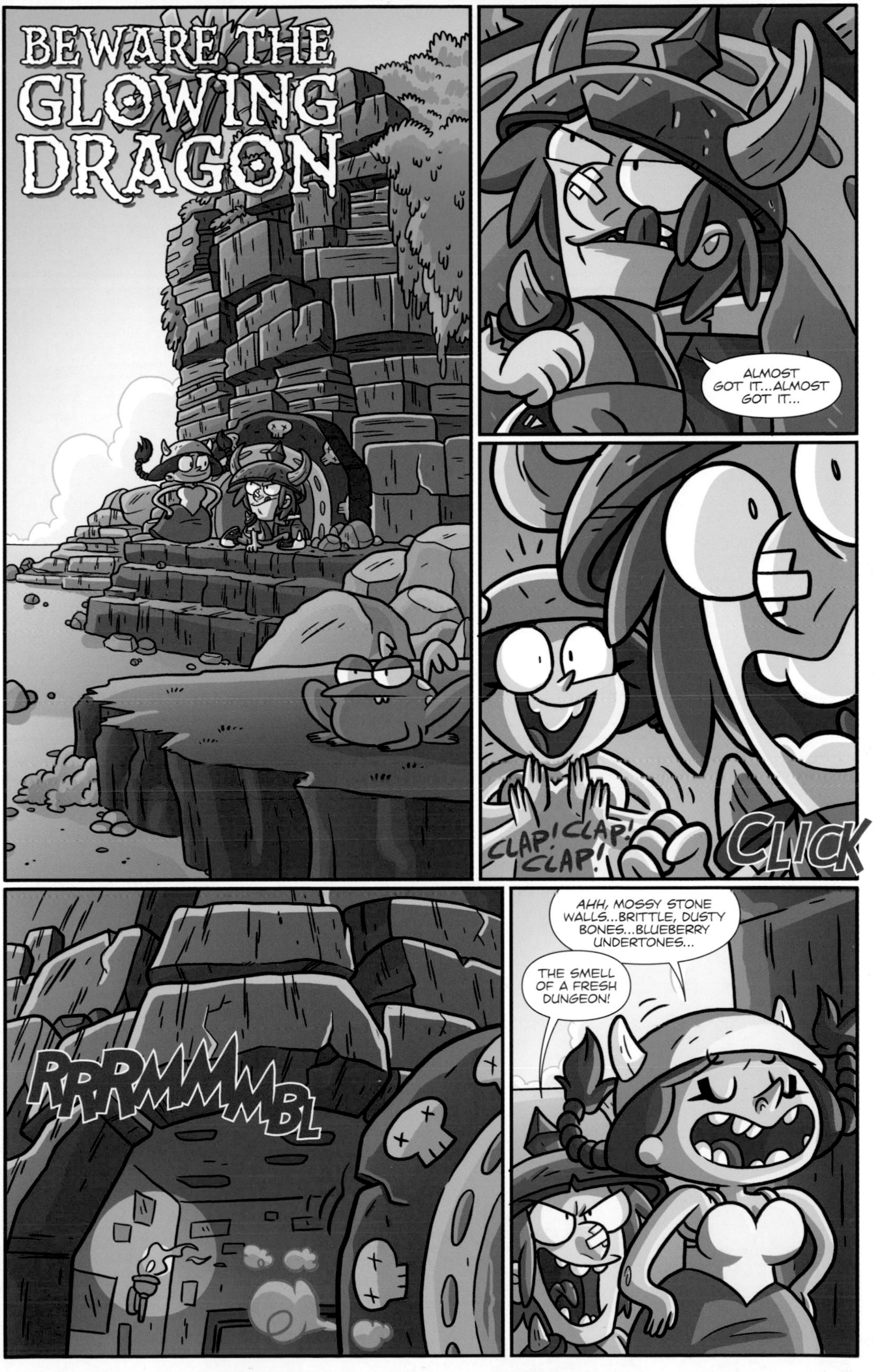
BEWARE THE GLOWING DRAGON
ALMOST GOT IT...ALMOST GOT IT...
CLAP! CLAP! CLAP!
CLICK
RRRMMMMBL
AHH, MOSSY STONE WALLS...BRITTLE, DUSTY BONES...BLUEBERRY UNDERTONES...
THE SMELL OF A FRESH DUNGEON!

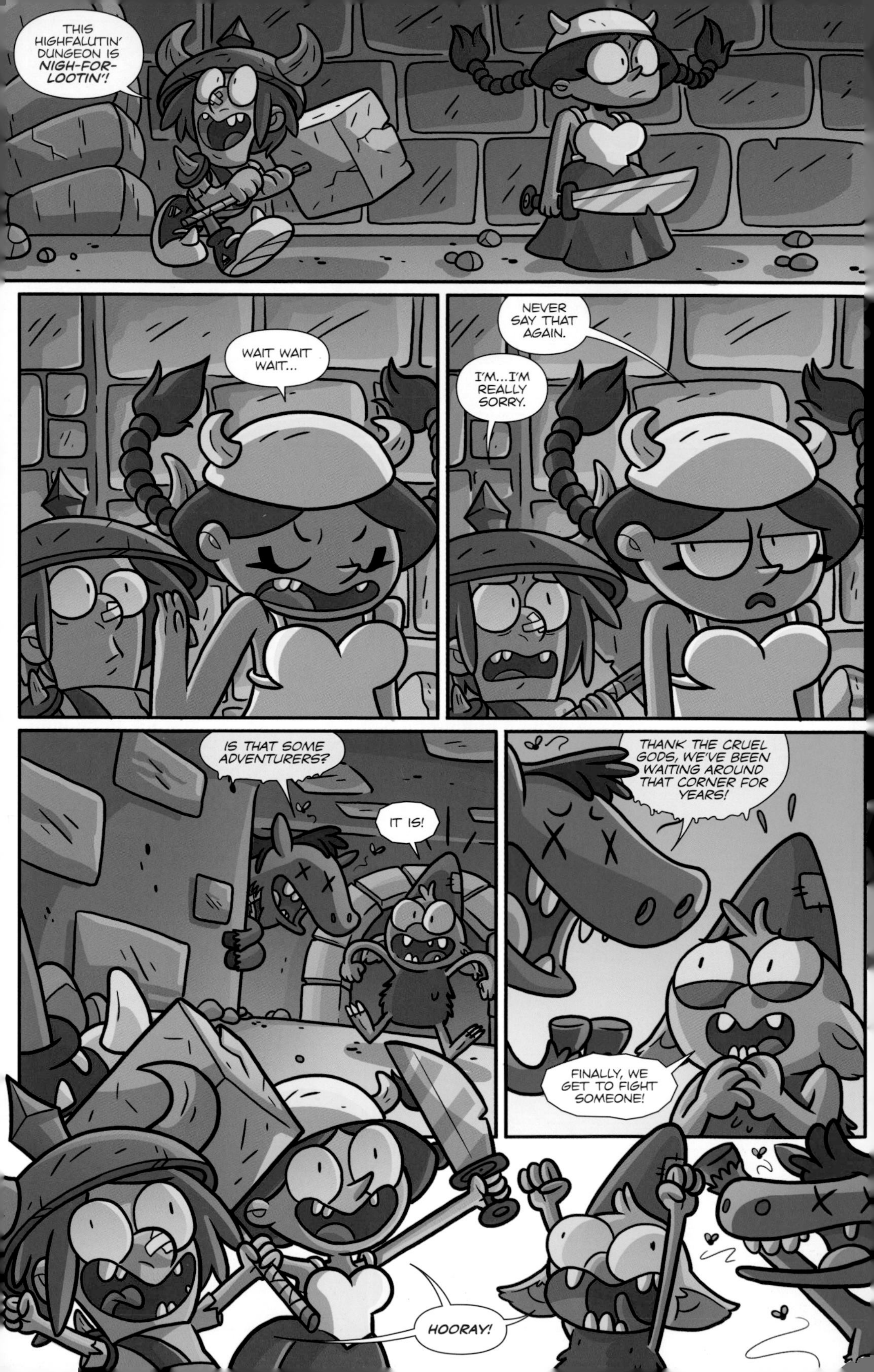
THIS HIGHFALUTIN' DUNGEON IS NIGH-FOR-LOOTIN'!
WAIT WAIT WAIT...
I'M...I'M REALLY SORRY.
NEVER SAY THAT AGAIN.
IS THAT SOME ADVENTURERS?
IT IS!
THANK THE CRUEL GODS, WE'VE BEEN WAITING AROUND THAT CORNER FOR YEARS!
FINALLY, WE GET TO FIGHT SOMEONE!
HOORAY!

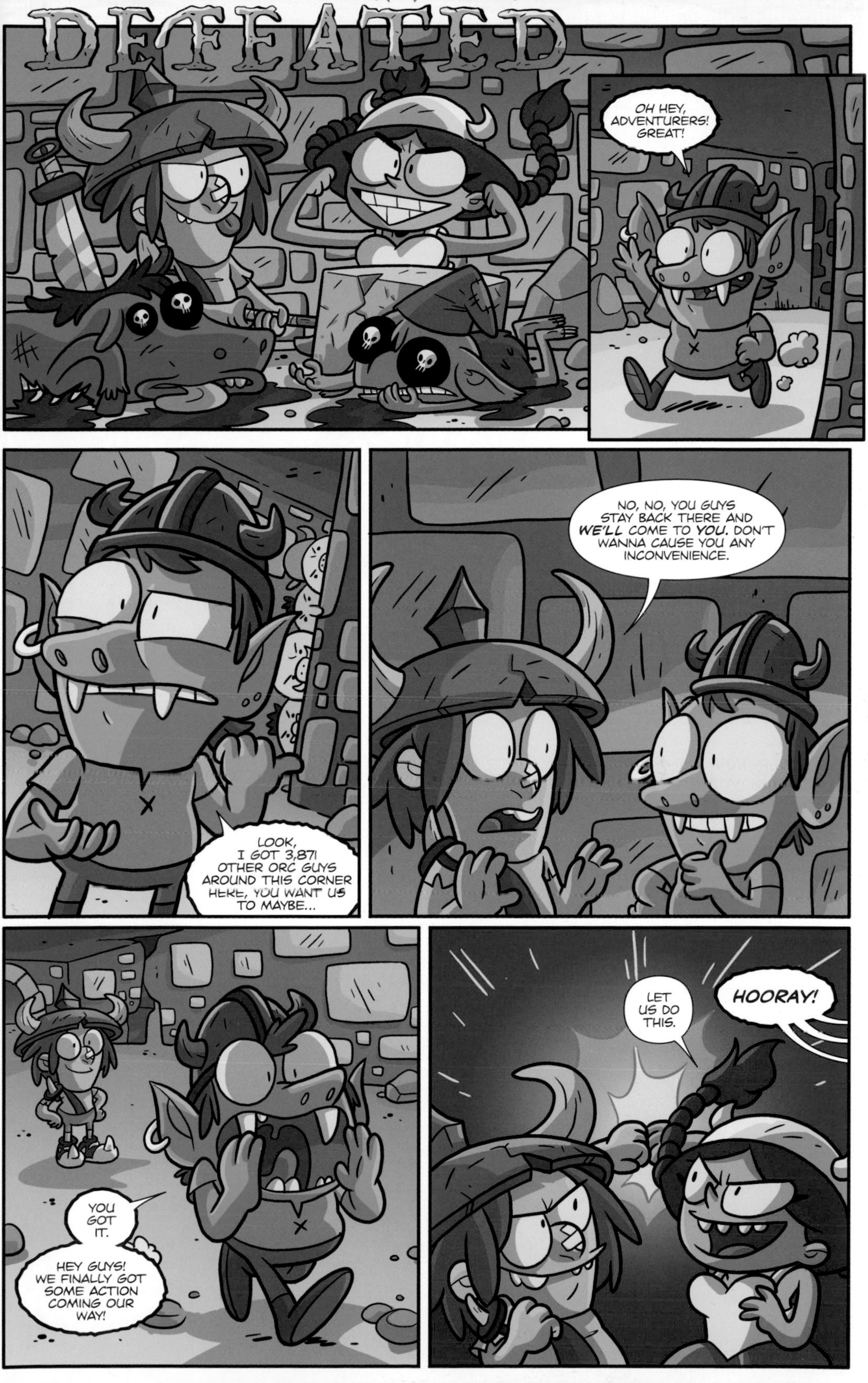
DEFEATED
OH HEY, ADVENTURERS! GREAT!
LOOK, I GOT 3,871 OTHER ORC GUYS AROUND THIS CORNER HERE, YOU WANT US TO MAYBE...
NO, NO, YOU GUYS STAY BACK THERE AND WE'LL COME TO YOU. DON'T WANNA CAUSE YOU ANY INCONVENIENCE.
YOU GOT IT.
HEY GUYS! WE FINALLY GOT SOME ACTION COMING OUR WAY!
LET US DO THIS.
HOORAY!

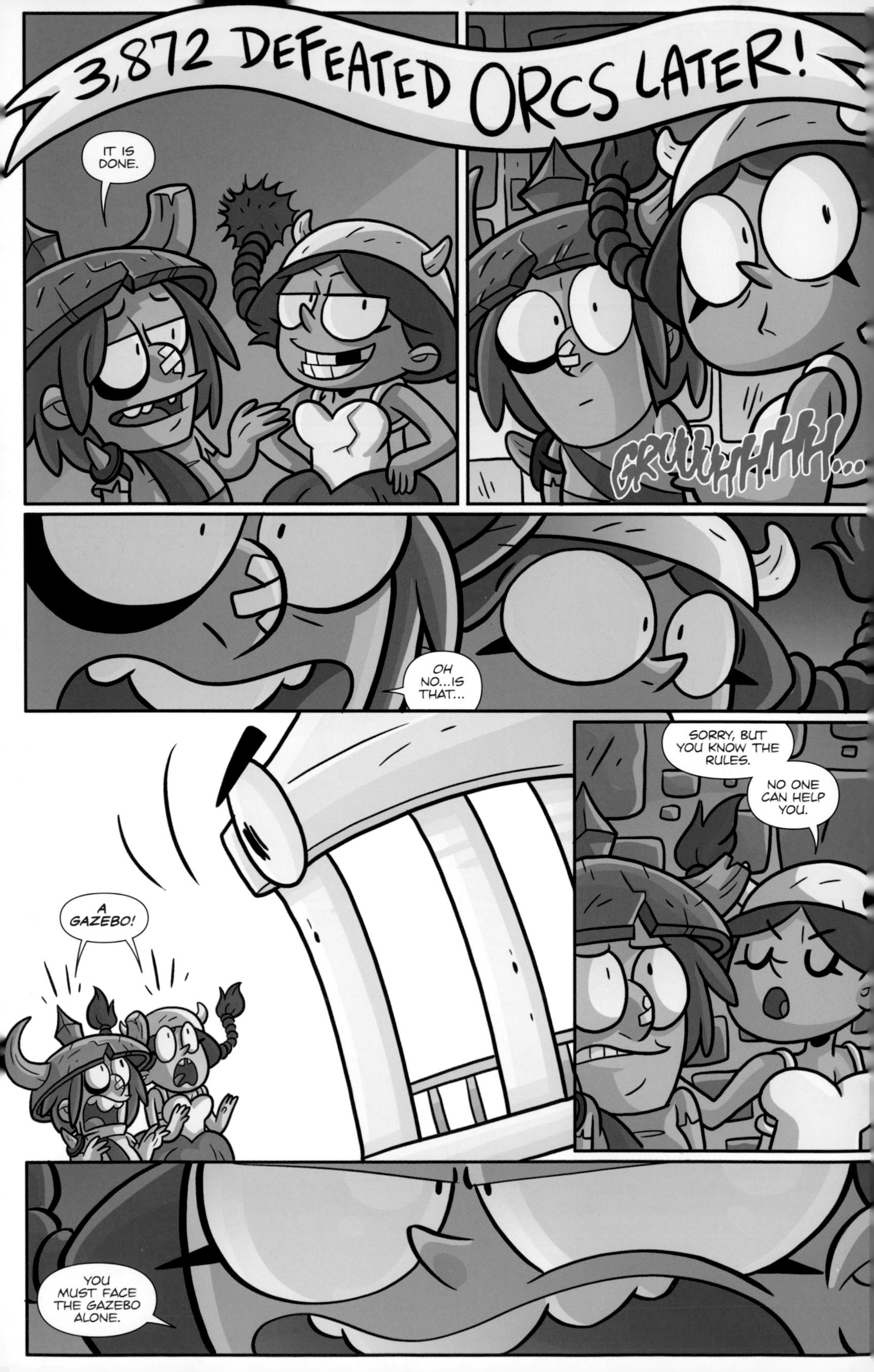
3,872 DEFEATED ORCS LATER!
IT IS DONE.
GRUUHHHH...
OH NO...IS THAT...
A GAZEBO!
SORRY, BUT YOU KNOW THE RULES.
NO ONE CAN HELP YOU.
YOU MUST FACE THE GAZEBO ALONE.

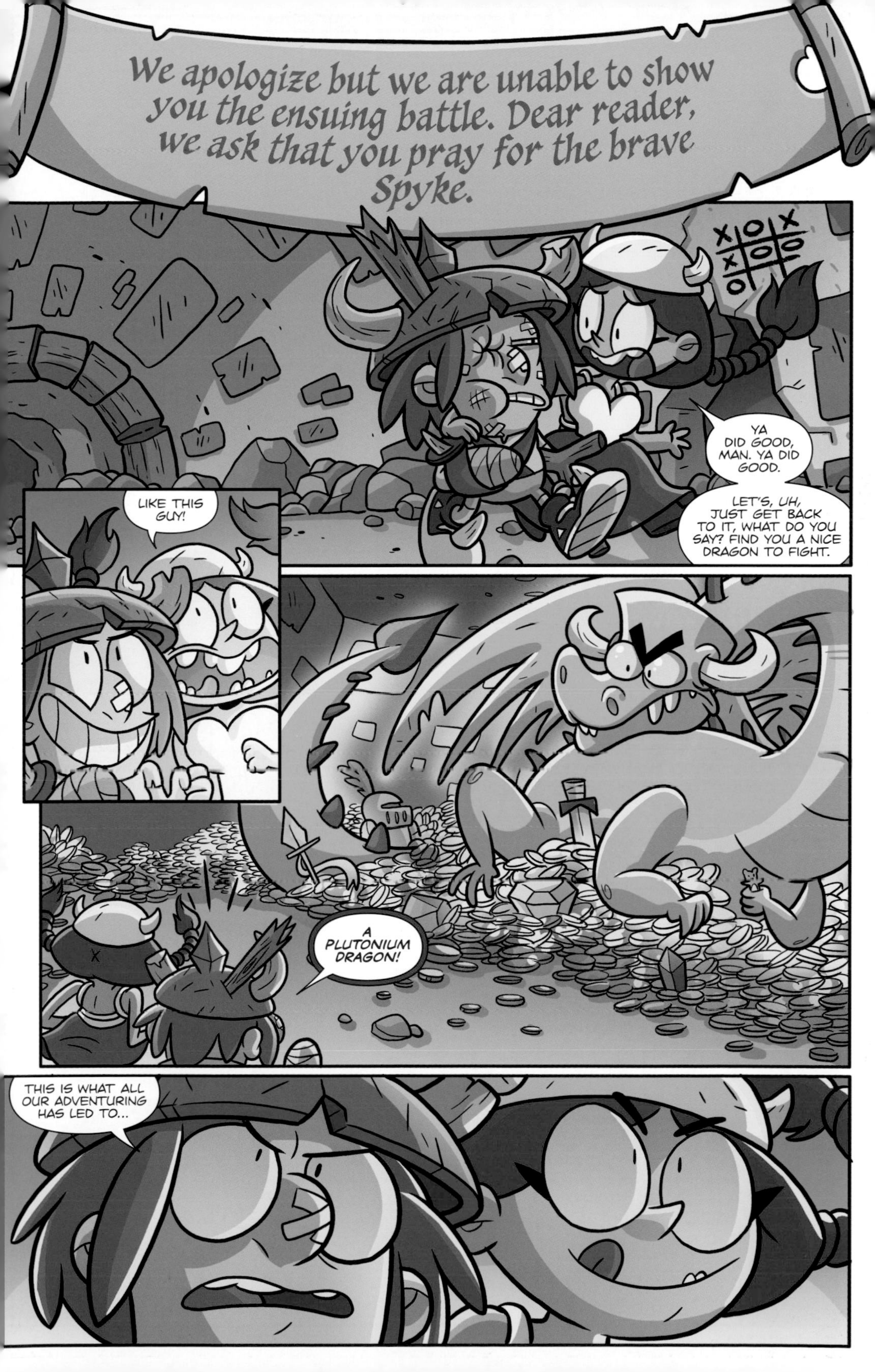
We apologize but we are unable to show you the ensuing battle. Dear reader, we ask that you pray for the brave Spyke.
YA DID GOOD, MAN. YA DID GOOD.
LET'S, UH, JUST GET BACK TO IT, WHAT DO YOU SAY? FIND YOU A NICE DRAGON TO FIGHT.
LIKE THIS GUY!
A PLUTONIUM DRAGON!
THIS IS WHAT ALL OUR ADVENTURING HAS LED TO...

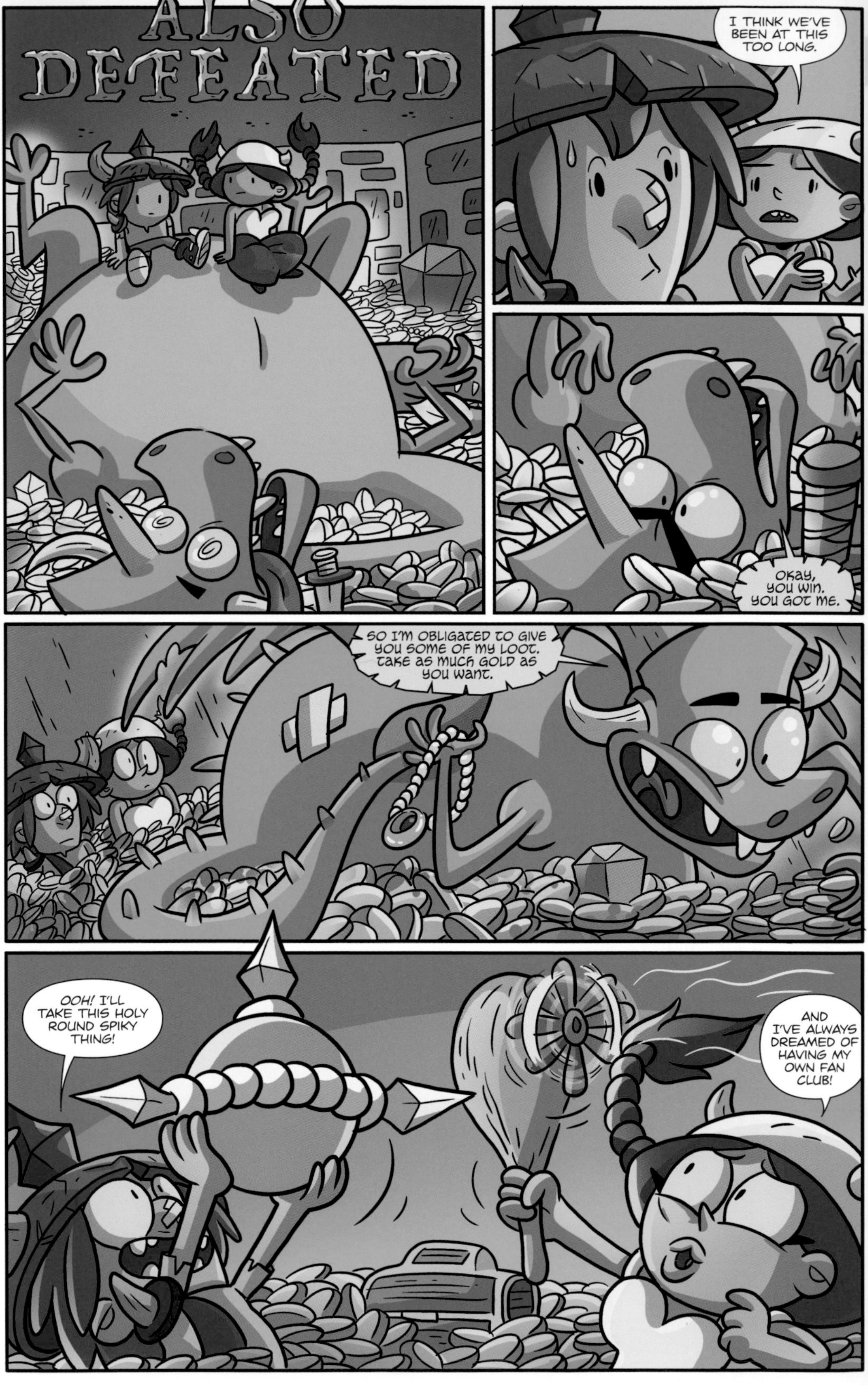
ALSO DEFEATED
I THINK WE'VE BEEN AT THIS TOO LONG.
OKAY, YOU WIN. YOU GOT ME.
SO I'M OBLIGATED TO GIVE YOU SOME OF MY LOOT. TAKE AS MUCH GOLD AS YOU WANT.
OOH! I'LL TAKE THIS HOLY ROUND SPIKY THING!
AND I'VE ALWAYS DREAMED OF HAVING MY OWN FAN CLUB!

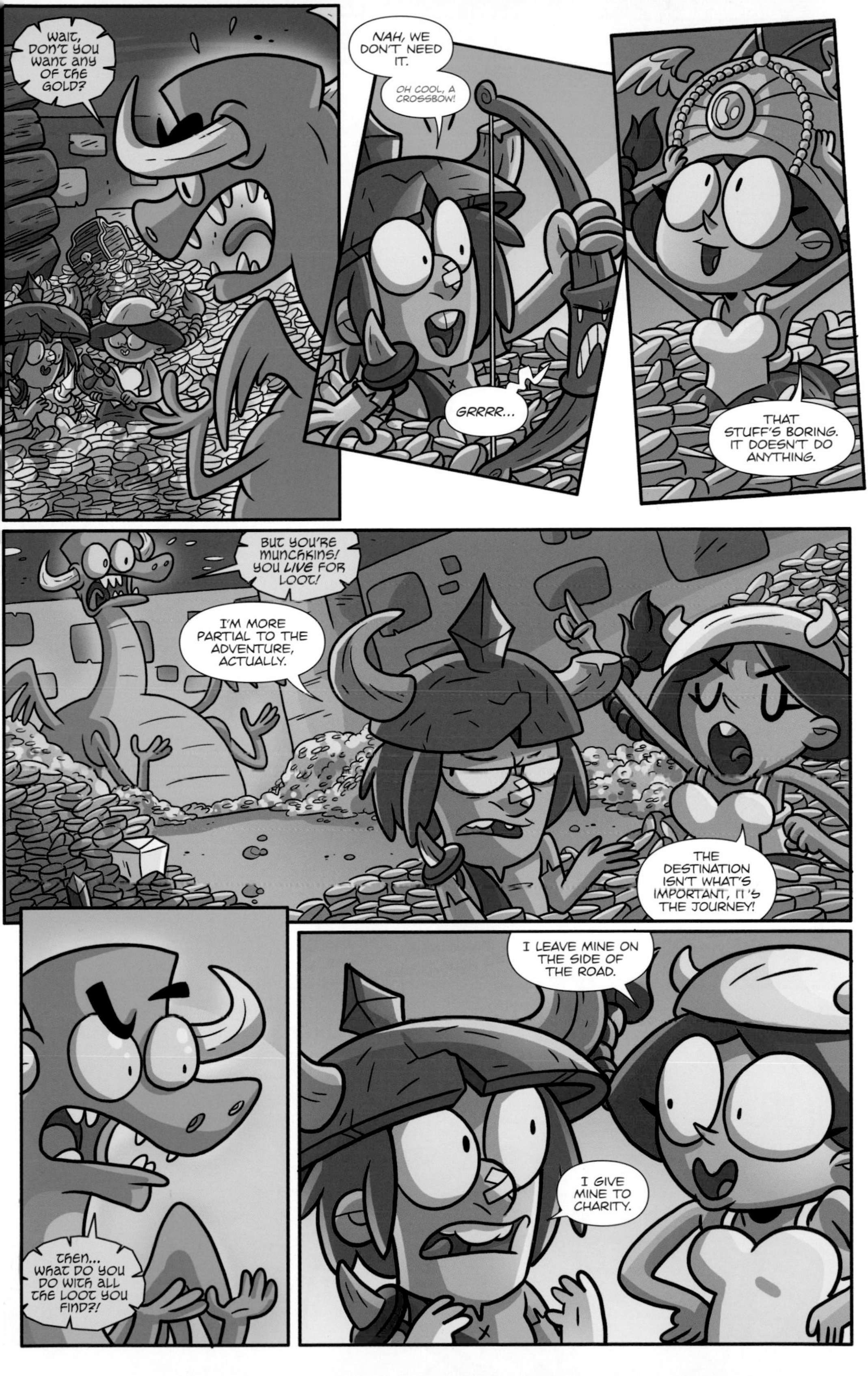
WAIT, DON'T YOU WANT ANY OF THE GOLD?
NAH, WE DON'T NEED IT.
OH COOL, A CROSSBOW!
GRRRR...
THAT STUFF'S BORING. IT DOESN'T DO ANYTHING.
BUT YOU'RE MUNCHKINS! YOU LIVE FOR LOOT!
I'M MORE PARTIAL TO THE ADVENTURE, ACTUALLY.
THE DESTINATION ISN'T WHAT'S IMPORTANT, IT'S THE JOURNEY!
THEN... WHAT DO YOU DO WITH ALL THE LOOT YOU FIND?!
I LEAVE MINE ON THE SIDE OF THE ROAD.
I GIVE MINE TO CHARITY.

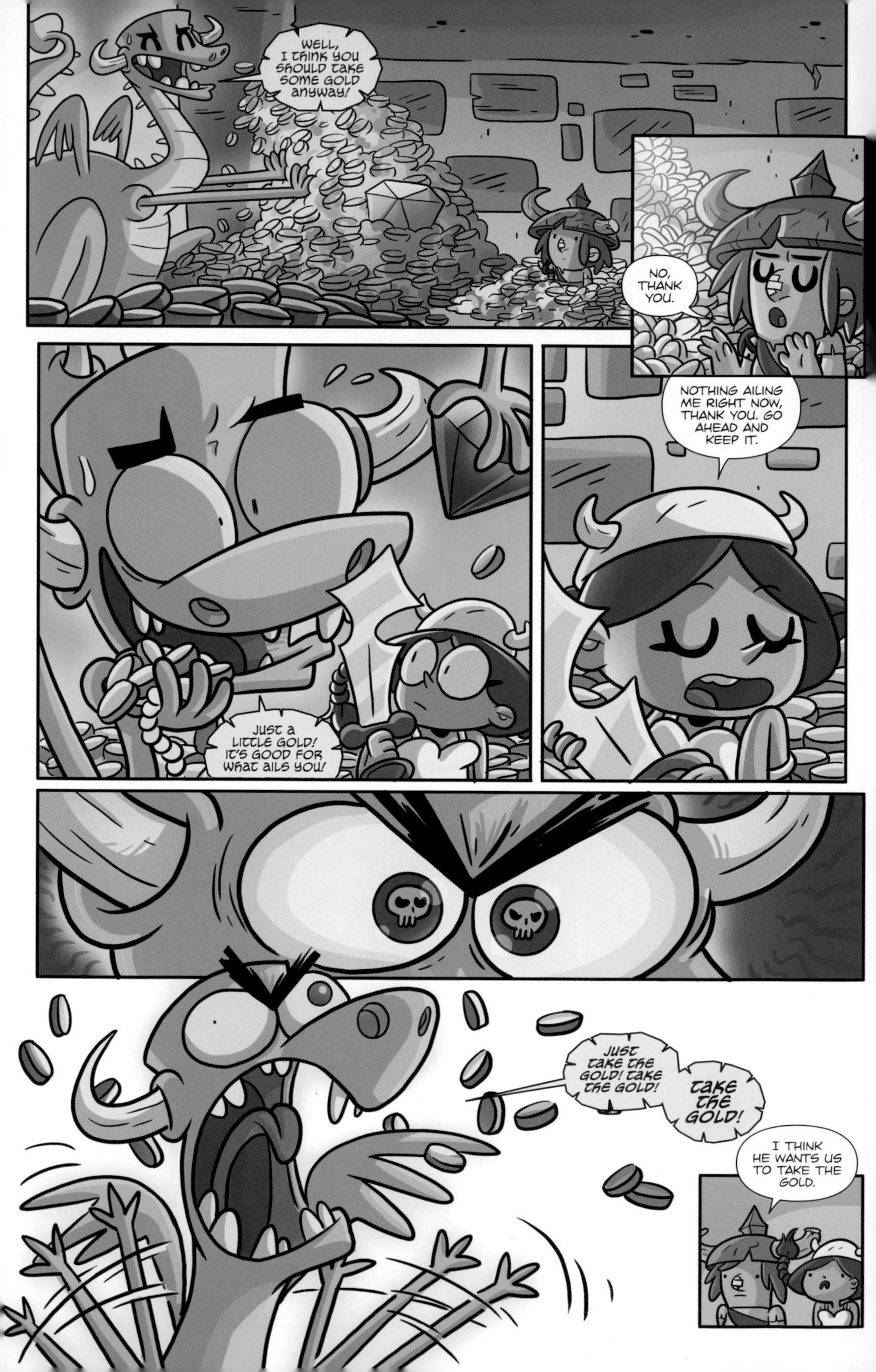
WELL, I THINK YOU SHOULD TAKE SOME GOLD ANYWAY!
NO, THANK YOU.
JUST A LITTLE GOLD! IT'S GOOD FOR WHAT AILS YOU!
NOTHING AILING ME RIGHT NOW, THANK YOU. GO AHEAD AND KEEP IT.
JUST TAKE THE GOLD! TAKE THE GOLD!
TAKE THE GOLD!
I THINK HE WANTS US TO TAKE THE GOLD.

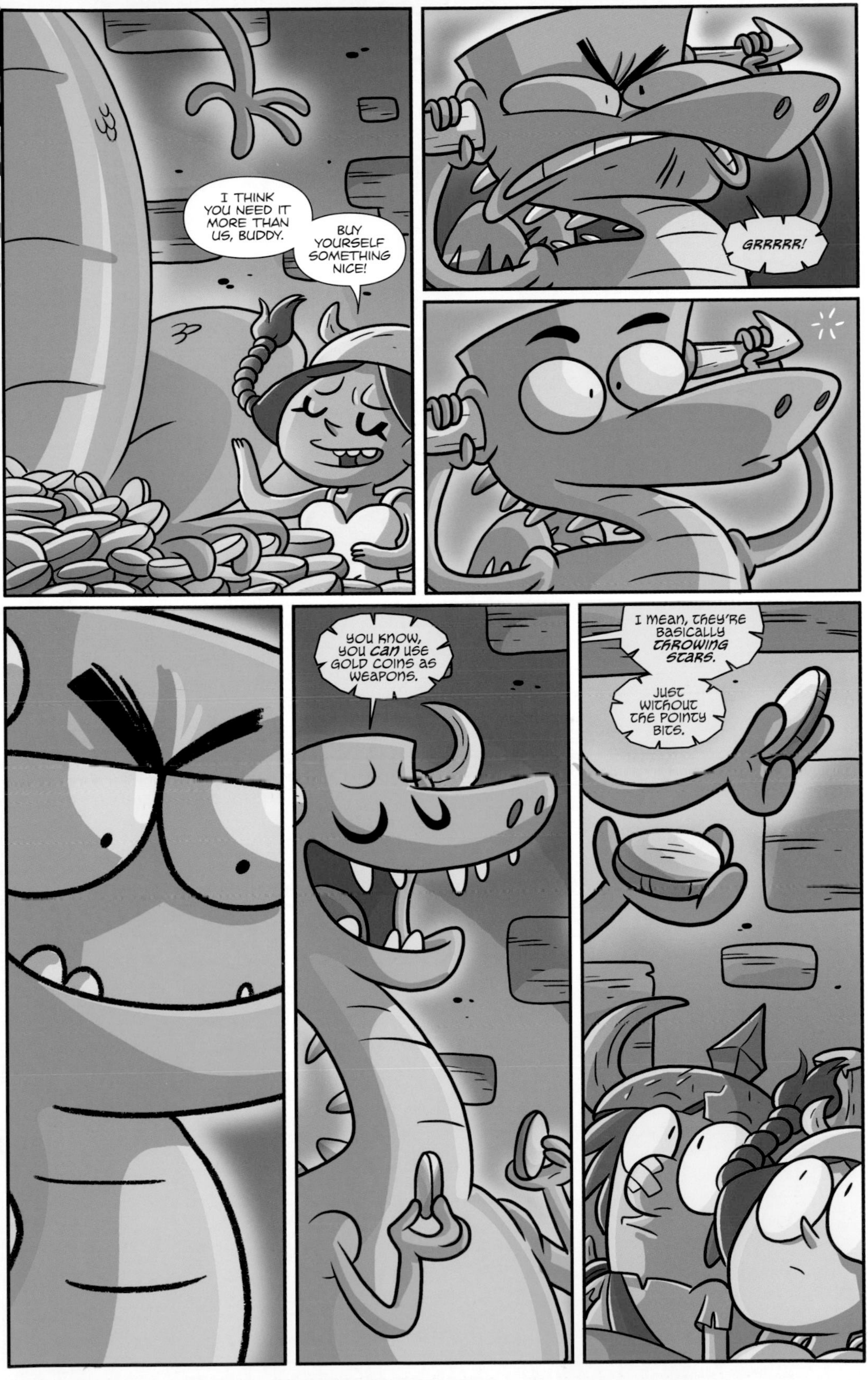

I THINK YOU NEED IT MORE THAN US, BUDDY.
BUY YOURSELF SOMETHING NICE!
GRRRRR!
YOU KNOW, YOU CAN USE GOLD COINS AS WEAPONS.
I MEAN, THEY'RE BASICALLY THROWING STARS.
JUST WITHOUT THE POINTY BITS.

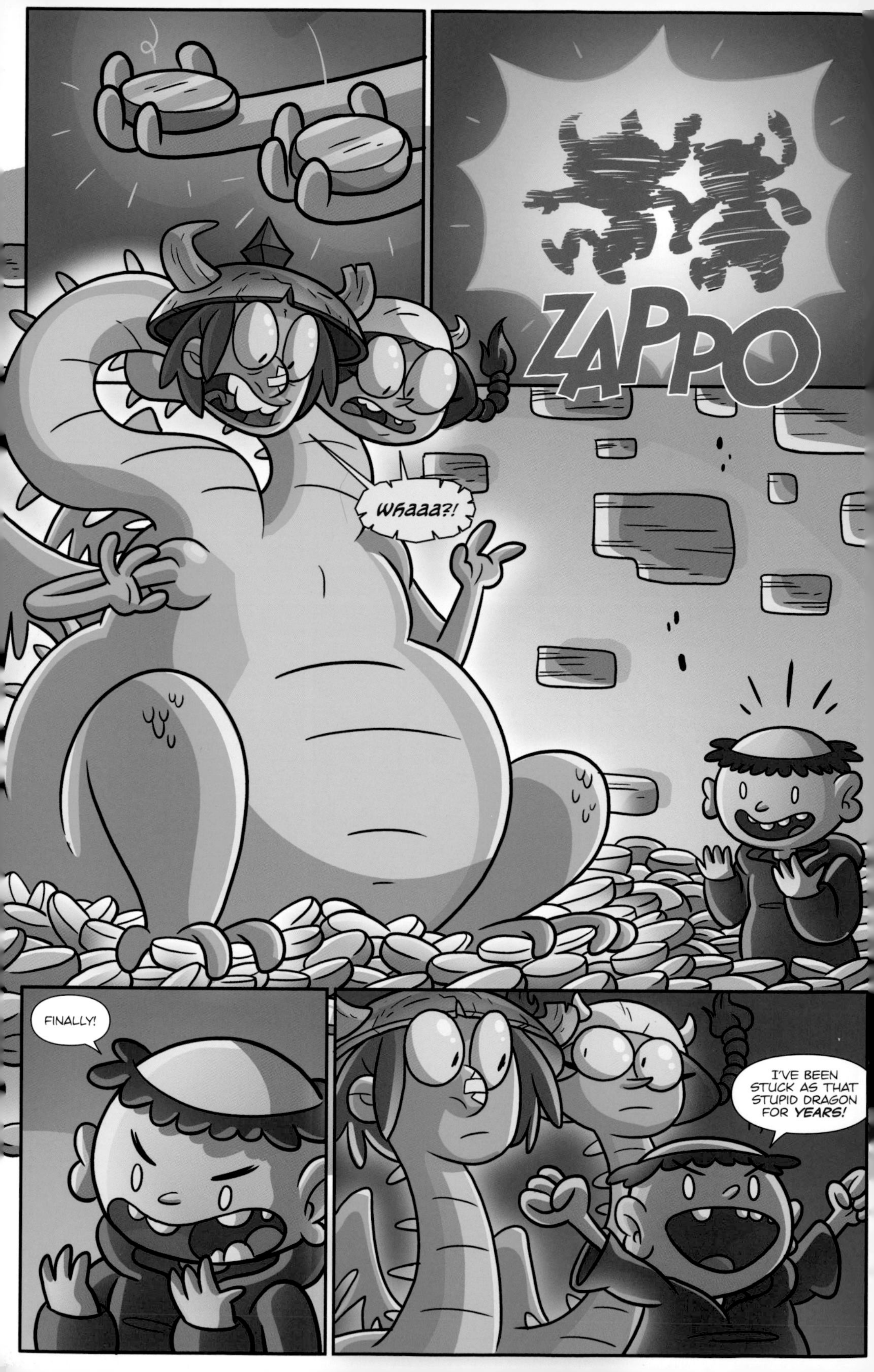
ZAPPO
Whaaa?!
FINALLY!
I'VE BEEN STUCK AS THAT STUPID DRAGON FOR YEARS!

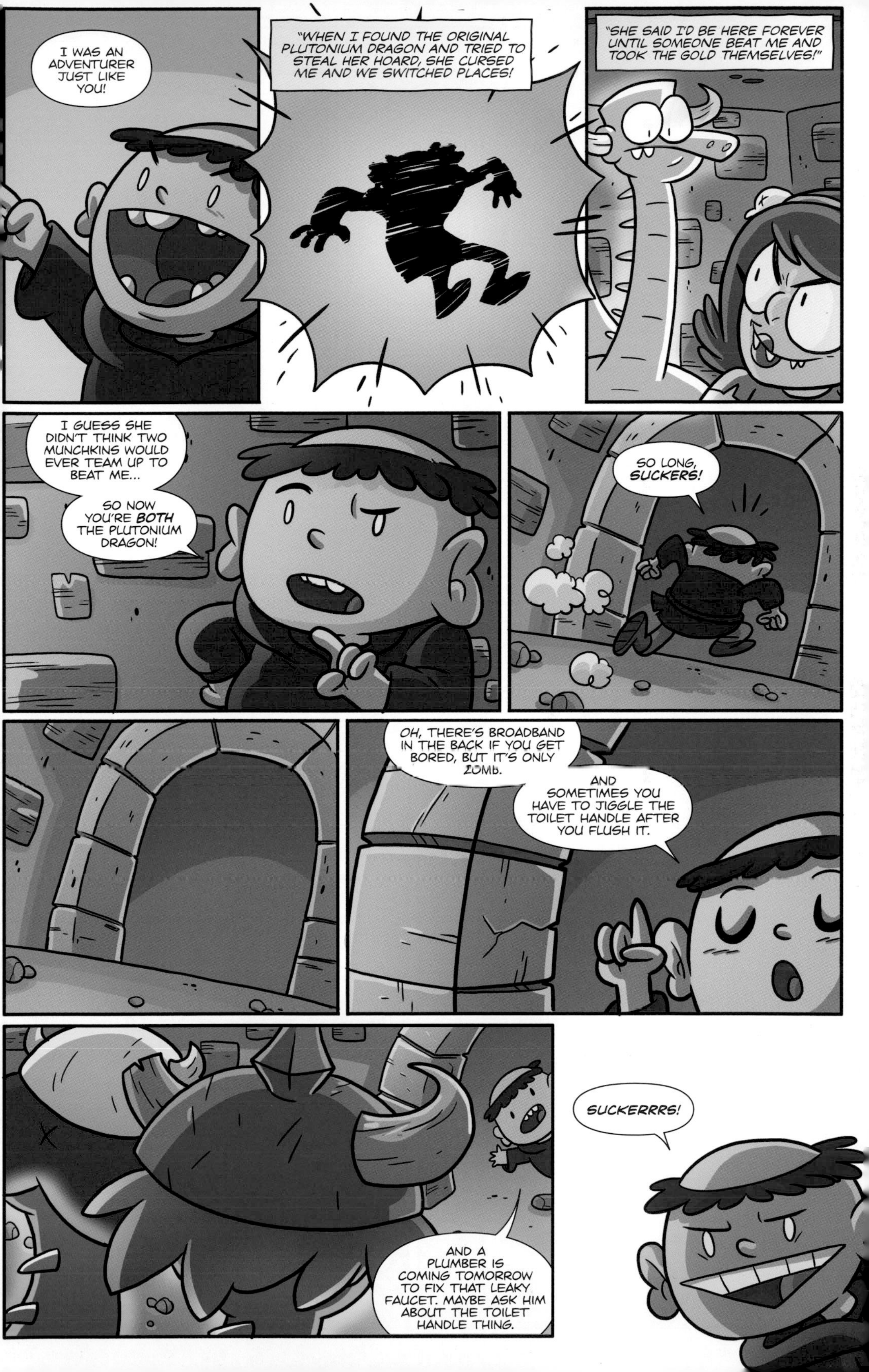
I WAS AN ADVENTURER JUST LIKE YOU!
"WHEN I FOUND THE ORIGINAL PLUTONIUM DRAGON AND TRIED TO STEAL HER HOARD, SHE CURSED ME AND WE SWITCHED PLACES!
"SHE SAID I'D BE HERE FOREVER UNTIL SOMEONE BEAT ME AND TOOK THE GOLD THEMSELVES!"
I GUESS SHE DIDN'T THINK TWO MUNCHKINS WOULD EVER TEAM UP TO BEAT ME...
SO NOW YOU'RE **BOTH** THE PLUTONIUM DRAGON!
SO LONG, **SUCKERS!**
OH, THERE'S BROADBAND IN THE BACK IF YOU GET BORED, BUT IT'S ONLY 20MB.
AND SOMETIMES YOU HAVE TO JIGGLE THE TOILET HANDLE AFTER YOU FLUSH IT.
AND A PLUMBER IS COMING TOMORROW TO FIX THAT LEAKY FAUCET. MAYBE ASK HIM ABOUT THE TOILET HANDLE THING.
SUCKERRRS!

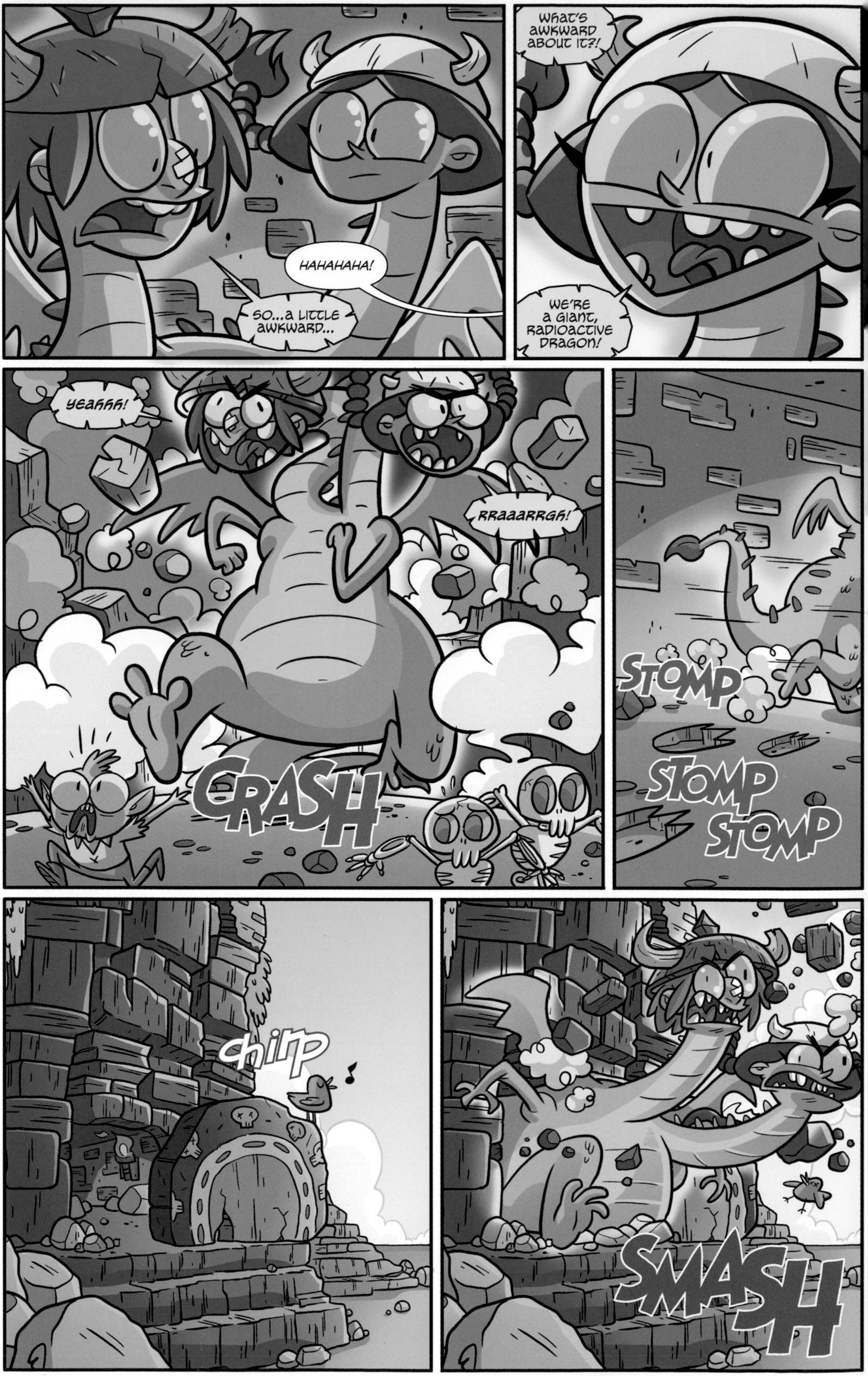
HAHAHAHA!
SO...A LITTLE AWKWARD...
WHAT'S AWKWARD ABOUT IT?!
WE'RE A GIANT, RADIOACTIVE DRAGON!
YEAHHH!
RRAAAARRGH!
CRASH
STOMP
STOMP
STOMP
CHIRP
SMASH

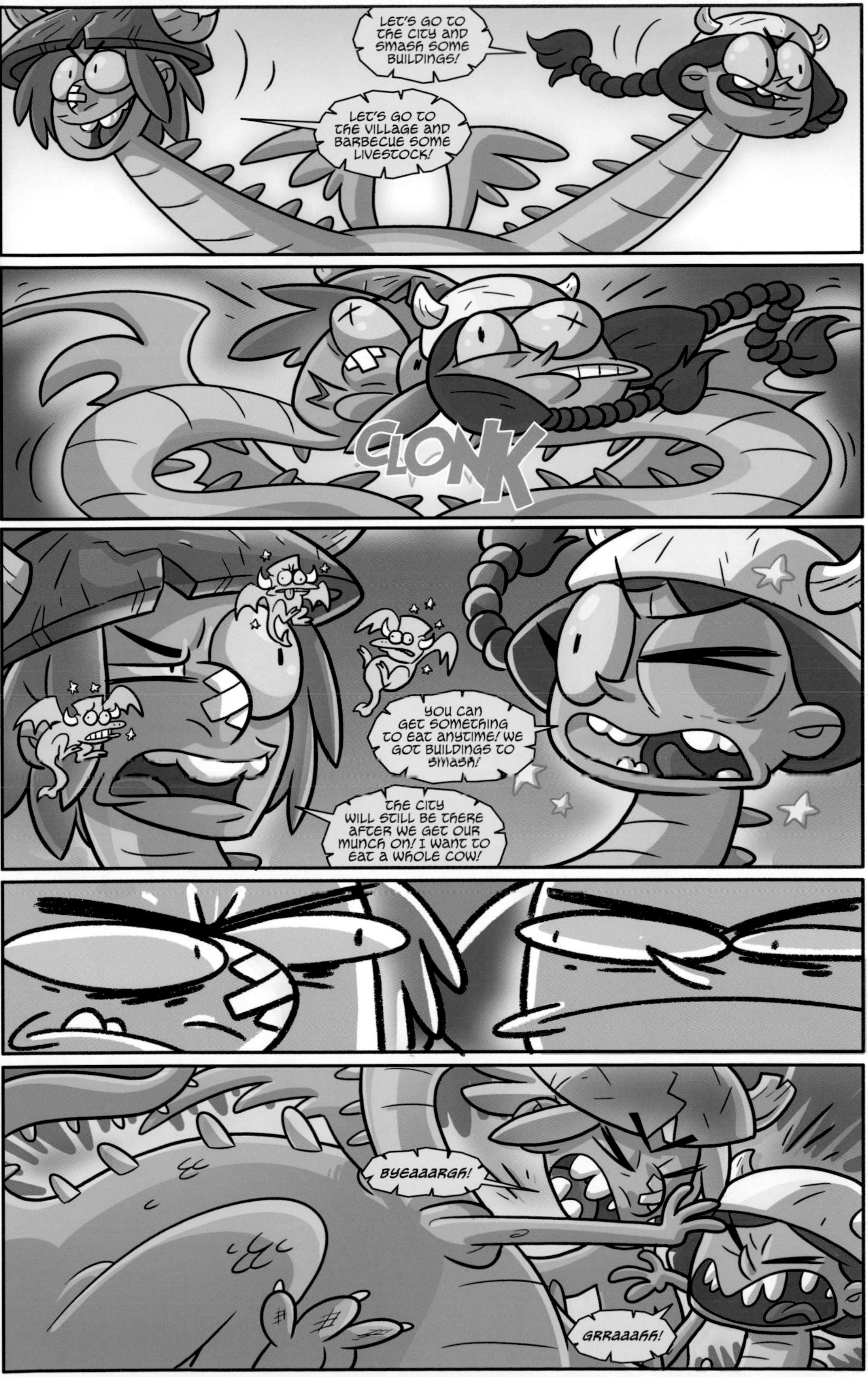
LET'S GO TO THE CITY AND SMASH SOME BUILDINGS!
LET'S GO TO THE VILLAGE AND BARBECUE SOME LIVESTOCK!
CLONK
YOU CAN GET SOMETHING TO EAT ANYTIME! WE GOT BUILDINGS TO SMASH!
THE CITY WILL STILL BE THERE AFTER WE GET OUR MUNCH ON! I WANT TO EAT A WHOLE COW!
BYEAAARGH!
GRRAAAHH!

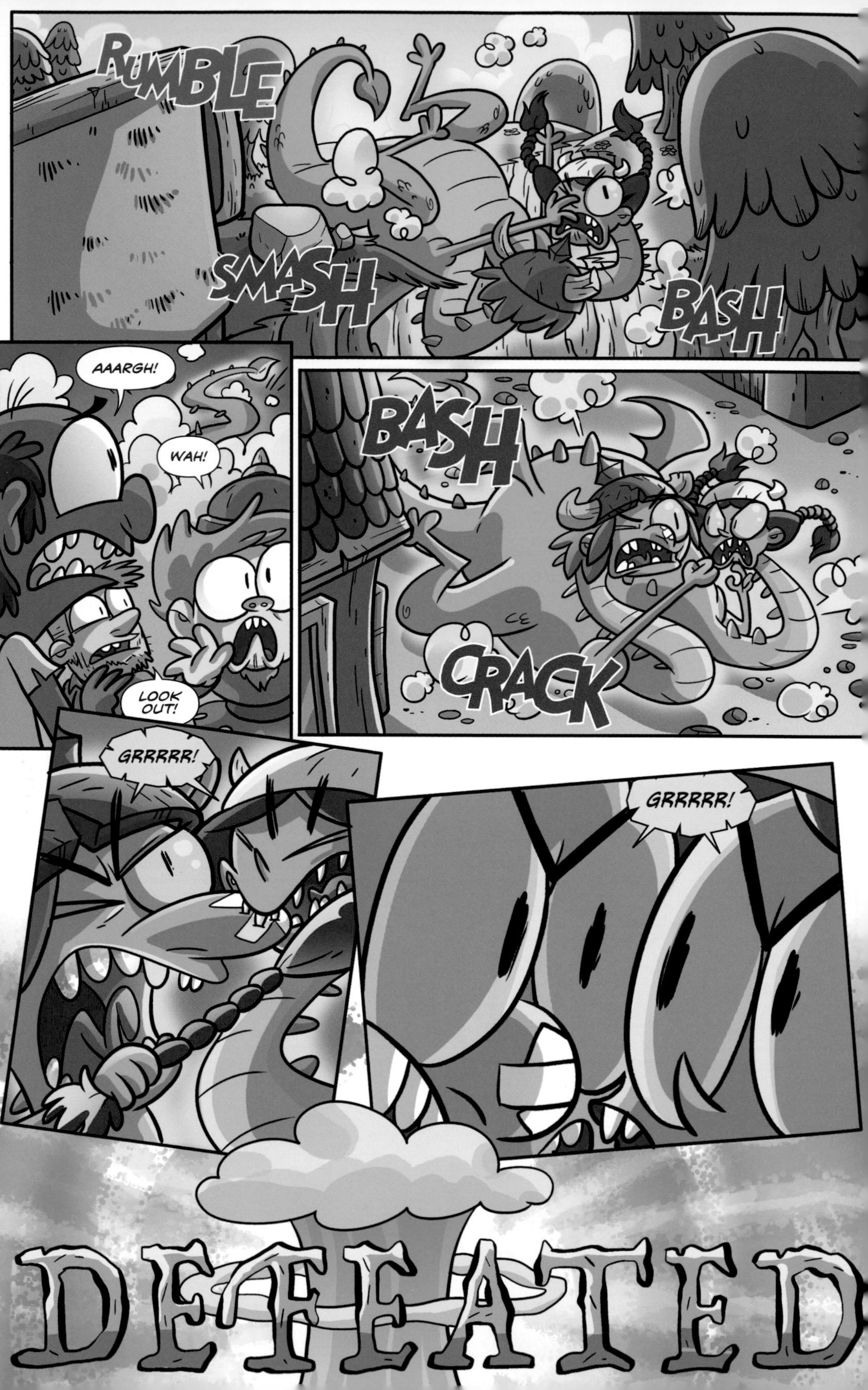
RUMBLE
SMASH
BASH
AAARGH!
WAH!
LOOK OUT!
BASH
CRACK
GRRRRR!
GRRRRR!
DEFEATED

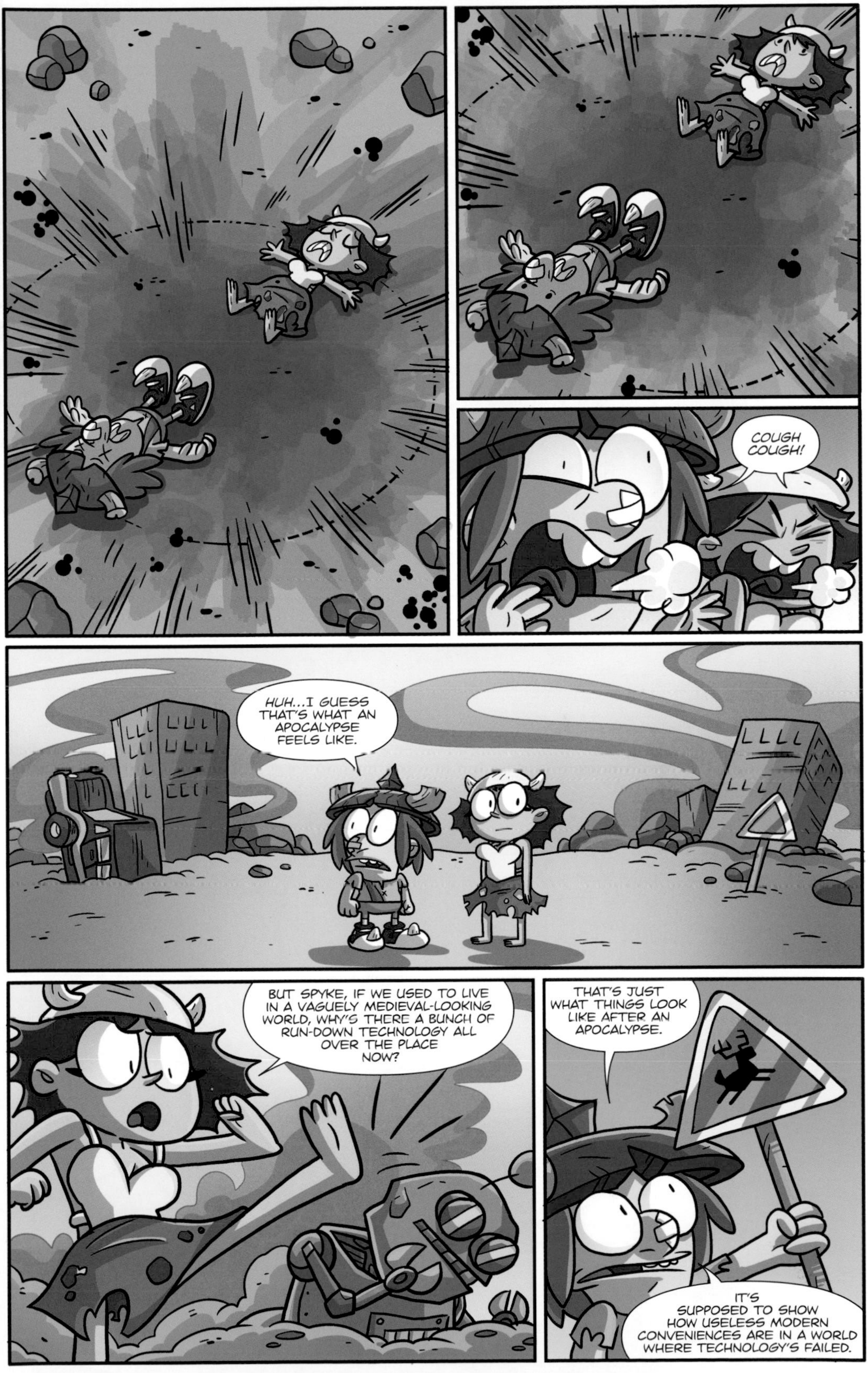
COUGH COUGH!
HUH...I GUESS THAT'S WHAT AN APOCALYPSE FEELS LIKE.
BUT SPYKE, IF WE USED TO LIVE IN A VAGUELY MEDIEVAL-LOOKING WORLD, WHY'S THERE A BUNCH OF RUN-DOWN TECHNOLOGY ALL OVER THE PLACE NOW?
THAT'S JUST WHAT THINGS LOOK LIKE AFTER AN APOCALYPSE.
IT'S SUPPOSED TO SHOW HOW USELESS MODERN CONVENIENCES ARE IN A WORLD WHERE TECHNOLOGY'S FAILED.

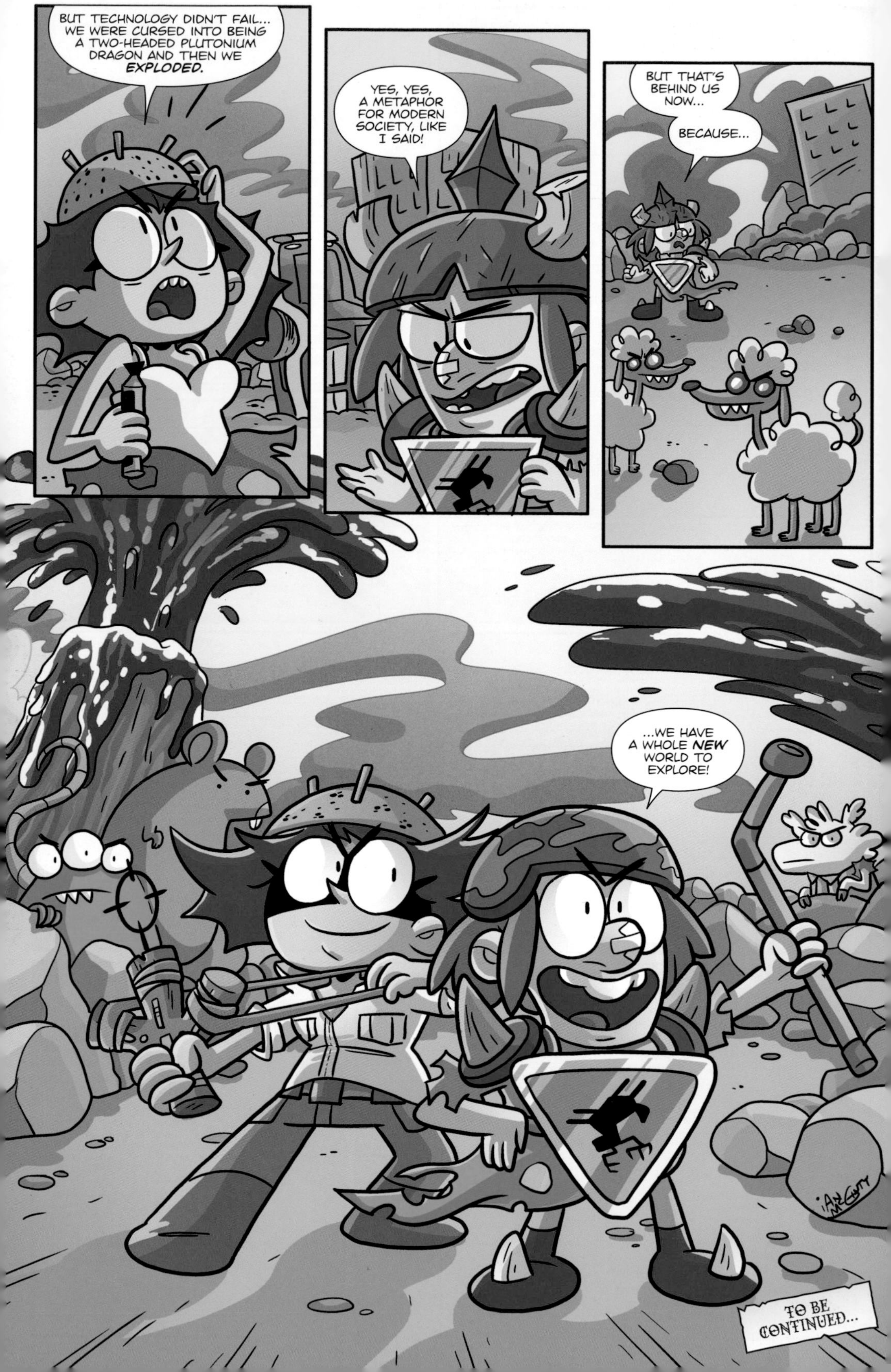

BUT TECHNOLOGY DIDN'T FAIL... WE WERE CURSED INTO BEING A TWO-HEADED PLUTONIUM DRAGON AND THEN WE ***EXPLODED.***
YES, YES, A METAPHOR FOR MODERN SOCIETY, LIKE I SAID!
BUT THAT'S BEHIND US NOW...
BECAUSE...
...WE HAVE A WHOLE ***NEW*** WORLD TO EXPLORE!
IAN McGINTY
TO BE CONTINUED...

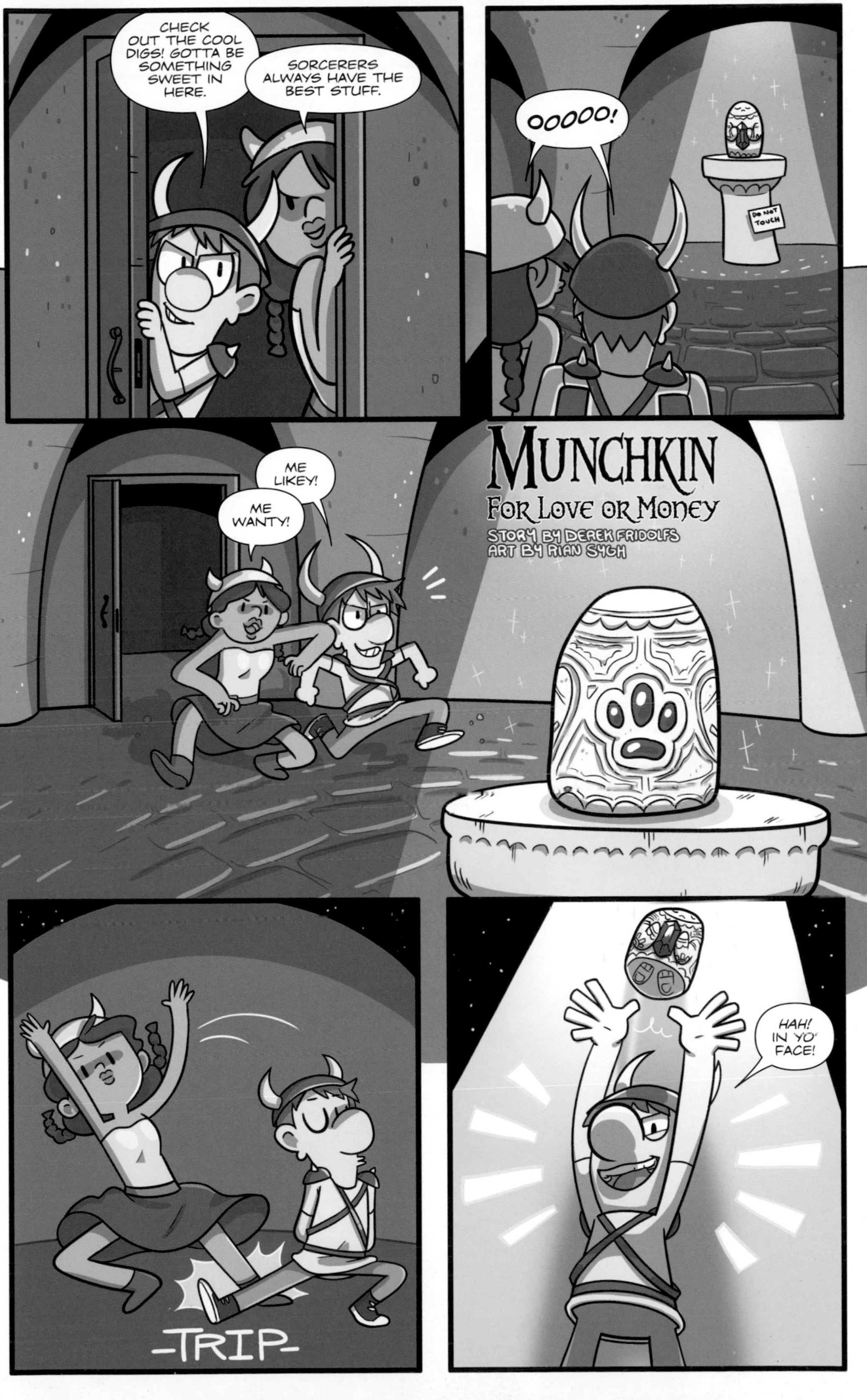
CHECK OUT THE COOL DIGS! GOTTA BE SOMETHING SWEET IN HERE.
SORCERERS ALWAYS HAVE THE BEST STUFF.
OOOOO!
DO NOT TOUCH
ME LIKEY!
ME WANTY!
MUNCHKIN
FOR LOVE OR MONEY
STORY BY DEREK FRIDOLFS
ART BY RIAN SYGH
-TRIP-
HAH! IN YO' FACE!

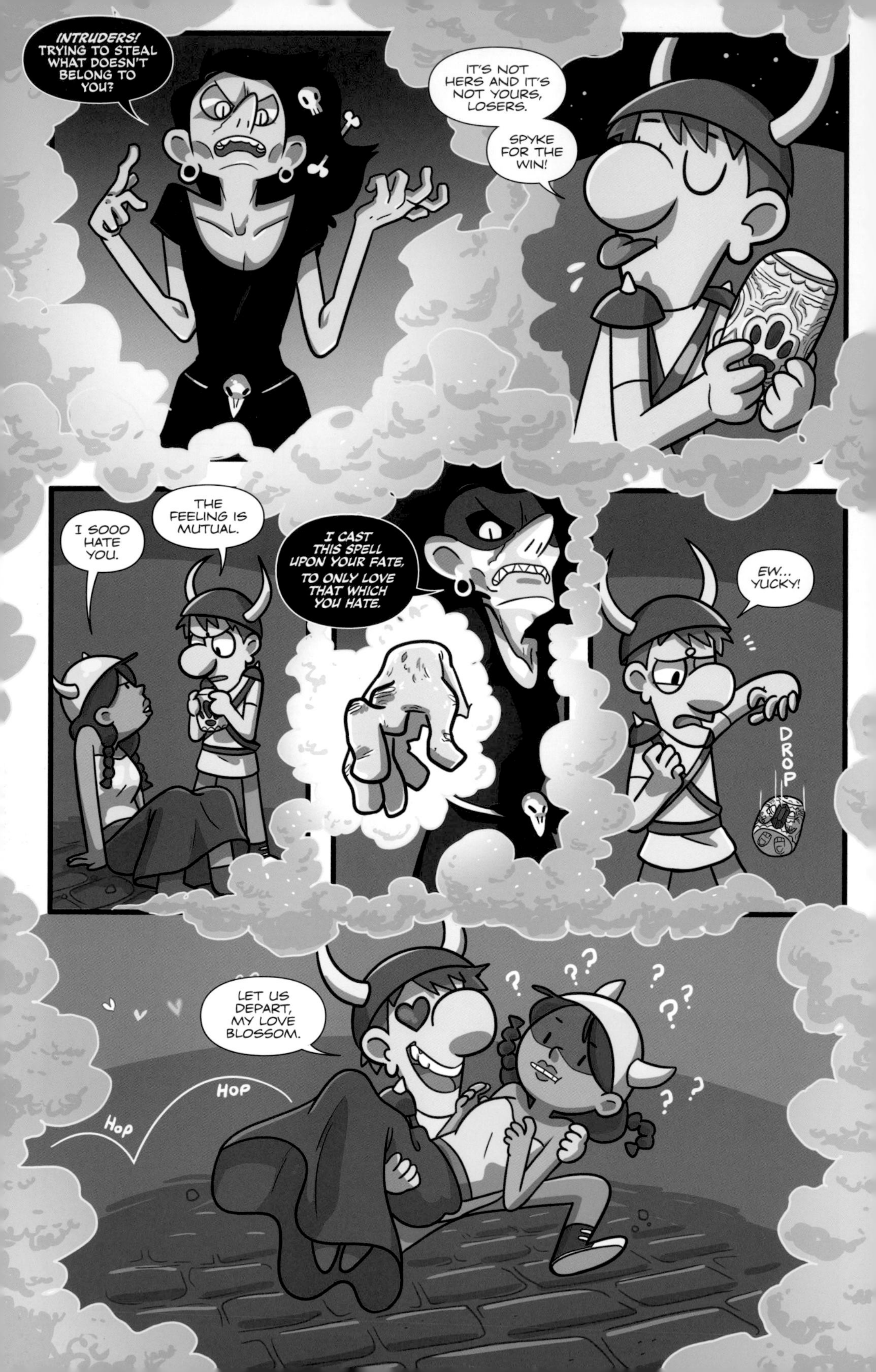
INTRUDERS! TRYING TO STEAL WHAT DOESN'T BELONG TO YOU?
IT'S NOT HERS AND IT'S NOT YOURS, LOSERS.
SPYKE FOR THE WIN!
I SOOO HATE YOU.
THE FEELING IS MUTUAL.
I CAST THIS SPELL UPON YOUR FATE, TO ONLY LOVE THAT WHICH YOU HATE.
EW... YUCKY!
DROP
LET US DEPART, MY LOVE BLOSSOM.
HOP
HOP

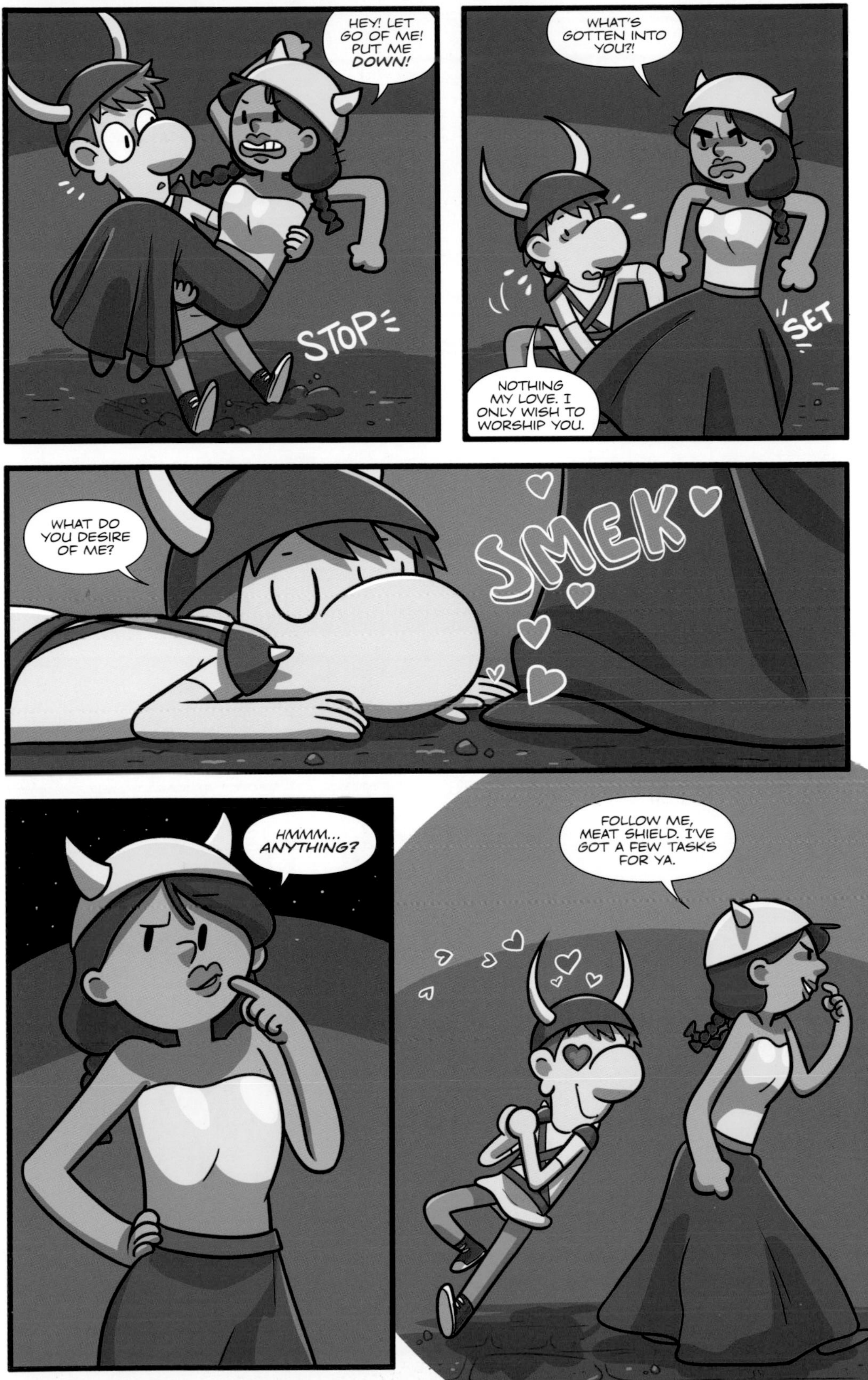
HEY! LET GO OF ME! PUT ME DOWN!
STOP
WHAT'S GOTTEN INTO YOU?!
SET
NOTHING MY LOVE. I ONLY WISH TO WORSHIP YOU.
WHAT DO YOU DESIRE OF ME?
SMEK
HMMM... ANYTHING?
FOLLOW ME, MEAT SHIELD. I'VE GOT A FEW TASKS FOR YA.

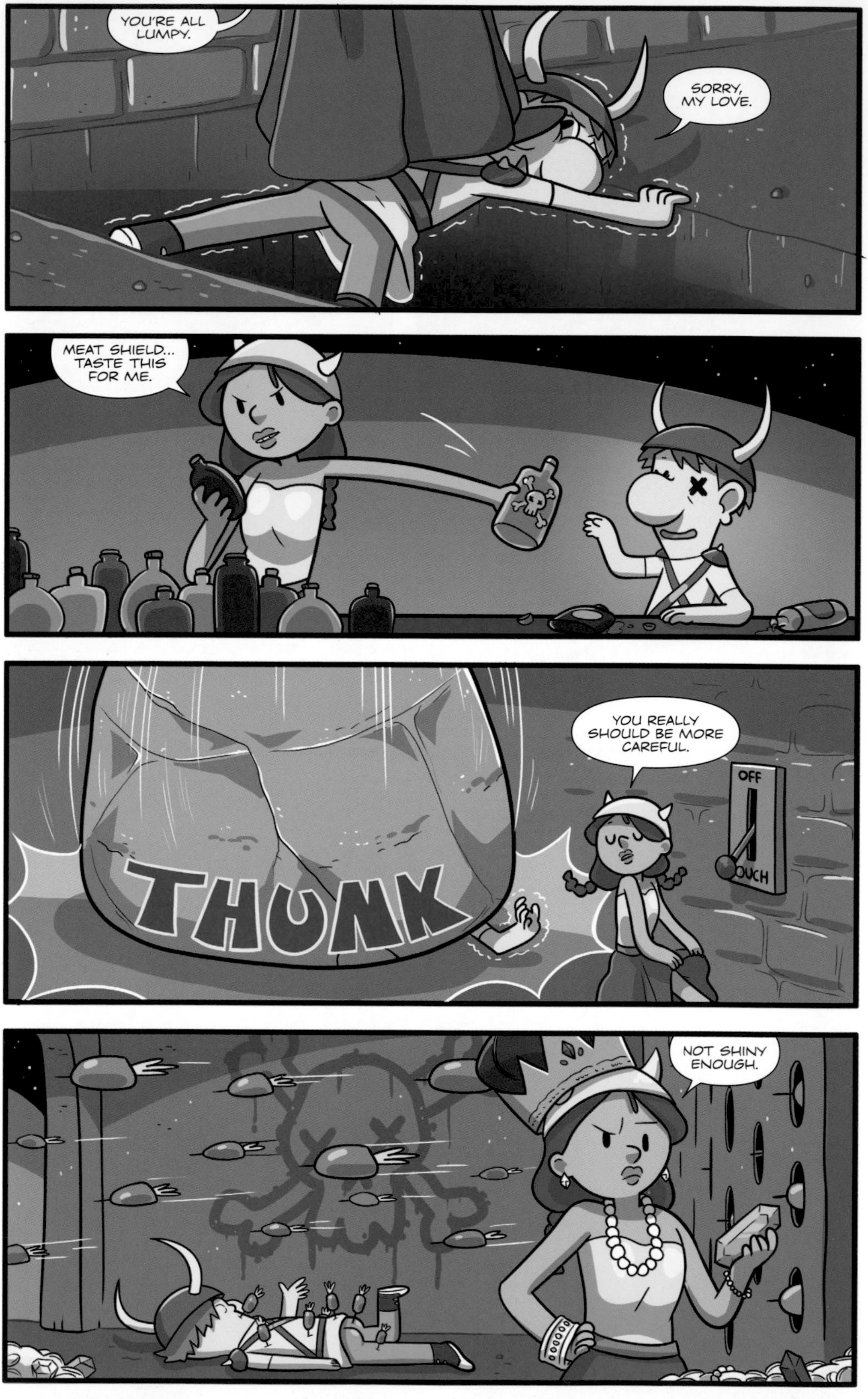
YOU'RE ALL LUMPY.
SORRY, MY LOVE.
MEAT SHIELD... TASTE THIS FOR ME.
YOU REALLY SHOULD BE MORE CAREFUL.
OFF
OUCH
THUNK
NOT SHINY ENOUGH.

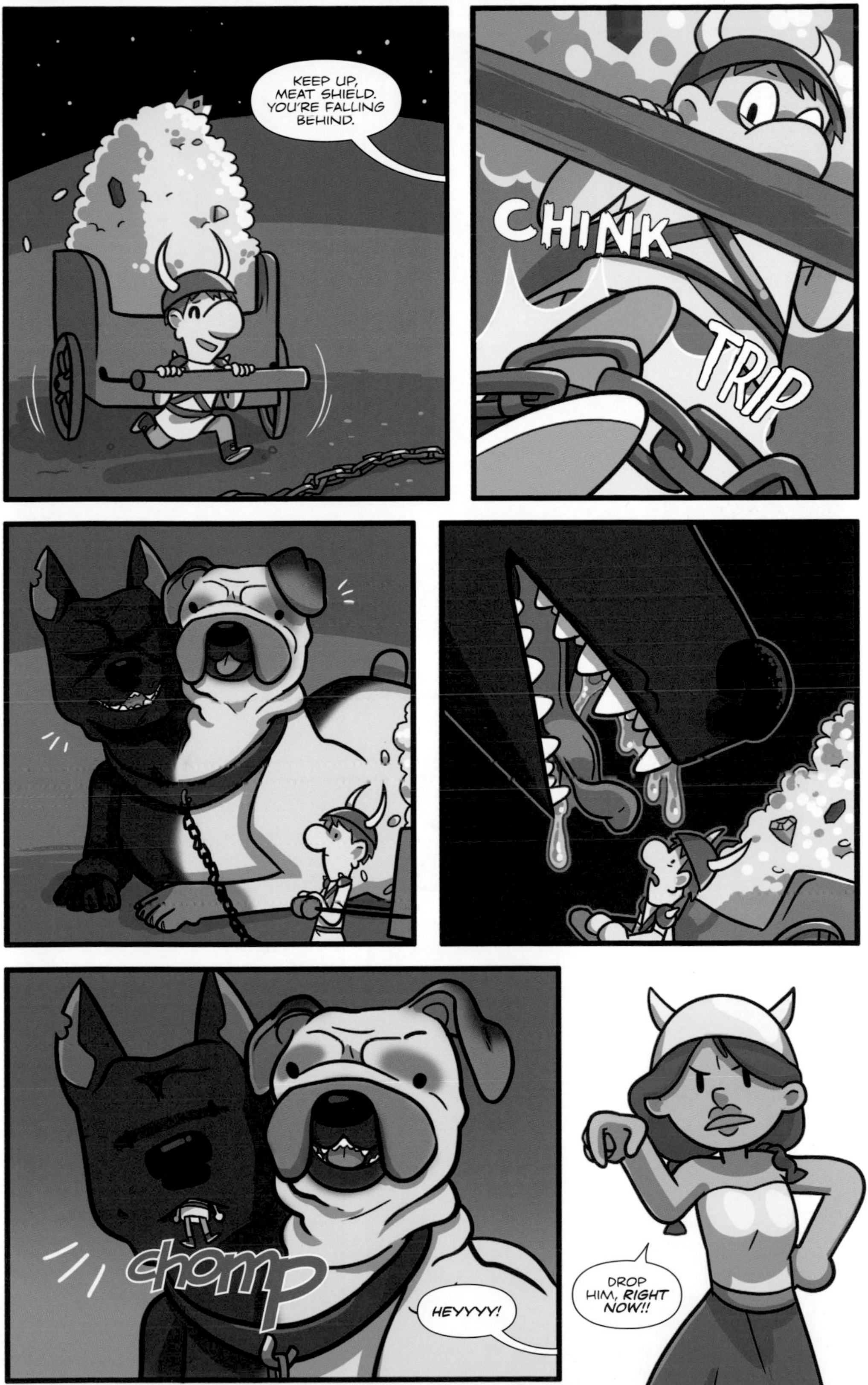
KEEP UP, MEAT SHIELD. YOU'RE FALLING BEHIND.
CHINK
TRIP
chomp
HEYYYY!
DROP HIM, ***RIGHT NOW!!***

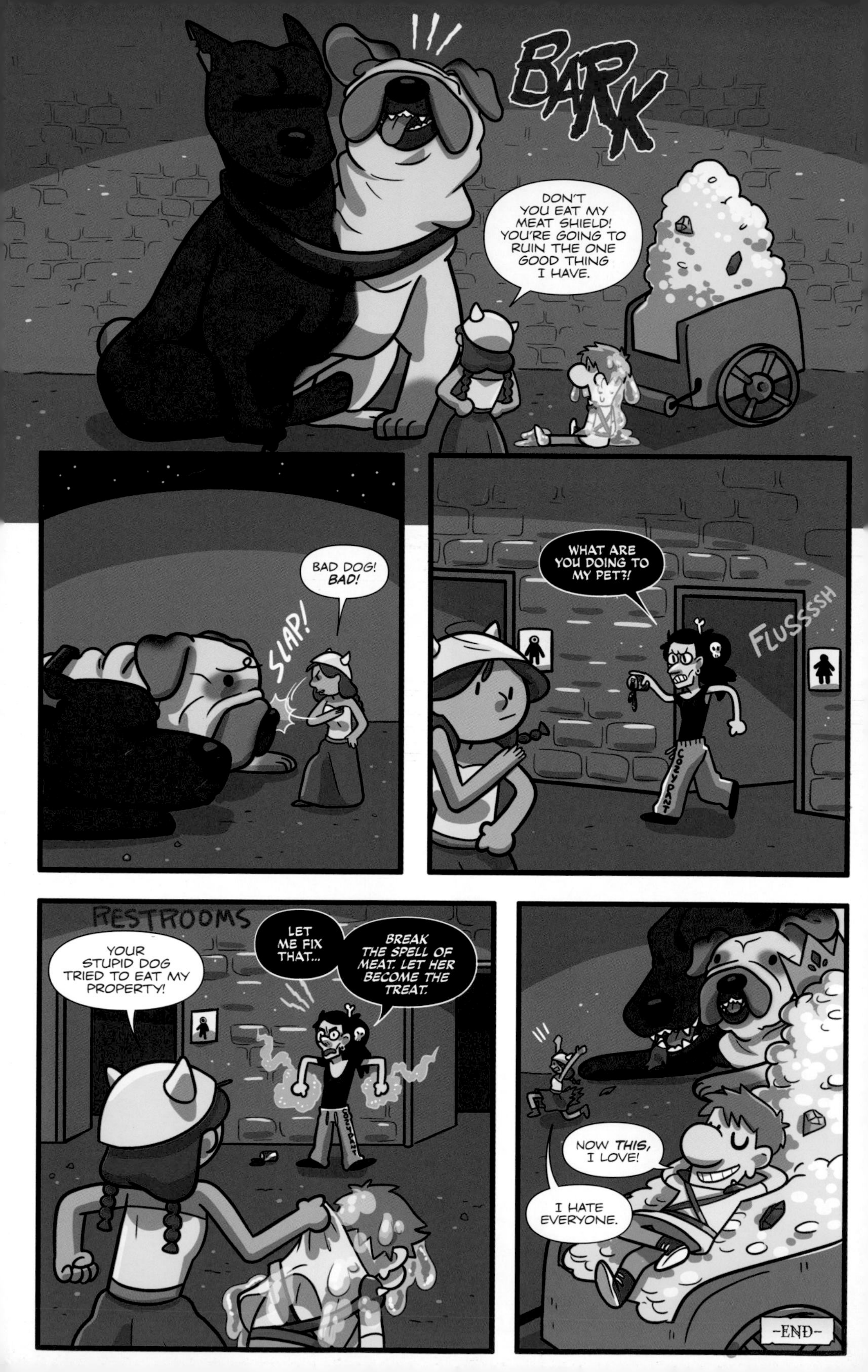

BARK
DON'T YOU EAT MY MEAT SHIELD! YOU'RE GOING TO RUIN THE ONE GOOD THING I HAVE.
BAD DOG! BAD!
SLAP!
WHAT ARE YOU DOING TO MY PET?!
FLUSSSSH
COZYPANT
RESTROOMS
YOUR STUPID DOG TRIED TO EAT MY PROPERTY!
LET ME FIX THAT...
BREAK THE SPELL OF MEAT. LET HER BECOME THE TREAT.
NOW THIS, I LOVE!
I HATE EVERYONE.
-END-

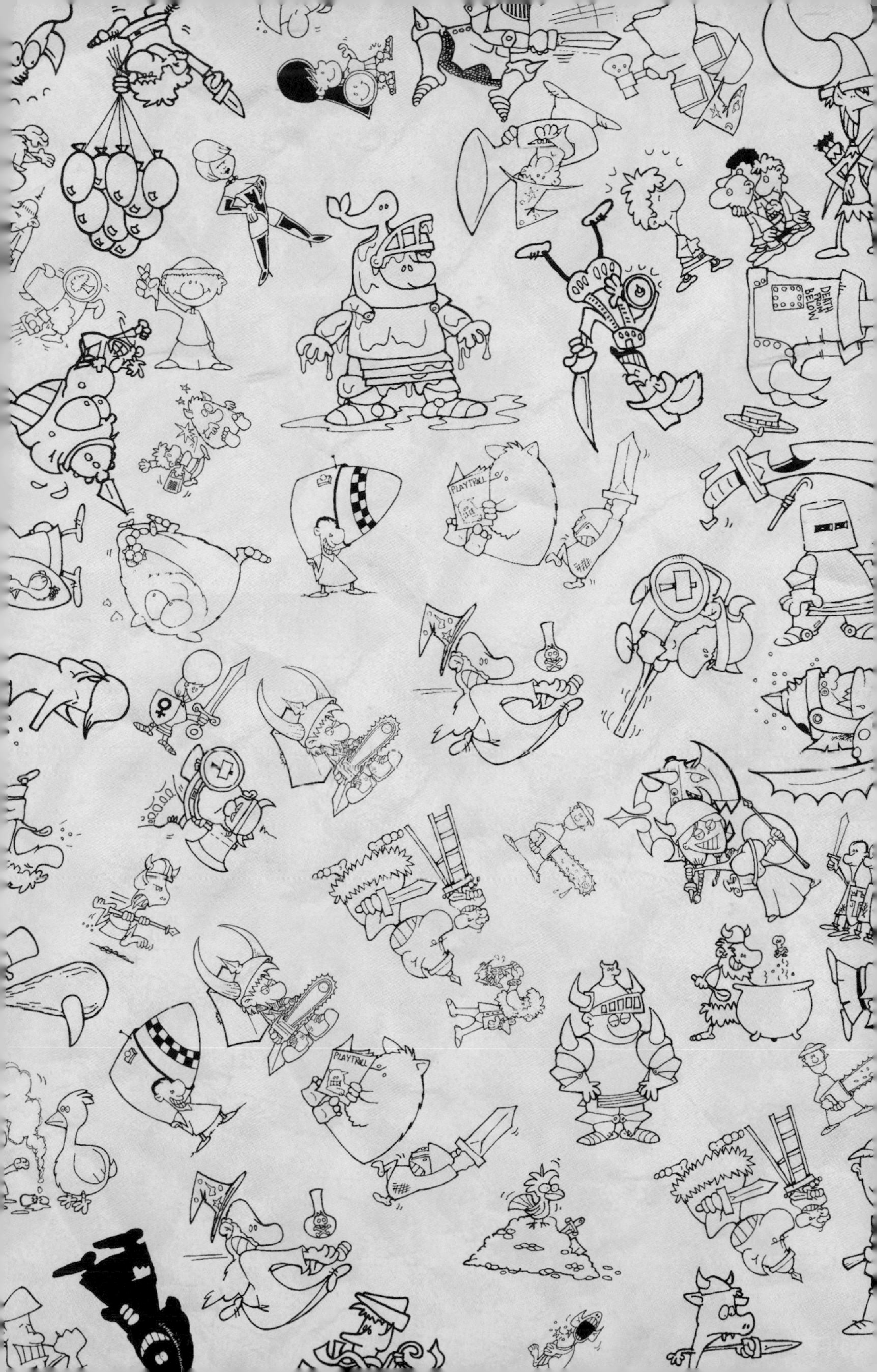
DEATH FROM BELOW
PLAYTROLL
PLAYTROLL

COVER
GALLERY

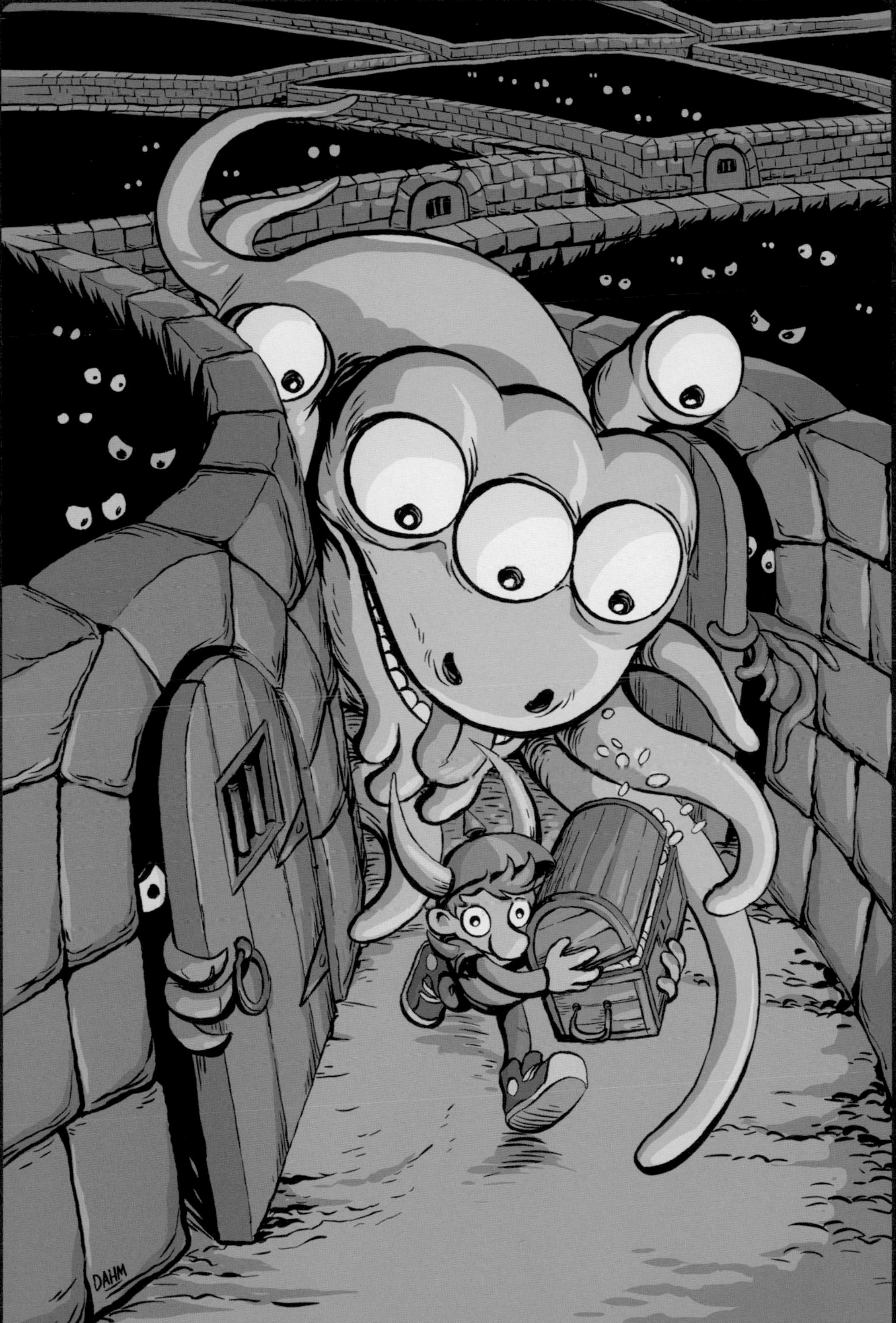
DAHM

Issue 5 Variant Cover by
Paul Maybury

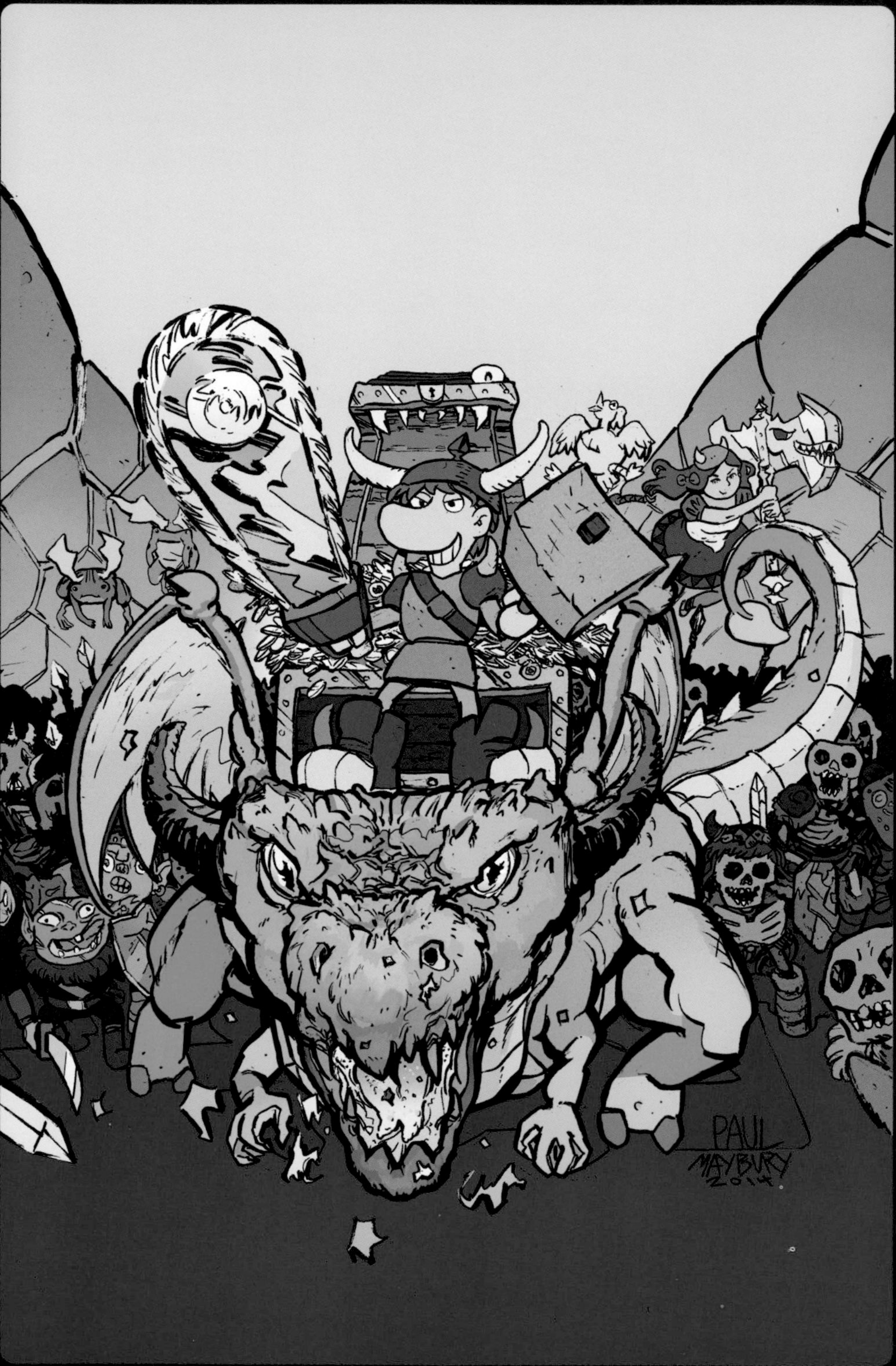
PAUL
MAYBURY
2014

Issue 6 Cover by
Rian Sygh

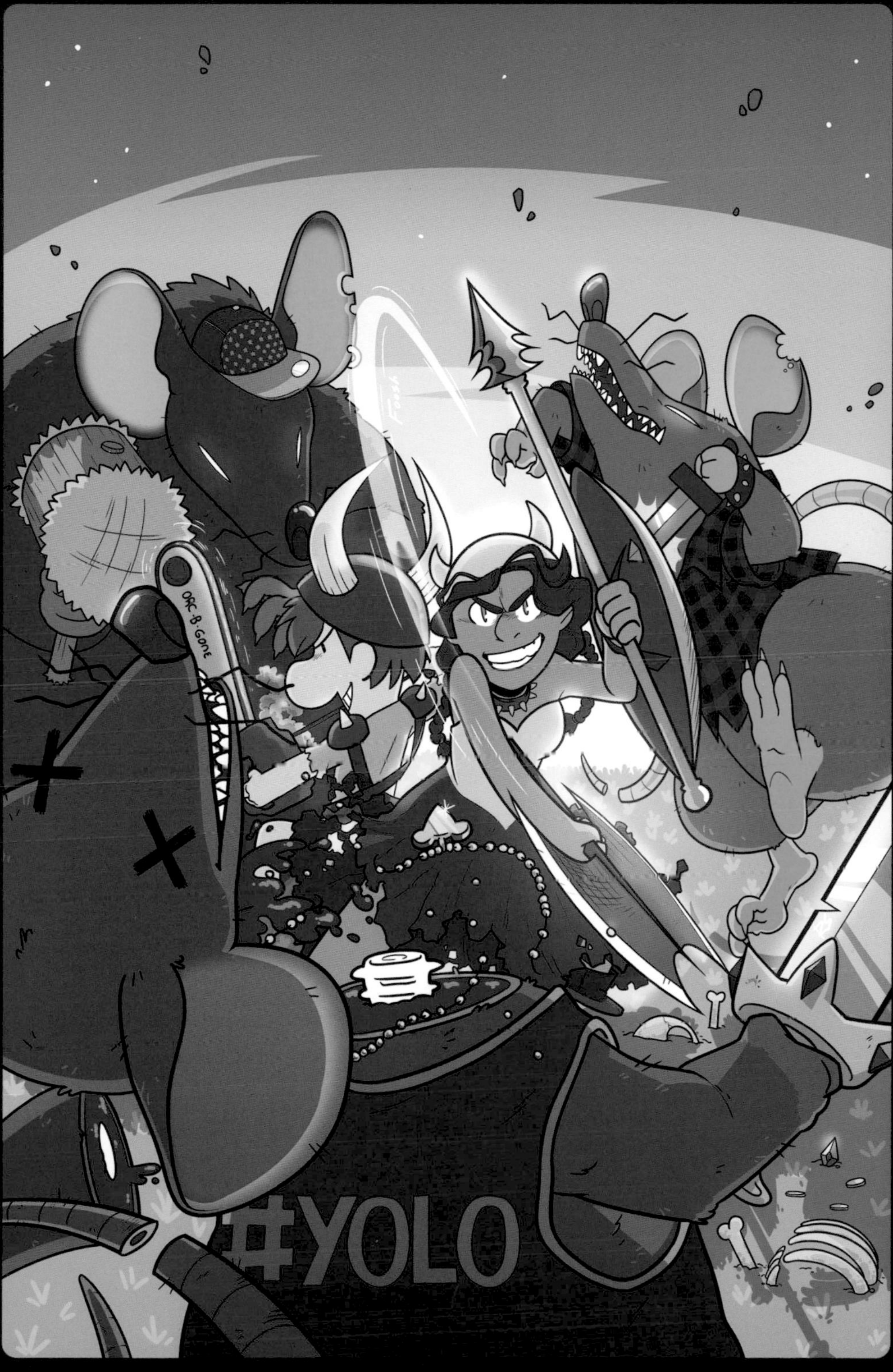
ORC-B-GONE
#YOLO

Issue 7 Cover by
Rian Sygh

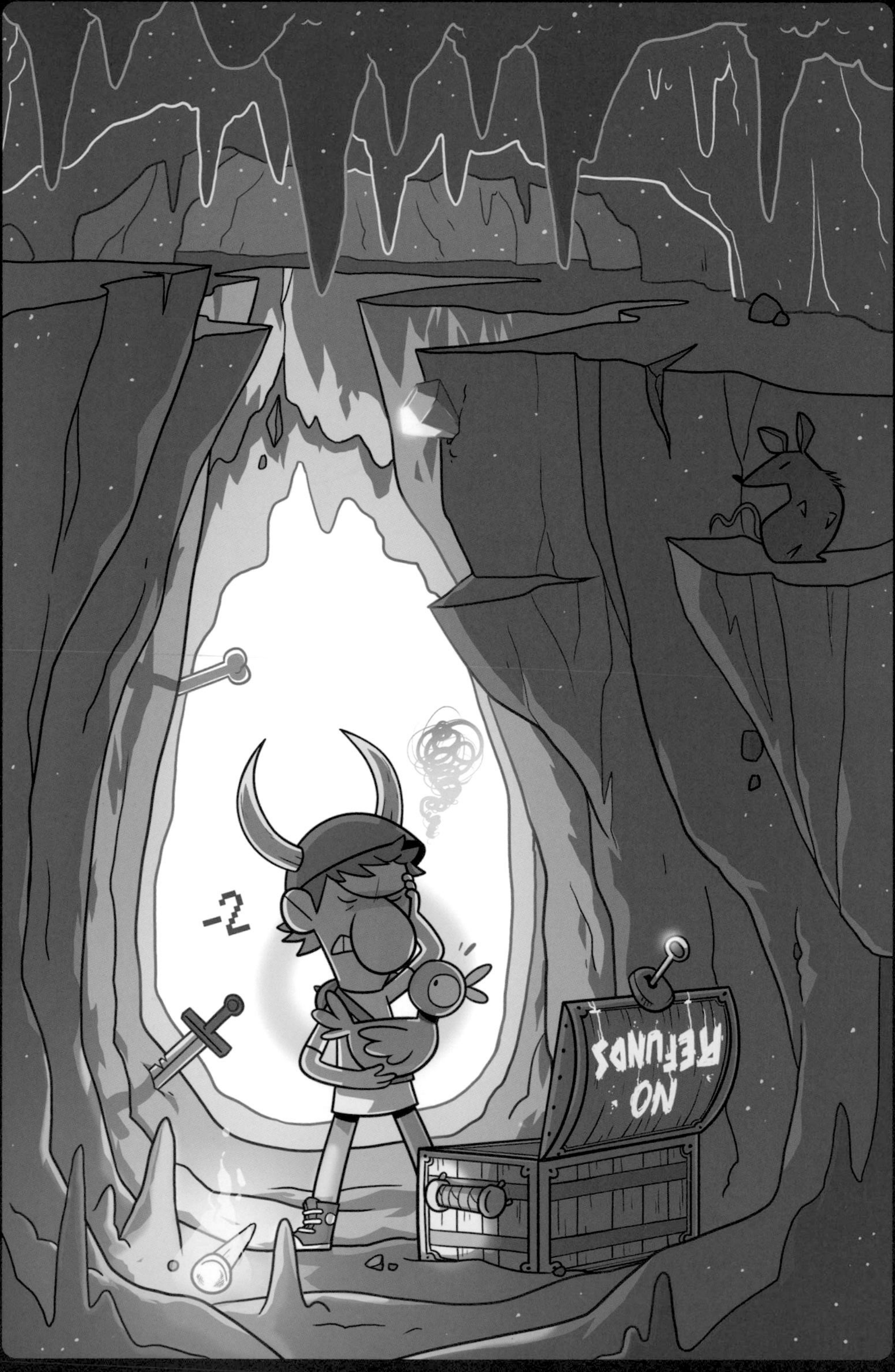
-2
NO REFUNDS

ISSUE 8 COVER BY
RIAN SYGH

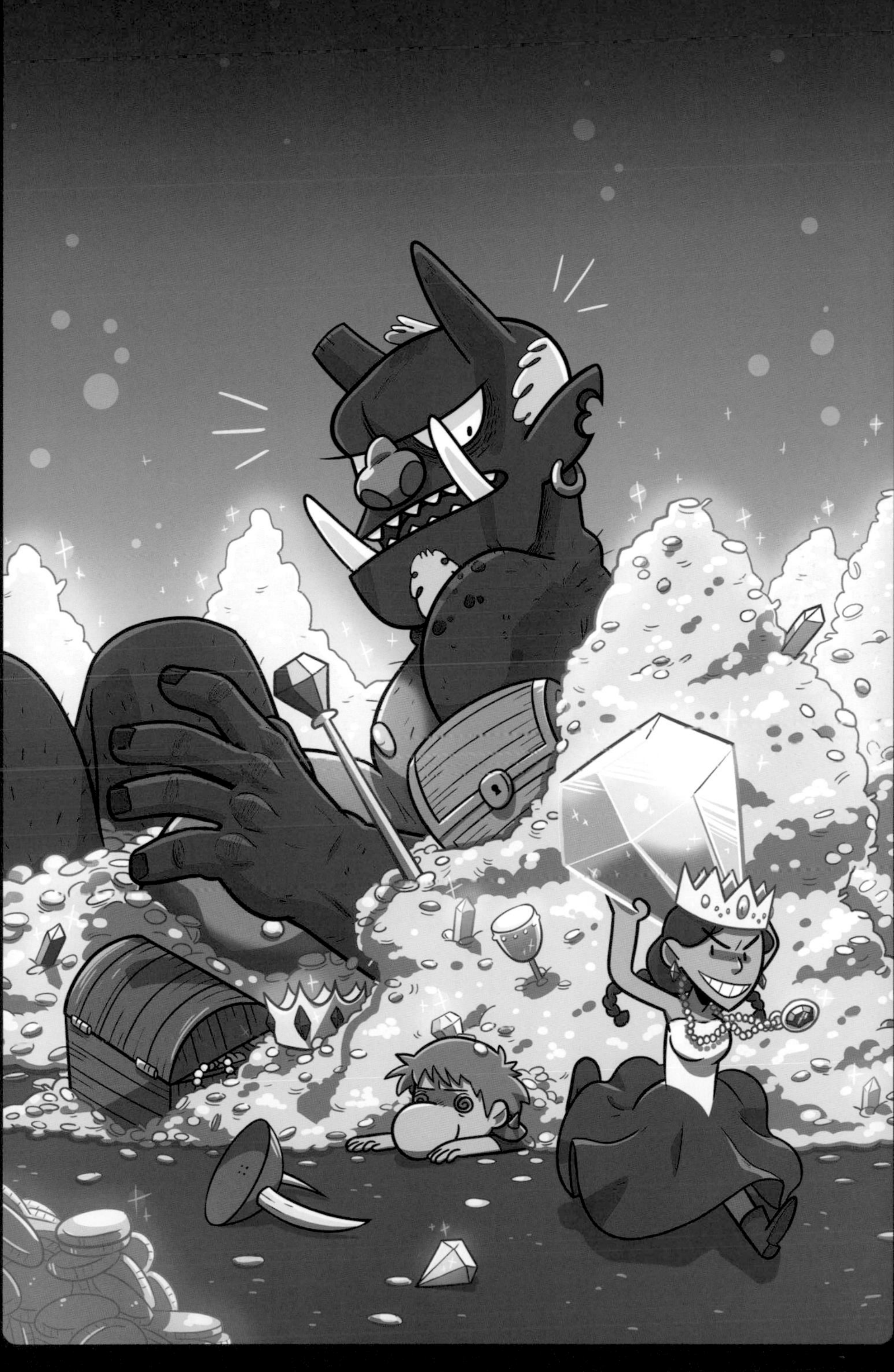

LEVEL 5
PALM TREE

If you kill the Palm Tree, instead of taking the level, you can keep it to give yourself an extra Hand. You get the Treasure either way.

Bad Stuff: Lose your best Hand item. If you don't have a Hand item, lose a level.

2 Treasures

munchkin.sjgames.com

BOOM! BOX ™

Not Usable by Elf
ELF-HELP BOOK

Play during any combat. The helper in this combat gains a level if the munchkin side wins. Usable once only.

400 Gold Pieces

munchkin.sjgames.com

BOOM! BOX™

ISSUE 7 BOOM! STUDIOS EXCLUSIVE CARD

CURSE!
TEMPORARY INANITY

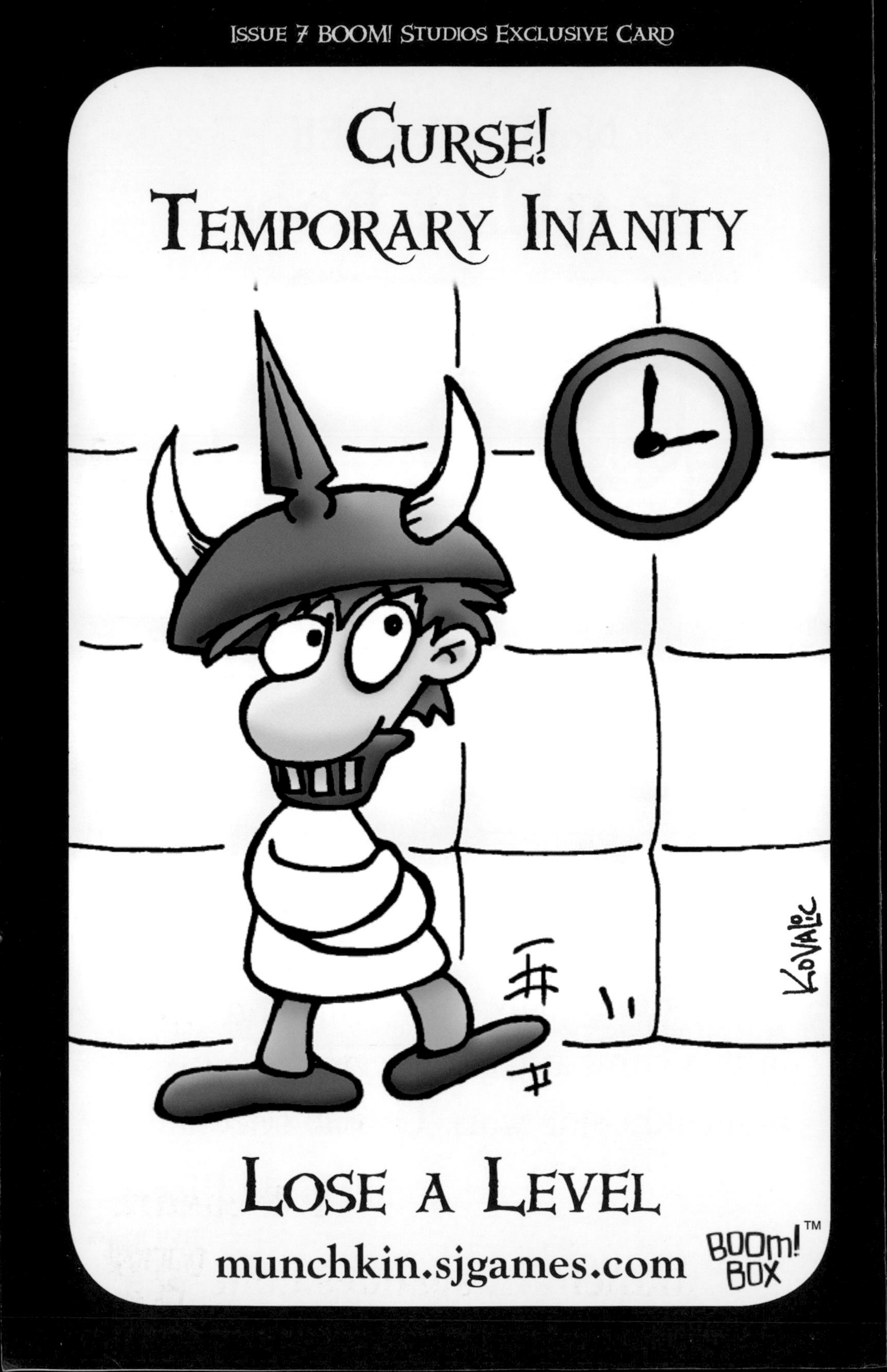
KOVALIC

LOSE A LEVEL

munchkin.sjgames.com BOOM! BOX™

ISSUE 8 BOOM! STUDIOS EXCLUSIVE CARD

LEVEL 1
BABY BOOMER

+5 against everyone *but* Kids. Adults always underestimate him.

TNT

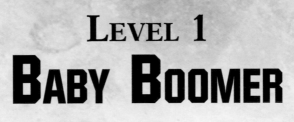

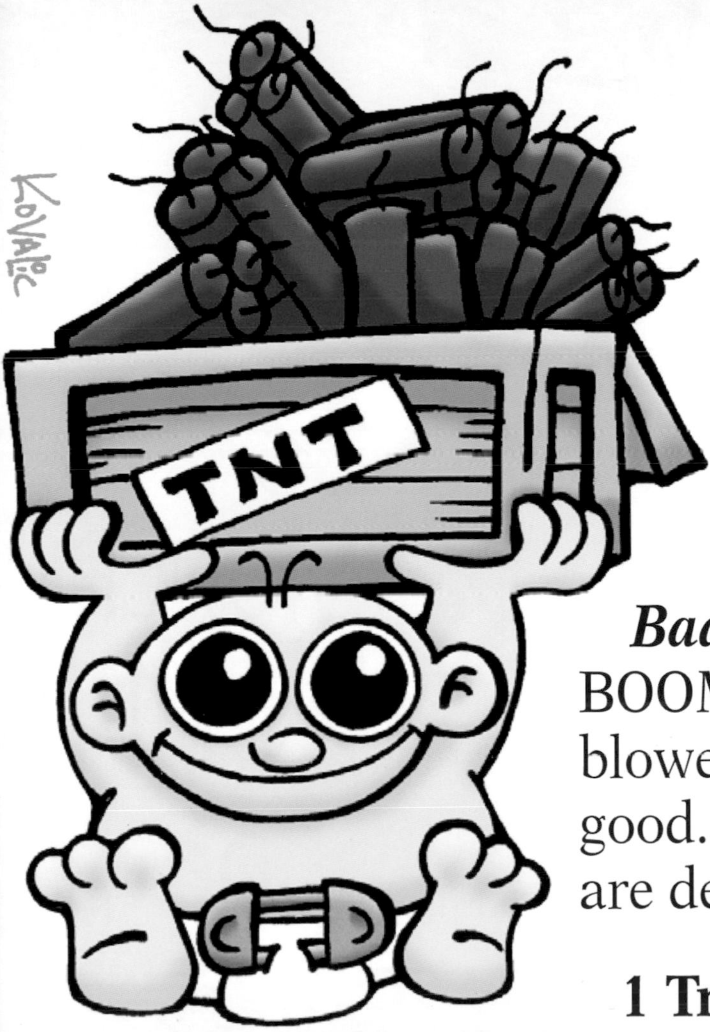

Bad Stuff:
BOOM! You blowed up good. You are dead.

1 Treasure

munchkin.sjgames.com BOOM! BOX™